D1327010

GLOBAL INVESTMENT RISK MANAGEMENT

GLOBAL INVESTMENT RISK MANAGEMENT

Protecting International Portfolios Against Currency, Interest Rate, Equity, and Commodity Risk

Edited by
EZRA ZASK

McGraw-Hill

New York   San Francisco   Washington, D.C.   Auckland   Bogotá
Caracas   Lisbon   London   Madrid   Mexico City   Milan
Montreal   New Delhi   San Juan   Singapore
Sydney   Tokyo   Toronto

Library of Congress Cataloging-in-Publication Data

Zask, Ezra.
    Global investment risk management : protecting international
portfolios against currency, interest rate, equity, and commodity
risk / Ezra Zask.
      p.   cm.
   ISBN (invalid) 0-07-135315-1
    1.   Investments, Foreign. I. Title.
HG4538.Z33   1999
658.15'5—dc21   99–29572

McGraw-Hill

*A Division of The **McGraw·Hill** Companies*

1 2 3 4 5 6 7 8 9 0 DOC/DOC 9 0 9 8 7 6 5 4 3 2 1 0 9

ISBN 0-07-135315-1

The sponsoring editor for this book was Stephen Isaacs, the editing supervisor
was Donna Muscatello, and the production supervisor was Elizabeth J. Strange.
It was set in Palatino by The Publishing Services Group.

Printed and bound by R.R. Donnelley & Sons Company.

This publication is designed to provide accurate and authoritative information
in regard to the subject matter covered. It is sold with the understanding that
neither the author or the publisher is engaged in rendering legal, accounting,
or other professional service. If legal advice or other expert assistance is required,
the services of a competent professional person should be sought.

—*From a Declaration of Principles jointly adopted by a Committee*
  of the American Bar Association and a Committee of Publishers.

McGraw-Hill books are available at special quantity discounts to use as premiums
and sales promotions, or for use in corporate training programs. For more information, please write to the Director of Special Sales, McGraw-Hill, 11 West 19th Street,
New York, NY 10011. Or contact your local bookstore.

 This book is printed on recycled, acid-free paper containing a minimum
of 50% recycled de-inked fiber.

C O N T E N T S

Chapter 12

Value at Risk for Asset Managers   187

Christopher L. Culp, *Managing Director, CP Risk Management, LLC*
Ron Mensink, *Quantitative Analytics Director, the State of Wisconsin Investment Board*
Andrea M.P. Neves, *Vice President, CP Risk Management, LLC*

Chapter 13

Trading Risks in International Investments—
Why Market-Neutral Strategies Sometimes Fail   215

Ezra Zask, *Manager, Gibson Capital Management, Ltd.*

Chapter 14

Managing Global Emerging Markets Risk   223

Richard J. Johnston, *Managing Director, OFFITBANK*
Jason L. Cook, *Senior Research Analyst, Emerging Markets Investment Group, OFFITBANK*

Chapter 15

Financial Meltdowns and Exchange Rate Regimes   237

Steve H. Hanke, *Professor of Applied Economics, The Johns Hopkins University*

Chapter 16

Asia Questions Risk?   245

Michael J. Howell, *Managing Director, CrossBorder Capital*

Chapter 17

Managing Latin American Investment Risk   269

Richard M. Johnston, *Managing Director, OFFITBANK*
Jason L. Cook, *Senior Research Analyst, Emerging Markets Investment Group, OFFITBANK*

Chapter 18

Appendix

David T. Beers is Managing Director of Standard & Poor's Sovereign Ratings Group. Based in London, he heads the global team of analysts who evaluate the credit standing of sovereign governments, sovereign-supported issuers, and multilateral lending institutions.

Prior to joining Standard & Poor's in 1990, Mr. Beers was an independent economic consultant, and before that, an economist at Salomon Brothers, specializing in the analysis of sovereign credits. Earlier, he worked at Bankers Trust Company, where he was responsible for evaluating country lending risks in the Asia-Pacific region.

Mr. Beers holds an M.S. degree in economics from the London School of Economics and B.A. degree in international relations from the University of Virginia. (CHAPTER 9)

Vinod Chandrashekaran, Ph.D. is a senior consultant in the Equity Research Group at BARRA Inc., Berkeley, California. He joined BARRA in July 1994 and has worked extensively on the latest version of BARRA's factor model for the U.S. stock market (US E3). His current research interests include studying the behavior of global stock markets from the risk and return perspective, investigation of improved methods for risk prediction over different horizons, and trading cost analysis and control. He received his Ph.D. in finance from the University of California at Berkeley in 1994. (CHAPTER 7)

Jason L. Cook joined OFFITBANK in January 1996 as a Research Analyst in the Emerging Markets Investment Group. From 1995 to 1996, Mr. Cook worked at First Commerce Corporation in the Credit Analysis Department, where he was responsible for performing financial statement projections and due diligence on commercial and individual clients. His experience also includes an internship at Grupo Elektra S.A., in Mexico. He holds B.A (1993) and M.B.A. (1995) degrees and an M.A. degree in Latin American Studies (1995) from Tulane University. (CHAPTERS 14 and 17)

Christopher L. Culp is Managing Director of CP Risk Management LLC in Chicago and Adjunct Associate Professor of Finance at the University of Chicago's Graduate School of Business. He has served previously as President of Risk Management Consulting Services, Inc., Senior Examiner (derivatives) at the Federal Reserve Bank of Chicago, research economist G.T. Management (Asia) Ltd. Hong Kong, and trading strategist at TradeLink LLC. Dr. Culp is Managing Editor of Institutional Investor's *Derivatives Quarterly* and Senior Fellow in Financial Regulation with Competitive Enterprise Institute in Washington, D.C. He holds a Ph.D. in finance from the University of Chicago Graduate School of Business and a B.A. in economics from The Johns Hopkins University. (CHAPTER 12)

Raymond T. Dalio is President, Chief Investment Officer, and a founder of Bridgewater Associates, Inc., which manages over $14.5 billion in currency overlay and global bond portfolios for institutional investors, principally large pension funds and central banks.

Since his graduation with an M.B.A. degree in finance from Harvard Business School in May 1973, Mr. Dalio has been managing currency exposures and advising investors on currency risk management in one capacity or another. In 1974, he was in charge of institutional futures business at Shearson Hayden Stone, where he advised companies on the management of their currency risks. In 1975, he left Shearson to form Bridgewater, which managed corporate currency and interest rate risks on a discretionary basis. In 1984–1985, Mr. Dalio designed the New York Futures Exchange's U.S. dollar contract. In 1985, he and Bridgewater began managing currency and global bond exposures for institutional investors, which has been the principal business of Bridgewater ever since. (CHAPTER 5)

Roger C. Gibson, CFA, CFP, is the founder and President of Gibson Capital Management, Ltd., a Registered Investment Advisor providing money management services for high-net-worth individuals and institutional clients nationwide. Gibson is well known as the author of *Asset Allocation: Balancing Financial Risk*, considered the industry standard on asset allocation. In 1998, *Dow Jones Investment Advisor*, the largest circulation magazine for financial advisors, awarded Gibson the Dow Jones Portfolio Management Award in the category of book publication for his significant contribution "to the art and science of portfolio management." Nationally recognized as an expect on asset allocation and investment portfolio design, Gibson is a frequent speaker at national educational conferences and is regularly quoted and featured in major financial publications. He serves on the Advisory Board and is a regular columnist on asset allocation for the *Journal of Retirement Planning* and is also a member of the Editorial Advisory Board of the *Journal of Financial Planning*. Gibson is a recipient of the Financial Writer's Award from Financial Planning magazine. He is also listed in *Who's Who in the World*, *Who's Who in Finance and Industry*, and was named by both *Money* magazine and *Worth* magazine as one of the top financial advisers in America. (CHAPTER 6)

Steve H. Hanke is a Professor of Applied Economics at The Johns Hopkins University in Baltimore and a columnist at *Forbes* magazine. He also serves as Chairman of the Friedberg Mercantile Group, Inc., in New York; President of the Toronto Trust—Argentina in Buenos Aires; and is a principal of CP Risk Management in Chicago, Illinois. Dr. Hanke is a member of the Steering Committee of The G-7 Council in Washington, D.C.; a Fellow at The World Economic Forum in Geneva; and a Distinguished Associate of the International Atlantic Economic Society. In June 1998, he was named as one of *World Trade* magazine's 25 most influential people for his contributions to the debates about currency boards and dollarization. (CHAPTER 15)

Joanne M. Hill is Co-Head of the Global Equity Derivatives Research Group at Goldman Sachs, which has repeatedly gained top ranking in industry surveys. She advises institutions in North America on strategies utilizing portfolio trading and equity derivative products and oversees the global research effort on these products. Dr. Hill has spent over 10 years at investment banks in a quantitative research capacity in the areas of asset allocation, fixed income, and equity products. Before coming to Wall Street, she was on the finance faculty of the University of Massachusetts (Amherst) and published extensively on modern portfolio theory topics and derivatives.

Dr. Hill is a member of the Review Board for the AIMR Research Foundation, the Board of the Futures Industry Institute, and the Board of Trustees of the Financial Management Association. She is a member of the Financial Products Advisory Board to the CFTC. She serves as the Managing Editor of *Derivatives Quarterly* and is on the editorial boards of the *Financial Analysts Journal* and *Financial Management*. She received her M.B.A. and Ph.D. degrees in finance and quantitative methods from Syracuse University, an M.A. in international affairs from George Washington University, and her undergraduate degree from American University. (CHAPTER 11)

Michael J. Howell is Managing Director of CrossBorder Capital, a London-based global investment advisor that specializes in asset allocation and emerging market analysis for institutional investors and governments. Mr. Howell has worked in the financial sector for nearly 20 years. He was previously Co-Head of Research at ING/Barings, responsible for the firm's investment strategy and equity research. Mr. Howell served as Research Director at Salomon Brothers between 1986 and 1992. He lives in London and is married with four children.

Richard M. Johnston joined OFFITBANK in 1992 and shares the responsibility as co-head of the Bank's investment activities in the emerging markets. Since graduating Middlebury College in 1980 with a B.A. in economics, Mr. Johnston has spent his entire business career involved with emerging markets finance. From 1980 to 1988, he was a member of the Latin American Group in the International Corporate Banking Division of Manufacturers Hanover Trust Company. During that time, he had a number of important assignments: primary responsibility for formulating and marketing Chile's comprehensive sovereign restructuring (1980–1984); managing the Bank's Venezuela operations (1984–1987); and managing the Bank's Mexican business activities and loan portfolio (1987–1988). Mr. Johnston joined Salomon Brothers in 1988, where he was a Vice President in the International Division and an architect in building the firm's entire emerging markets business. He has been deeply involved in pioneering the issuance of new emerging markets securities in the U.S. and euro-markets and in introducing many institutional investors to the merits of investing in the emerging markets. He has lived in Amsterdam, Bogotá, Buenos Aires, Caracas, Frankfurt, London, Mexico City, Santiago, and Tokyo. He is a shareholder of OFFITBANK and member of the Management Committee. (CHAPTERS 14 and 17)

Ira G. Kawaller, President of Kawaller & Company, LLC, assists companies in their use of derivatives and managing financial risks. Prior to founding Kawaller & Co., Mr. Kawaller headed the New York office of the Chicago Mercantile Exchange, with prior employment at J. Aron & Company, AT&T, and the Board of Governors of the Federal Reserve System. He received a Ph.D. in economics from Purdue University in 1976, and he has held adjunct professorships at Columbia University and Polytechnic University. (CHAPTER 10)

Ron Mensink is the Quantitative Analytics Director at the State of Wisconsin Investment Board, where he guides analytical activities related to asset allocation, performance measurement, and risk measurement. He earned his M.B.A. in finance from the University of Wisconsin at Madison and is a Chartered Financial Analyst. (CHAPTER 12)

Ranga Nathan is Senior Vice President of Global Risk Management at Sakura Dellsher, Inc. in Chicago. He was previously a principal at Waldner & Co., listed for 15 years by *Euromoney* as a leading currency advisor. His clients have included multinational corporations and institutional investors across North America and Europe. For more than 15 years Mr. Nathan has structured and supervised the management of clients' currency exposures. Before his tenure at Waldner, he held positions at Citibank (Asia) and Chase Manhattan Bank (Europe). He is currently a member of the Editorial Board of *Derivatives Quarterly*. (CHAPTER 8)

Andrea M.P. Neves is Vice President of CP Risk Management, LLC, a financial risk management consulting firm based in Chicago. Ms. Neves specializes in various approaches to risk measurement, volatility analysis, and managerial risk consulting. Her clients have included insurance companies, commercial banks, institutional investors, international non-financial corporations, electric utilities, and futures, options, and securities exchanges. Prior to joining CPRM, Ms. Neves was Senior Technical Consultant at Risk Management Consulting Services, Inc. Other experience includes work at a derivatives litigation support firm and research for the Center for the Study of Futures and Option Markets. Ms. Neves holds an M.S. in physics an M.A. in economics, and is currently pursuing an M.B. A. from the University of Chicago, concentrating in analytical finance. (CHAPTER 12)

Todd E. Petzel is Executive Vice President and Chief Investment Officer of Commonfund. Prior to joining Commonfund, Dr. Petzel was the Executive Vice President, Business Development, of the Chicago Mercantile Exchange. Dr. Petzel holds A.B., A.M., and Ph.D. degrees from the University of Chicago. He has taught at Macalester College and Stanford University. In 1982, he joined the Coffee, Sugar and Cocoa Exchange in New York as chief economist. In 1988, he became Vice President, Financial Research, for the Chicago Mercantile Exchange. While in Chicago, Dr. Petzel also taught finance classes at The University of Chicago's Graduate School of business. Dr. Petzel is the author of the book, *Financial Futures and Options: A Guide to Markets, Applications, and Strategies,* and numerous articles and reviews. He serves as referee for a number of journals devoted to economics and finance and as editor of *Derivatives Quarterly*. (CHAPTER 2)

Steven A. Schoenfeld is the Head of International Equity Strategies at Barclays Global Investors (BGI), where he and his team are responsible for the management of $52 billion in non-U.S. index investments. Prior to joining BGI in 1996, Mr. Schoenfeld worked at the International Finance Corporation (IFC), where he helped develop the IFC Investable (IFCI) Emerging market Indexes and structured the first index funds based on the IFCI Indexes. Before joining IFC, he worked in the derivatives industry, including three years trading Japanese stock index futures at the Singapore International Monetary Exchange (SIMEX). Mr. Schoenfeld was a Fulbright Scholar in Economics at the National University of Singapore, holds a B.A. from Clark University, and receive his M.A. from the Johns Hopkins University School of Advanced International Studies. He is the author of *The Pacific Rim Futures and Options Markets*. (CHAPTER 4)

Istvan Szoke is a founding partner and Managing Director at Eastern Heritage Capital, a Geneva-based investment advisor specializing in central and eastern European investments. Prior to that he was an analyst and assistant portfolio manager covering eastern Europe at Vontobel Asset Management. Mr. Szoke began his career at Bankers Trust, where he worked in corporate finance in Budapest and London and later in the equity group in New York. He holds a B.A. in economics/business from the Budapest University of Economics and an M.B.A. from the Wharton School of the University of Pennsylvania. Mr. Szoke is a native Hungarian. (CHAPTER 18)

Lee R. Thomas is Managing Director and the Senior International Portfolio Manager at Pacific Investment Management Company (PIMCO). He holds B.A. and Ph.D. degrees in economics from Tulane University. (CHAPTER 3)

Maria E. Tsu is Vice President of Equity Derivatives Research at Goldman Sachs, and has been with the firm since early 1994. She focuses on U.S. equity benchmark issues and applications of derivative products in active investment strategies. She has a background in engineering and a Masters degree in Economics with a quantitative finance focus from Virginia Tech.

Richard Vogel is a Managing Director and founding partner of Eastern Heritage Capital, a Geneva-based investment advisor specializing in central and eastern European investments. Prior to that, he was Vice President responsible for European equity research and portfolio management at Vontobel Asset Management, where he managed international equity portfolios in excess of CHF450 million. He began his career at the Boston Consulting Group in London, where he worked on corporate restructuring in eastern Europe. Mr. Vogel holds a degree in business and economics from the University of St. Gallen and an M.B.A. from the Harvard Business School. (CHAPTER 18)

ABOUT THE EDITOR

Ezra Zask is President of Ezra Zask Associates, Inc. He is a Manager for Gibson Capital Management, Ltd., a Registered Investment Adviser that provides comprehensive money management services with a disciplined asset allocation methodology for high-net-worth individuals and institutional clients. He is also a principal of CP Risk Management, LLC, a leading risk management consulting company. Mr. Zask held senior capital market positions with Manufacturers Hanover Trust Company and Mellon Banks. He has started and managed currency, market-neutral, and emerging market debt hedge funds and taught at Columbia and Carnegie-Mellon Universities. He is active in the investment arena as a writer and speaker. Mr. Zask received a B.A. degree from Princeton University and an M.A. from Columbia University. He is married to Judith Linscott and has a daughter, Anna, and lives in Lakeville, CT. (CHAPTERS 1, 13, and APPENDIX)

C H A P T E R   1

Global Investment Risk Management

Ezra Zask
Gibson Capital Management, Ltd.
Lakeville, Connecticut

THE ELUSIVE GAINS OF INTERNATIONAL INVESTMENTS

The allure of foreign investment has been with us for centuries, as has the risk of these investments. The constant search for high returns and diversification of investments (along with the opportunities of foreign travel) has long beckoned investors. In the past generation this has led to an immense growth in investment outflows from the U.S., Japan, and Europe. These outflows have come from a broad range of investors, including banks, hedge funds, mutual funds, funds managers, pension funds, and insurance companies. It is estimated that the international allocation of large institutional investors now approaches 10 percent.

Relying on the twin pillars of modern portfolio theory, high returns and diversification, academic and professional writings have reinforced this international movement. Three benefits are normally cited in support of international investment:

1. Non-U.S. equities represent approximately two-thirds of the world's market capitalization and are therefore too large to ignore.
2. Economic growth has, on average, been higher outside the U.S. over the past two decades. Since returns often follow growth, global investment appears warranted.

1

3. International investment should provide diversification benefits for U.S. investors, since the forces driving the international markets differ from those that affect the U.S. markets.

The assumption behind these theories is that adding international exposure to a portfolio will normally reduce its risk without lowering returns.

Critics of the global investment paradigm emerged before the crisis of 1997–1998. The promise held out by international investment has proven difficult to find. One has only to compare the returns of the S&P 500 to the EAFE (J.P. Morgan Europe, Australia, and Far East Index of industrial country stock markets) between 1988 and 1997 to question the potential benefits of international diversification (Table 1–1).

Figure 1–1 shows the relationship between the equity markets of the developing countries (Emerging Market Free Index), the U.S. (S&P 500), and the industrial world excluding the U.S. (EAFE). Several conclusions emerge. First, the U.S. stock market has outperformed the others over the 1987–1998 time period. Second, the emerging countries' stock markets experienced considerably greater volatility than those of the industrial world.

T A B L E 1–1

Annual Returns from EAFE and S&P
1988-1997

Year	EAFE	S&P 500
1997	2.10%	33.40%
1996	6.36	22.96
1995	11.55	37.58
1994	8.06	1.32
1993	32.94	10.08
1992	-11.85	7.62
1991	12.50	30.47
1990	-23.30	-3.10
1989	10.80	31.69
1988	28.59	16.61
Average 10-year return	6.56	18.05

F I G U R E 1–1

Emerging Market, S&P 500, and OECD Equities

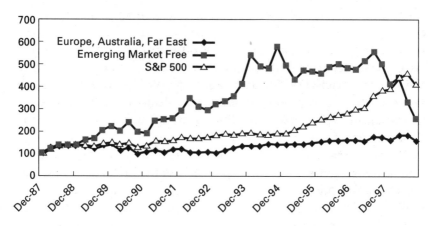

Similar conclusions emerge from an examination of Figure 1–2, which shows that the U.S. bond market has provided a higher U.S. dollar return than either the emerging markets (as measured by the Emerging Market Bond Index) or the industrial world excluding the U.S. (as measured by the Merrill Lynch Global Government Bond Index).

F I G U R E 1–2

Total Bond Returns in U.S. Dollars

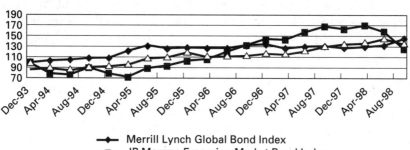

RISKS IN THE BOND, EQUITY, AND CURRENCY MARKETS

The additional risk of investing in overseas markets has long been obvious. Indeed, it has been often said that the risk premium paid to holders of sovereign debt is well-earned. Global economic crises have occurred with regularity. In recent times, they include the energy crisis (1973), debt default (1982), stock market collapse (1987), european currency devaluation (1992), Mexican devaluation (1994–1995) and the Asian crisis precipitated by the devaluation of the Thai baht in 1997.

These crises have greatly increased the volatility of international investments. Equally important, as the crisis of 1998 clearly indicates, the periodic crises are normally accompanied by a dramatic increase in correlation in the price movement between countries. For example, the stock and bond markets of most nations moved in tandem throughout most of 1997 and 1998 in response to common global forces. Needless to say, this undermined one of the key "benefits" of international investment: portfolio diversification.

Additional drawbacks often cited include higher expenses (transaction, management, and custody fees), tax issues, and operational issues (disclosure, accounting, etc.). In addition, there are added political and currency risks that heavily influence returns from international investing and which can also result in higher volatility."

However, the size and extent of these risks appear to have increased in recent years. This increase can be explained by the increase in the size and number of actors in the global financial arena; the tremendous increase in the funds available for investment; the rapid rise of derivatives and structured products; and the technological revolution that has allowed funds to flow around the world at lightning speed.

Several chapters deal with the growing risk in the major global investment markets. Stephen Schoenfeld describes the risks in the equity markets, especially in emerging markets, as well as the prospects for the future. Lee Thomas describes the risks of the global bond markets, especially in relation to currency risk, which is more important for fixed-income returns. He then places this risk in the context of optimal portfolio diversification and reveals that foreign bonds provide value to portfolio managers. Ray Dalio outlines the currency risks of international investments and suggests a framework for hedging these risks.

RISK MANAGEMENT OVERSIGHT

The upheavals of the past decade have highlighted the importance of risk management organization, systems, policies, procedures, and behavior. The combination of larger investment positions, leverage, derivatives, and market volatility have made billion-dollar losses by banks, institutional investors, and hedge funds all too common. Often, the cause is a risk management system that failed to adequately control risk.

Several chapters address the organization of risk management for two of the most important actors in the international investment arena: institutional investors and hedge funds. In "Institutional Use and Control of the Investment Process," Todd Petzel provides a detailed set of elements of a risk management program for institutional investors. He points out that an effective program needs to be implemented in the context of the institution's risk and investment objectives. He also highlights a number of investment pitfalls that are often overlooked by institutional investment managers.

INTERNATIONAL INVESTMENTS, ASSET ALLOCATION, AND PORTFOLIO DIVERSIFICATION

Roger Gibson and Vinod Chandrashekaran explore international investment from the standpoint of asset allocation and portfolio optimization. They seek to answer the question of what role international investment plays in an optimal investment portfolio. Mr. Gibson uses asset allocation analysis to show the essential role of international investment in an investment portfolio. His analysis uses a longer-time horizon than many investors to make his argument that international investments do fulfill a significant role in improving the asset allocation of portfolios. Mr. Chandrashekaran advocates the use of a systematic approach to portfolio construction as a risk management tool. He examines the use of marginal contribution analysis and optimal portfolio construction as aids to quantitative risk management.

RISK MANAGEMENT STRATEGIES AND TECHNIQUES

These describe the leading approaches to global investment risk management. Two themes emerge overall. The first involves the abundance and diversity of risk management strategies that are now available to portfolio managers. The second is the extent to which the continuous crises in global investments have caused us to rethink and rework these strategies.

Currency Risk Management

As Ray Dalio points out in Hedging Currency Risk, one gets two exposures from international investments: the underlying asset and the currency. Currency risk has a stronger effect on foreign bonds than on foreign stocks because bond markets are less volatile than stock markets. There has probably been more ink spilt on the pros and cons of currency hedging for investment portfolio than most other topics in international finance. Mr. Dalio provides a trenchant review of the rationale behind currency hedging and the relevant benchmarks and decision criteria that need to be analyzed.

In Management of Currency Fluctuations Associated with International Investments, Mr. Ranga Nathan analyzes the impact of currency fluctuations on overall investment returns. He then examines the conditions under which a currency overlay program is warranted. Finally, he describes methods of measuring the effectiveness of active overlay programs.

Ira Kawaller looks at the use of derivatives in Hedging the Currency Exposure of a Nondollar Portfolio. His discussion focuses on the currency risks and opportunities afforded by the euro, a topic that is only beginning to be addressed by funds managers.

Country Risk Analysis

In the 1970s and early 1980s, country risk analysis was the pre-dominant tool for managing international lending and invest-ment risks. The emerging country debt crisis of the 1980s, which most country rating programs failed to predict, reduced the use-fulness of these programs for decision-makers. However, the events of this decade, which clearly have country risk factors as their focus, have led to a resurgence of country risk analysis. However, the contagion and volatility of the 1990s seemed to spare few countries, no matter how high their risk ratings. As the IMF reported in September 1998, "Sound management of fiscal and monetary policies provides no guarantee against major eco-nomic crises."

David T. Beers provides a comprehensive introduction to the Standard & Poor's sovereign credit ratings, which cover local and foreign currency debt issued by governments in 77 countries. The ratings use both quantitative and qualitative factors to capture economic and political risk. An important distinction is made between *economic risk,* which addresses the government's ability to repay its obligations, and *political risk,* which addresses the sov-ereign's willingness to repay debt.

Value at Risk for Asset Managers

One of the few truly new risk management tools to have come along in the past decade is value at risk (VaR). It has now become widely accepted by banks, institutional investors, government regulatory agencies, and central banks as the most promising starting point for market risk measurement. Along with stress testing and scenario analysis, VaR promises to become more widely used in the future.

However, VaR is also one of the most misunderstood techniques. Christopher L. Culp, Ron Mensick and Andrea M.P. Neves provide an introduction to VaR in their chapter, Value at Risk for Asset Managers. They then discuss the use of VaR to monitor managers, portfolios, and hedging programs; define a formal system of risk targets, and implement a risk budget.

The Uses of Derivatives in Investment Risk Management

Derivatives are widely used to hedge the market risk of domestic investments. However, their use is more limited in the international sphere because of the limited number of instruments available, their lack of liquidity, and their expense.

However, the volatility of the markets has led to great strides, especially in the use of derivatives to hedge equity risk in developed markets. Joanne Hill and Maria Tsu address these issues in their chapter, Equity Derivatives Strategies and Risk Management.

Relative Value Strategies and Investor Psychology

It is perhaps incongruous to place relative value strategies in the hedge section of this book, given the losses suffered by Long Term Capital Management, a major user of this approach. However, relative value (or market neutral) strategies have a long heritage as risk management tools. They use the relationship between two or more instruments whose value is related through price correlation as a reinforcing hedge, which at times is highly effective.

In my own chapter, entitled Trading Risks in International Investments—Why Market-Neutral Strategies, I describe the application of relative value strategies and focus on a main threat to this type of strategy: investor psychology, especially as it relates to the risk perception and risk tolerance of investors.

EMERGING MARKETS AND THE LESSONS OF THE PRESENT CRISIS

Each crisis in international investments reveals a new set of risks and the present crisis is no exception. This section describes the crisis in the emerging markets in the context of the lessons learned for risk management strategies. Richard Johnston, in his chapter on Managing Global Emerging Markets Risk, details the risks of investing in emerging countries and some implications for risk management.

Boom and Bust of Emerging Markets

While the proximate cause of the Asian crisis and its aftermath will be debated for a long time to come, the major outlines are relatively clear. Between 1985 and 1995, Asia enjoyed dramatic economic growth fueled by hundreds of billions of dollars in foreign capital inflows which reached a high of $300 billion in 1996. Unfortunately, this growth was accompanied by sharp increases in stock and land prices; increases in short-term borrowing from abroad, much of it in foreign currencies; and the allocation of capital to nonproductive projects, the result of "crony capitalism."

After the mid-1990s a series of external shocks (the devaluation of the Chinese remnimbi and the Japanese yen and the slowdown in growth of the Japanese economy) led to deteriorating external accounts and overvalued currencies in Asia. There is a real difference of opinion as to the cause of the subsequent spread of the crisis. One school points to a "crisis mentality" and changing perception of risk among investors as the major cause of the crisis. An alternative view blames the weaknesses in Asia's financial system and crony capitalism, in which implicit government guarantees against failure removed incentives for effective risk management by many actors.

In Asia Questions Risk, Michael J. Howell makes a subtle and original argument that liquidity matters most in determining the value of stock markets in emerging markets. In the 1990s, this growth in liquidity was greatly magnified by foreign capital inflows that led to "regional overproduction, which was exacerbated by a demand slowdown in Japan and China."

Then Richard Johnston presents an overview of the risk of investing in Latin America in his chapter, Managing Latin American Investment Risk. In his discussion of risk management strategies, Johnston points out that derivatives have only limited use in this region. Instead, he argues for a full understanding and close monitoring of fundamental risks and appropriate asset allocation decisions to control risk.

New Risks Emerge

One of the interesting facets of financial crises is their revelation of new risks (or newly important risks). The present crisis has given us at least two examples. First, there is *contagion risk*, in which seemingly unrelated countries (at least from a trade and investment standpoint) nonetheless suffer from a related crisis. For example, the currency devaluation in Thailand in July 1997 caused a tidal wave that affected all markets within a matter of months. Contagion risk has two main effects: (1) it increases the correlation of movements among markets around the world, and (2) it increases the volatility and duration of market movements.

The term moral hazard refers to the risk that investors, creditors, and debtors will make decisions on the (false) belief that a safety net exists in the form of a lender of last resort to cover their losses should they make a mistake. The argument is often used that the Asian crisis was at least partly a result of the expansion and misallocation of credit, based on the assumption that banks, local governments, OECD nations, and the IMF would provide a safety net. There were three notable outcomes of these assumptions: higher capital inflows and loans; lower interest rates; and a reduction in due diligence and credit analysis. In other words, moral hazard risk led to a breakdown of effective risk management at many levels of the global financial system.

Exchange Rate Regimes

The world has experienced three waves of speculative attacks on fixed exchange rate regimes recently: the European Monetary System (EMS) crisis of 1992–1993, the Mexican meltdown and "tequila hangover" of 1994–1995, and the "Asian flu" of 1997–1998. Steven Hanke discusses recent trends and proposed remedies for the risky currency market in a chapter called Financial Meltdowns and Exchange Rate Regimes. Mr. Hanke raises the question of whether the free flow of funds and full currency convertibility are necessarily the best course for emerging markets.

Perhaps the greatest lapse in risk management was the massive borrowing by all actors and investors in local currencies without foreign exchange hedges. This was based on the belief that pegged exchange rates were equivalent to government guarantees against currency devaluation. After devaluation, these actors become insolvent, negating the supposed boost to exports of currency devaluation.

To some extent, the story of the past decade has been a reciprocal relationship between the emerging and industrial nations in which the latter provided capital and technology and the former adopted the capitalist economic model, including the removal of controls on capital movements. As long as the emerging markets experienced rapid growth and an improved standard of living, this tradeoff worked. However, the severe setback of 1997 and 1998 continues to threaten a backlash; witness the renewed interest in *capital controls and currency intervention.*

One of the arguments for currency intervention and currency boards revolves around the extent to which countries that stood outside the free flow of money (especially China and India) were able to avoid contagion. Also important is the price they have paid for this avoidance.

One of the most powerful arguments for a currency board flows from John Maynard Keynes' observation in 1923 that a nation can only have two of the following three things: free movement of capital, fixed exchange rates, and independent monetary policy. Countries that tried all three failed. Most recently, South Korea, Thailand, Malaysia, and Indonesia have failed and wound up with devalued currencies and high interest rates. Currency boards are an attempt to allow a nation to pursue an independent monetary policy while fixing exchange rates.

CHAPTER 2

Institutional Use and Control of the Investment Process

Todd E. Petzel
Executive Vice President and Chief Investment Officer
Commonfund
Westport, Connecticut

Institutional investors are, in theory, very different from other individuals in their outlook and approach to the world markets. Pension funds and endowments are supposed to be very long-lived institutions, unaffected by the life-cycle considerations that affect most investors. They are also primarily oriented toward investing, making it much more likely that they will have access to the best tools and information with which to manage these funds.

Does this change their behavior? In many ways it does, but in other ways the individual decision makers behind this institutional money suffer from many of the same human failings that characterize most investment activity. This chapter describes the objectives and tools of the institutional money manager and then outlines some of the key elements of a risk management program for an institutional investor. Along the way, many potential pitfalls will be identified.

INVESTMENT TOOLS

Pension funds and endowments have slightly different investment objectives. An endowment has an infinite time horizon, and its objective is to help supply resources to the university or foundation it supports. It is a rare academic institution that collects all of its revenue from its endowment, and it is more often the case that the endowment supplies less than 10 percent of the school's operating budget.

Pension assets have a much more dedicated purpose. In defined contribution plans, there is no other source of wealth. In other plans, there is the possibility that substandard investment returns could be augmented by additional firm contributions, but the general expectation is that each program should be self-sustaining. This makes pension funds different from most endowment programs in that the liability side of the equation is much clearer. Total return to meet the obligations to the retirees must be secured.

Despite these differences, there are many more similarities. Neither fund should be terribly affected by short-term volatility. Both funds should be invested primarily in equities. The long-term orientation of the investments opens up the possibility of placing less liquid securities in the portfolio and consequently earning a premium from this illiquidity.

Institutional investors were among the first participants in hedge, private capital, and venture capital funds. They recognized the virtue of diversification, while attempting to enhance returns with these less popular strategies. As pioneers with these strategies, institutional investors also began to become familiar with their potential risks.

The core of any institutional investor portfolio is still comprised of marketable stocks and bonds. A generation or two ago, a typical U.S. portfolio would consist in its majority of government bonds and high-grade corporate debt mixed with large-cap U.S. stocks. There was a belief that one could spend the "income," which led portfolios to be overweighted in fixed income due to the generally higher interest rates relative to dividend yields.

It was not until the concept of total return was widely accepted that this began to change. It is hard for many people to imagine that total return was ever a new concept, but for many plans well into the 1970s and 1980s there was a clear distinction between capital gains, which could not be spent, and income, which could. As more and more institutions built spending rules based on a percentage of their endowments' value, there was no logical reason to stay overweighted in bonds.

Optimizations and simulations became relatively common-place tools to analyze the expected risk and return of a portfolio. As more analysis was applied to the problem, it became clear that long-term institutional investors should have a decided tilt toward equities. Throughout the 1980s and 1990s the share of equities in institutional portfolios climbed.

As portfolios shifted more toward equities, questions were raised about how the efficiency of the portfolio could be further improved. Since liquidity needs are not high for all the portfolio of an endowment or pension fund, the opportunity to diversify into less-liquid nonmarketable securities existed. Institutional investors were among the first, along with high-wealth individuals, to explore the areas of hedge funds, private capital, and other nontraditional asset classes.

Hedge funds first appeared as limited partnerships designed to appeal to sophisticated investors who wanted to exploit the stock evaluation skills of the manager. The theory was simple. In the course of analyzing stocks, managers would find both good stocks and bad stocks. A traditional manager would be constrained to buy only the good stocks, while avoiding the bad stocks. Why not use all the information? Buy the good companies, sell short the bad, and collect "alpha" in both directions. In the process, the short position would provide a cushion against market declines. Hence the name, hedge funds.

Since these simple beginnings, the notion of a hedge fund has really outgrown its name. Hedge fund managers still largely employ partnership structures, but the range of investment strategies varies widely. Long and short strategies are still the bedrock of the approach, but no longer are managers constrained to marketable securities or even equity-based strategies.

Today, there literally are as many styles of hedge funds as there are creative managers. Some are quite conservative long/ short equity managers with limited leverage, whereas others take highly levered macro bets on currencies, interest rates and sometimes even commodities. As the experience of the third quarter of 1998 showed, some funds that were taking what they perceived to be low-risk positions found themselves in uncharted territory and with significant losses. Belatedly, some institutional investors learned that it is vitally important to look behind the return numbers to determine what really is going into the portfolios.

The other instance of active diversification came in the area of private and venture capital. Public participation in these programs remains limited, but institutional investors have come to discover that dedicating a small part of their portfolios to these investments can produce significant additional return, while also providing good diversification benefits. Illiquid investments should carry a premium for that illiquidity, and who is in a better position to reap these returns than long-lived pensions and endowments?

A small number of institutional investors have begun to explore other alternatives as well. Long-only commodity plays are designed to be an inflation hedge. Some of these investments come in the form of structured notes based on a commodity index. Others are more-focused strategies involving oil and gas, or timberland. Actively managed futures accounts are used by some in much the same way as hedge funds. The desire is to have returns based on the expertise of the managers and to enjoy those returns at times when other asset classes may be doing poorly.

RISK MANAGEMENT

Know Your Objectives

There are many challenges associated with executing an institutional investment program. Primary among them is the clear articulation of an investment perspective. Whether talking about the entire portfolio or a single strategy within it, the first step is to identify one's objectives in terms of expected return and tolerable risk.

Most institutional investors approach this task with a variety of tools derived from modern portfolio theory. As previously mentioned, portfolio optimizers and simulators allow for an analytical game of "what if." Asset classes can be combined in various ways to estimate how the portfolio will behave over different time horizons. As long as the future generally approximates the past, these tools can provide very helpful descriptions.

The biggest challenge in using any of these tools is assessing the reasonableness of the assumptions behind the models. It may seem obvious that the expected return and risk assumptions are critical parameters driving the outcomes. But perhaps more subtle is the covariance matrix of returns, which can produce the result that a high-risk, low-return asset is a good investment as long as it is sufficiently uncorrelated (or better yet, negatively correlated) with the other asset groups.

Here, historical statistics over a very long period are quite useful. If possible, one should make sure that observations are obtained over several full market cycles. But after the analysis is done on historical data, it is also useful to ask the question, "What if these data are wrong?" In particular, at times of great stress in the markets, correlations between asset classes tend to increase. A useful exercise is to rerun the optimizer or simulator after raising the correlations between all asset classes. If the projected optimum mix is decidedly different, it is a red flag that your model is not stable and the projections should be taken with a grain of salt.

Once there is a degree of consistency in the model's output, it is possible to target an asset mix that accords with one's risk/return preferences. Knowing the right amount of risk is one of the hardest problems of the institutional investor. For a pension fund, one has a good idea of the liability side of the equation, making the estimation of the probability of shortfall a little easier. But for endowments, there is a less formal link between the asset and liability sides. Trustees want endowments to grow over a very long time horizon, but as long as the demands on the endowment are somewhat nebulous, it is hard to determine just how much risk is appropriate.

Know Your Investments

Setting target objectives is tough enough. But the next step can be even harder, and that is really knowing the investments within the asset mix. Large cap U.S. stocks seem easy, but what is the beta of the portfolio? Does the manager favor a momentum, growth style, or is he a bottom-up, value-stock picker? If outside managers are used, it is usually a good idea to diversify across managers, but only if there are gains from diversification. Picking two or three managers who are essentially doing the same thing does nothing but maximize fees.

Moving beyond simple stock portfolios, the task of knowing the investments becomes more challenging. A bond portfolio needs to be checked for duration, convexity, and any implied options that would make the convexity relationship potentially unstable. If anything in the previous sentence is not readily identifiable, then the investor would do well to enlist the aid of a qualified consultant to assist in evaluating the portfolios. Great mistakes were made in early 1994 by people who thought they owned simple bond and mortgage portfolios but found they had implicitly written options that cost them millions of dollars when interest rates jumped.

Additional complications arise when investors use derivatives. Here, the nature of the payoffs under all possible outcomes must be known. Are the risks linear, or do they change with different possible outcomes? Is leverage a necessary, or even desirable, part of the investment? What collateral is being posted by the counterparties to secure performance? How often is the position marked to market, and in what form will calls for additional collateral be made? Are all the counterparties creditworthy, and what can be done to monitor this on an ongoing basis?

If one has nontraditional assets in the portfolio, additional complications arise. Private partnerships used to invest in private and venture capital typically are structured as limited liability vehicles that limit the amount of investors' potential losses. But they often couple limited liability with limited liquidity by demanding a lockup period for the investment. Hedge funds also use this mechanism, and many of those programs are very reluctant to divulge the investments being made. A black box can be very profitable, but the investor must satisfy himself that the hedge fund manager is investing in a way consistent with the overall risk/return profile, or take the chance of being surprised when adversity strikes the portfolio.

Increasingly, institutional investors are demanding—and receiving—more transparency in these portfolios. This is another example of how the sophistication of institutional investors is growing. Rare today is the institutional money manager who is completely content to hand over assets to an outside manager and not stay on top of the investment strategy and execution.

This is not to say that the investor directs the investments. When this happens, it makes for a very bad relationship between the outside manager and the investor. The act of hiring a manager should define a division of labor. The manager manages and the investor oversees. If there is ever a significant gap between performance and expectation, the relationship should be terminated, but this gap should be based on a very complex set of criteria that extends well beyond simple returns. An investor who terminates a manager for "bad performance" without knowing what the strategy was or how effectively it was being pursued probably was predestined for disappointment.

Get Prices Right

Getting accurate prices on all the investments in a portfolio can be a daunting task. One should be completely comfortable only with the prices of liquid marketable equities, bonds, and exchange-traded derivatives. Everything else needs to be closely examined and checked, if possible, against secondary sources.

Usually the safest source of good pricing data is your custodian. Large-scale, world-class custodians are forced to deal with an extremely wide array of securities, and that fact requires them to have access to accurate bids in most markets. They also have the ability to compare data from many managers and brokers, which helps them identify potential problems. But even the best custodians don't get all the prices exactly right.

One might suppose that the manager has an incentive to see that the portfolio is accurately priced. This may be true in the long run, but in the short run there are many temptations leading to deviation from this rule. From direct incentive pay to the indirect marketing benefits of having high valuations, there are ample reasons for a manager to not want to knock down the price of less liquid items in the portfolio. In these cases, it is incumbent upon the investor to scrutinize the valuations closely.

Perhaps the most obvious case of pricing difficulties happened in February 1994, when, after a rapid run-up in interest rates, the Granite Fund posted a profit. Practically every other fixed-income fund posted a loss that month, and upon closer inspection, it seems the Granite Fund should have too. This fund had taken on a complicated set of spread trades involving mortgage tranches, and had then applied leverage.

In its prospectus to potential investors, Granite disclosed that it would be trading in sometimes very illiquid securities for which bids were sometimes unavailable. At such times, the fund reserved the right to evaluate the portfolio according to theoretical prices based on its proprietary formulas. This is known as *marking to model* as compared to *marking to market*. In February 1994 the entire interest rate world came tumbling down, and the mortgage investments in which Granite invested were particularly hard hit. With bids evaporating, Granite exercised its option to use its model and for a month reported that it was prospering. A month later, the entire $600 million invested in the fund was gone.

In such cases, the institutional investor should have the wherewithal to get better information. The first red flag should have been the nature of the portfolio, with the leverage in less liquid securities. This is a warning signal that prices of these instruments must be watched closely. The second and most obvious warning signal came from the aberrant returns in a single month. When every fund in the world is losing money except one, hard questions should be asked. A savvy investor might have been able to avoid the problems if the pricing questions had been identified early (and if the terms of the partnership allowed relatively easy withdrawals).

As one moves to nonmarketable securities that are in partnerships with long lockups, the situation changes a bit. While it is always better to have accurate readings on prices, the benefit here is minimal compared to marketable securities. On an investment that has eight more years of a lockup, it is virtually useless to spend any time determining whether your fund has an internal rate of return of 6 percent or 7 percent for the last quarter. The total return will be determined by the flow of funds back to the investor and not on some interim mark. By entering into such partnerships, one is implicitly agreeing to these terms. Investors who are disturbed by these features probably should not have these investments in their portfolios.

Off-exchange derivatives pose yet another set of pricing problems. Swaps and off-exchange options can be highly customized, and it is mandatory that the terms of these deals be completely understood or the pricing will be suspect. One should never rely completely on one's counterparties for the evaluation of an off-exchange derivatives deal. They may represent a major, multinational bank or broker and have vast capabilities in this area, but they are also on the other side of the trade. Marking these derivatives to market, especially if the deal contains leverage, is a key line of defense against surprises. Fortunately, as swaps have become more standardized and there is a slowly growing movement toward active collateralization of such deals, getting good prices has become easier. But there is always more to do.

Institutional investors are very different from individual investors in this area of risk management. It is not unreasonable to demand, and receive, sufficiently detailed data so that judgments of pricing can be made. This really is beyond the abilities and resources of most individuals. The biggest errors come on the institutional side when the investors fall prey to the thought that the approach used by individuals is good enough.

Double-Check the Checkers

Even institutional investors have limitations on their resources in risk management. You hire managers, who in turn deal with brokers. These brokers then deal with custodians for some securities and a network of brokers for other investment instruments. At each point in the transaction chain, there are strong incentives for the participants to protect themselves by checking the accuracy of each transaction. However, mistakes and worse do occur, and it is important to look for additional measures of control.

Most funds hire an accounting firm to audit their funds, though in some types of programs this is not required. When institutional investors hire external managers, one of the first things to check is the degree of auditing oversight. Some funds ask their auditors to do a complete census of their investments, checking for the existence and accurate pricing of each investment in the portfolio. Increasingly, however, some audit engagements approach the fund audit by sampling across the fund. Close work is done on a serious percentage of the assets, with the remainder of the time spent verifying the procedures affecting all the assets.

. A priori, one would expect that the census approach is more thorough, but it is also very much more expensive. The statistical approaches have demonstrated their effectiveness in many applications. The choice between the two depends in part on the type of assets being examined. If the funds are invested in marketable equities traded at the NYSE or on the national market and held in custody at a major custodian, there is less likelihood of a problem. Funds that have private transactions or derivatives (especially off-exchange, where there is no clearinghouse) would be more susceptible to problems from a sampling approach.

In every transaction of this type, a certain degree of delegation occurs. How much to rely on auditors is a decision that depends on many factors. The auditor's resources and experience with the type of program under examination is a critical factor. The degree of controls in place at the custodian and broker are also important. In short, there is no easy answer on how much to delegate, but in the end, the fiduciaries need to satisfy themselves that the combination of internal and external resources is more than sufficient to cover the risks of operational error or fraud.

Relying too much on internal staff can be a source of problems, especially if the incentives are not properly aligned. The worst situation occurs when people responsible for trading also are responsible for the operational aspects of the trade. If the traders are also the risk managers, there is ample opportunity for incentives to be grossly distorted. It is important to have clear separation of functions and a reporting chain that provides enough independence so that if problems are identified, they won't be suppressed.

This was most evident when Barings Bank collapsed under the weight of unauthorized trading losses in its Singapore office. There was, at least in principle, a division of labor between the traders and the back office. However, the woman who ran operations was married to the head trader, who in turn oversaw the entire branch office. It seems apparent in retrospect that this was an undesirable arrangement, but at the time Barings had what it perceived was a profitable operation and didn't want to upset the structure in place.

Independent risk managers can add significantly to the ability to check the checkers. In principle, a risk officer should report directly to the CEO or some other high-ranking officer of the company outside the areas of potential risk. This person should be of sufficient seniority that the people in trading and operations cannot "trump" his or her decisions. Like the outside auditor, the risk manager needs to have a clear path to the board of directors in the unlikely event that officers higher in the direct line are the source of the problem.

The old definition of risk manager was fairly narrow and referred to insurance programs. Today, the term has taken on a broader meaning. Present-day risk officers should not be checking every trade ticket or confirmation. Instead, they should be assessing the thoroughness of procedures both inside and outside the company. Since risks can take many forms, it is important to work in investments, operations, marketing, and the legal and regulatory areas. It is also important to instill a culture of risk management in all employees. This is not something that is the exclusive domain of a few specialists. Everyone needs to participate actively in the formulation and execution of sound risk management practices.

At the end of the day, many people inside and outside the firm will be checking for the accuracy and integrity of the investment process. Having checkers for the checkers is a very good way to minimize opportunities for error or fraud. These problems will never be avoided completely, but if they can be identified early in the process, the likelihood of significant damage will be small.

Simulate Risks

The most important thing any investor can do is ask the question, "What can go wrong?" Most individuals are fairly limited in their analytical abilities to attack this question in detail, but there is still a purpose to be served in fitting investments with expectations and risk tolerance. For the institutional investor, there are many tools to help with this task.

Value-at-risk (VaR) models have been used by the trading community for many years now as a convenient way to measure exposures on a trading desk or firm-wide level. VaR relies on historical relationships of returns and correlations to estimate how big a loss one might expect, say, 5 percent of the days in a year. It does this by running the portfolio through a simulator based on past events and looking at the distribution of returns.

VaR is a powerful tool in that it looks at the risk of a portfolio with all of its subtle interactions across investments. It has allowed many large trading firms to more accurately assess risks, deploy capital, and identify trading areas that could not be justified based on risk-adjusted returns. Designed for such trading firms, it has more recently been applied to investment portfolios with long horizons.

Extending VaR to portfolios has its own issues that go well beyond the scope of this chapter. However, it is easy to see that a system built to assess one-day risks has to be modified somewhat to ask questions about portfolios over a quarter or a year. Because of autocorrelation within time series and shifting cross-correlations across asset classes, it is not possible to simply extrapolate from a database of daily returns. Either strong assumptions have to be made or the analysis has to be repeated using weekly, monthly, and quarterly returns to identify possible discrepancies.

Even after that is done, the results of a VaR analysis are not really complete. One might receive a strong indication that one could lose at least X dollars 5 percent of the time, but there is no real clue as to what the ultimate downside might be. There is always benefit in asking the question, "How much can I lose?"

An example from the early part of the decade is illustrative. For many years in the late 1980s and early 1990s, groups of European nations worked to keep their currencies in alignment, hoping to lay the groundwork for a common European currency. Exchange rates could move within a narrow band, but if they drifted too far, central banks would act in the market to put things back on target.

If the system of currency links was going to work in the long run, macroeconomic policies for the countries would have had to be more coordinated than in fact they were. Interest rates varied across countries, and investors tried to exploit this. For example, people would buy Italian bonds and then turn around and hedge the dollar/lira currency risk by selling D-marks forward.

Why D-marks? Because with lower interest rates in Germany, the cost of hedging in the cross currency was lower than hedging against lira directly. As long as the two currencies moved in tandem according to the policy, the strategy would work.

It didn't. Despite months of statistical evidence that showed the lira and D-mark closely linked, in August and September of 1992, the system broke apart. The world recognized that the lira was overvalued relative to the D-mark. Italian interest rates jumped as their currency fell. Short positions in D-marks also lost money. In short, all the possible trades went bad. The statistical hedge fell apart badly, and many hundreds of millions of dollars were lost.

Looked at through the VaR lens, these trades looked very low-risk. After all, for many years these relationships had been in place. Only when there was a shift by the European central banks away from defending unreasonable exchange rates were the risks fully known. By then it was too late for these investors, but it might not have been if they had used a bit more foresight.

After completing a VaR analysis, the investors might then have asked what else beyond their statistical experience could happen to these trades. In particular, since the currency bands were a political construction, it would have been logical to ask what would happen if the political winds shifted. In such an environment, it is not necessary to guess the probability of the event, but only to assess the impact if it occurred. If those "what if" games had been played, it is possible that these positions might not have been established, or would have been established on a more modest scale.

Many other examples of similar events can be described. In 1994, when interest rates moved quickly up by 200 basis points, few statistical models predicted the impact of such a large move. In the third quarter of 1998, some hedge fund managers placed highly leveraged bets on the basis of statistical relationships, which promptly blew up when Russia defaulted on its debt and credit spreads around the world expanded beyond those seen in many years. The funds that survived were those that had simulated much worse events than had previously been experienced and kept the risk to reasonable levels.

The conclusion here is that statistical modeling can be a powerful tool to assess risk in a portfolio, but it should not be the only tool. Simulating extreme events, in essence, stress-testing the portfolio, supplements the statistical modeling and gives another way to evaluate risk. In the end, those portfolios that have prepared themselves for extreme, low-probability events should be in better shape when periods of extreme volatility surface.

INVESTMENT PITFALLS

The section above on risk management gives guidance for institutional investors in several general areas. It does not, however, talk about common pitfalls in the investment practice that fall somewhat outside the traditional definition of risk management. This section just as easily could have been labeled "Keep a Healthy Skepticism," because in each of the subsections below, the pitfall comes from being too trusting.

Don't Buy on Reputation Alone

Possibly the easiest pitfall for any investor to succumb to is to hire a manager or buy a security based on the reputation of the person recommending it. This is just as true for institutional investors as it is for individuals, but it is less forgivable for the former. Institutional investors should have the resources for the due diligence necessary to go beyond a well-placed recommendation.

Examples of errors of this type abound, and they date back as far as one wants to explore. Tulip bulbs in the seventeenth century and fictional parcels of Louisiana in the nineteenth century were sold to middle- and upper-class citizens with the justification that other smart (and rich) people were doing it. In more recent times, New Era was marketed as an investment fund combined with a charitable enterprise. It was in fact a Ponzi scheme. Scores of reputable institutions were taken in by it, largely on the basis of the quality of the investor list.

The institutional investor can and should use every source of information available to him or her. This includes recommendations from others who have a demonstrated track record in the area. However, it is essential to remember that no matter how smart others are, it is the fiduciaries of a fund who have the responsibility to their investors. If funds are lost because of a lack of due diligence, it will be little comfort that other reputable people took losses too.

Don't Follow the Numbers

When is the time to go into an asset class or to hire an individual manager? For institutional investors with a long horizon, the answer is probably when it is most out of favor. Buying silver in 1980 at $40 an ounce as a hedge against inflation was probably at the opposite end of this spectrum. It typifies the kind of momentum investing that almost invariably leads to substandard returns. Yet people persist in wanting to follow the numbers.

In the early 1990s, emerging markets had very little following, and as these markets matured and the underlying economies grew, fantastic annual returns were recorded for several years. By 1994 the word had gotten out, and hundreds of millions of dollars came pouring in. At first it worked, and the new money bid equity prices up even higher in these countries. Eventually, however, the reality of good, but not astonishing, growth came home to rest and the markets retreated. In 1997 and 1998 many emerging markets struggled, and returns were strongly negative.

Does that mean 1998 was the time to buy? It may have been if there was fundamental growth potential available for these countries. What is more obvious, however, is that by 1993, there was way too much capital chasing too little true value, and stock prices in many markets had reached extreme levels. The suggestion here is not that one should avoid all active markets. Rather, it is an admonition that investing well after a run has started tilts the risk/return ratio well toward the risk side.

Similar admonitions exist for hiring managers, but here the analytics are much harder. Suppose a manager has beaten his benchmark for three straight years and rests squarely at the top of the peer-group rankings. It is very tempting to attribute all the performance to skill and expect this performance to continue. However, another hypothesis could be that the manager tilts a certain way within the stated style (tech stocks, for example, among large-cap growth stocks), and that the tilt has been in

favor recently. The question then becomes whether the manager
will tilt away at the right time when the substyle falls out of favor
or persist and suffer poor performance.

A good example of this comes from high-yield bond managers after 1994. As credit spreads narrowed in U.S. junk bonds,
some managers reached for incremental yield by adding a significant percentage of emerging market debt to their portfolios. In
fact, virtually all the "top" managers in 1997 participated in this
trend. If one had invested based solely on the numbers, one
would have been positioned to get really hurt when Russia
defaulted on its debt in August of 1998.

Great numbers can also mask great risk. There isn't a manager in existence who will step up to the plate and say, "I just took
some really big bets last year, and they all came in." Instead, the
story is always about how thoughtful the analysis was behind
the returns. When looking at manager returns, one should examine the big gains just as critically as the big losses. Sometimes
the big gains are simply huge bets that worked, and in the future,
that might not always be the case. Keep a skeptical eye on all
performance.

It is critical to look behind the numbers and decide what is
driving the returns. Separating skill from luck is the hardest task
in evaluating managers. One will never be successful doing it if
all the emphasis is on recent performance. It sounds counterintu-
itive, but you might do better looking among the managers whose
styles are out of favor, with the understanding that most approaches ebb and flow through time.

Don't Shift Your Time Reference

There is a great temptation to take one's eye off the relevant ball.
For long-term investors like pensions and endowments, this often
means trying to time the market based on short-term variation in
the market. If one is a day trader, it is suicidal to accept losses on
the theory that the position will straighten out in a few days or
weeks. It is equally foolish for endowments to shift across asset
classes every few months or quarters.

Market timing requires two right decisions: when to get in
and when to get out. Most investment committees of endowments

meet only a few times a year, and it would be remarkable if all the critical decision points coincided with the meeting dates. There are many professional staffs of pension funds who are given authority to make asset shifts at their discretion, but this is the exception rather than the rule in the world of endowments.

Even when there are full-time staffs, the track record is mixed. Some studies show that more than 90 percent of the inter-fund variation in return can be traced to long-term asset alloca-tion. Individual security selection and market-timing decisions contribute very little. In such a world, the expected incremental gain is modest at best.

But one should not lose sight of the potential costs. Every time a portfolio is sold and another is bought, costs are incurred. These can range from less than 100 basis points to more than 200 basis points, depending on the assets being traded. It is extremely expensive to transition international stock, and great emphasis should be placed on trying to minimize these expenses.

The endowment or pension fund that shifts into a trading mode will likely find itself with a few right market calls, a few wrong ones and massive transaction costs. It is better to spend one's effort determining the best long-term mix and staying with it. Market volatility is always a potential distraction, but it is a distraction that should be avoided.

Don't Fail to Oversee the Managers

This may seem obvious, but a common failing is to be lulled into a false sense of security by good returns. A management process that relies too heavily on returns as a determinant of oversight activity will probably be disappointed at some point.

One investment committee chairperson I know, who is ex-tremely knowledgeable about the business, did most of the man-ager selection for the school endowment. The staff at the school had many responsibilities other than oversight of managers. Collectively, they relied on the numbers and word of mouth to stay on top of managers.

One of their managers was a well-known large-cap manager, who had a solid track record. One day, the investment committee chairperson read in the paper that this manager was sitting on almost 50 percent cash, because valuations in the market were high and the manager couldn't really find anything to buy.

The manager was fired from the account because there was an expectation that the account would generally be fully invested. The school had hired a stockpicker, and not a market timer. The chairperson felt very satisfied with the process.

But it wasn't as good as it could have been, and it could have been a lot worse. First, the system of oversight relied on triggers from the returns data, which the committee didn't see more often than quarterly. If the manager had performed adequately in the short term, there may have been no inquiry as to the source of the returns. It is almost certainly the case that if the chairperson hadn't read about the manager in the paper, no inquiry would have been made.

The kind oversight that needs to be exercised on a continuing basis is pretty boring stuff. Look at the stocks versus the guidelines. Check the cash in the portfolio. Look for concentrated positions. Such oversight is boring because portfolios don't change all that quickly, but they can and do change. The school in the case just described was fortunate that the manager made such a big move into cash that it made the papers. A more likely event is "style drift" that remains undetected for quarters until significant losses pile up. Ongoing oversight must be part of the process.

Avoid the Illusion of Liquidity

The third quarter of 1998 brought this message home dramatically. Many markets appear liquid when they are going up. Buyers and sellers interact easily and transactions of considerable size can be absorbed without difficulty. But this is not always the case. At times of market stress, liquidity shrinks dramatically, adding additional stress to short-run positions. If significant leverage is applied, the problem is amplified, because calls for additional collateral can force trades earlier than is desired.

Long Term Capital Management (LTCM) was a victim of this illusion in 1998, just as the practitioners of portfolio insurance were in October of 1987. Dynamic market strategies almost always have as an underlying assumption the ability to enter or exit the market near a specific target. When liquidity dries up, the assumption fails.

Institutional investors can actually use this to their advantage. The long-term perspective of their investments allows them to ride out liquidity problems and perhaps even to add to their portfolios at bargain-basement prices. The pitfall to avoid is investing with managers who overestimate the liquidity in their markets, use too much leverage, or underestimate the sensitivity of their portfolios to liquidity concerns. Solving this problem goes back to the discussion above about really knowing one's investments.

SUMMARY

Risk management for institutional investors is not significantly different from sound practice for traders or other investors. The long-term orientation of the portfolios, however, gives these investors some latitude that others lack. This can be a strong advantage if the institutional investor maintains perspective and a healthy skepticism about all elements of the investment process. There is no recipe to avoid all losses, but a thoughtful, well-executed program can minimize the damage from the inevitable.

Reducing Risk Using Global Bond Diversification

Lee R. Thomas
Managing Director and Senior International Portfolio Manager
Pacific Investment Management Co.
Newport Beach, California

There are two potential reasons for owning foreign bonds. Many investors think that foreign bonds are risky ways of enhancing returns. It is quite the opposite: foreign bonds can reduce risk by diversification, even if you hold a passive portfolio. However, a passive portfolio of foreign bonds will probably not outperform (or underperform) the U.S. market in the long run. In other words, the main reason for holding foreign bonds is the risk reduction you get from strategic diversification. Foreign bonds can reduce the risk of a bond portfolio without reducing its expected return.

Before turning to the strategic arguments for holding foreign bonds—the focus of this chapter—there is another reason for holding foreign bonds, tactical return enhancement. Using foreign bonds opportunistically to enhance return is a question of being in the right foreign market at the right time. In other words, opportunistic use of foreign bonds depends on being able to "find alpha."

Global managers have more opportunity to add alpha than domestic-only investors do. Why? One reason is that if you are managing a global bond portfolio, you have many markets to choose from. Including emerging markets, a global manager can monitor about 30 bond markets around the world. It's hard to imagine that if you look at 30 markets, you are not going to find a single one somewhere that is not mispriced.

There is another reason to believe that global bond managers can consistently find value. Most of the world's bond markets are still dominated by their respective domestic investors. For example, most U.S. bond money is invested in U.S. bonds; most Japanese money is invested in Japanese bonds; and most French bond money goes into French bonds. Most investors are not yet global investors. As a result, yields in different markets may be inconsistent. In other words, global investors stand to profit from the myopia of domestic-only investors.

USING FOREIGN BONDS STRATEGICALLY

To illustrate that foreign bonds can be a diversifying and risk-reducing addition to U.S. portfolios, let's take a look at how a mixed portfolio of U.S. Treasury bonds and foreign bonds would have performed in the past. Figure 3–1 shows the historic return and risk of mixed U.S. and foreign bond portfolios, where the percentage allocated to foreign bonds varies from zero to 100 percent. Frankly, the results for unhedged foreign bonds are discouraging. We know from portfolio theory that diversification should be a potent way to reduce risk. Looking at Figure 3–1, you can see that the risk is least when only about 20 percent of the portfolio is held in foreign bonds. Moreover, the resulting reduction in risk is negligible, compared to buying just the U.S.

You can also see from the chart that historically, foreign bonds did produce a higher total return. However, that certainly does not guarantee that foreign bonds will have a higher return than U.S. bonds during the next 20 years. Historical returns are not good predictors of future returns. You certainly would not want to add foreign bonds to your portfolio just because they beat U.S. bonds during one particular historic period.

The strategic justification for holding foreign bonds is long-run risk reduction, and in terms of risk reduction, the unhedged results in Figure 3–1 are discouraging. The problem is that as you diversify away some of your interest-rate risk, you add a great

F I G U R E   3–1

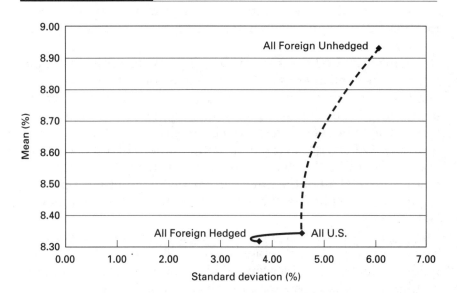

deal of exchange-rate risk to the portfolio. When you replace some U.S. bonds with German bonds, the interest-rate volatility of the portfolio falls because U.S. and German interest rates are not perfectly correlated. Unfortunately, at the same time, you introduce mark exchange-rate risk into the portfolio. When you replace some more U.S. bonds with Japanese bonds, the interest-rate volatility of the portfolio falls again, but again you introduce a new risk to the portfolio, yen exchange-rate risk. This exchange-rate risk accumulates in the portfolio and eventually neutralizes the effect of reduced interest-rate risk. Figure 3–1 shows that this happens when about 20 percent of the portfolio is allocated to foreign bonds. Thereafter, adding more foreign bonds to the portfolio increases its volatility because the added exchange-rate risk overwhelms the risk reduction afforded by diversification.

The problem is that a foreign bond is a package of bundled interest-rate and exchange-rate exposures. For the purpose of diversifying a U.S. portfolio, you want the interest-rate exposure but not the exchange-rate exposure. Exchange-rate risk is like toxic waste, an unwanted byproduct of the diversification process.

Fortunately, it is inexpensive and easy to unbundle foreign bonds' interest-rate and exchange-rate risks and strip away the exchange-rate risks of foreign bonds before using them to diversify U.S. bond portfolios.

Currency-hedged foreign bonds have roughly the same interest-rate exposures as unhedged foreign bonds, but they have negligible exchange-rate risk. Let's repeat the experiment shown in Figure 3–1, but this time using currency-hedged foreign bonds instead of unhedged foreign bonds to diversify the U.S. bond portfolio. Otherwise, everything is the same. There is no active management of either the bonds or the currency. All of the currency is hedged all of the time, and the bonds represent a passive foreign index. As before, the foreign allocation will vary from 0 to 100 percent.

Figure 3–1 helps to show the results of the new experiment. There are two important things to notice. First, the amount of risk reduction that is available, compared to not diversifying your U.S. bond portfolio, is substantial. By diversifying your portfolio into hedged foreign bonds, you can reduce its risk by almost half. That reduction in risk does not involve any reduction in total return. In fact, during this 20 year period, the total return to diversified portfolios was greater than the total return to the U.S.-only portfolio. Be warned however, this should not be taken as a prediction that foreign bonds will outperform U.S. bonds in the future. The second thing to note is that the percentage allocation of foreign bonds that minimizes the portfolio's overall risk is much greater. In Figure 3–2, the risk-minimizing allocation to foreign hedged bonds is substantial, about 80 percent of the portfolio. This is even greater than the foreign allocation in most global bond benchmarks, which is about 65 percent.

Do these findings make economic sense, or are they due to chance alone? Obviously, this question is key, since we are not so much interested in the past as we are in the future. If the results shown in Figure 3–1 are due to chance alone, they should not be expected to repeat going forward.

First, let's consider why diversified portfolios had substantially less risk than the undiversified portfolios in Figure 3–1, at least when the bonds were currency hedged. Diversification worked because U.S. and foreign interest rates were not perfectly

FIGURE 3–2

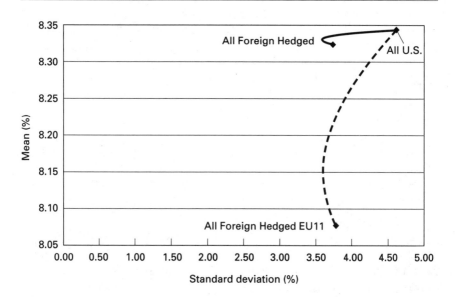

correlated. Going forward, we expect the same. Interest rates are driven by monetary policy and business cycles. One reason the world has adopted flexible exchange rates is to give central banks in different countries monetary autonomy, that is, the ability to control their own monetary policy. Going forward, we expect central bankers to use that autonomy to set local interest rates that are appropriate to local business conditions. Moreover, looking around the world today, there is certainly no reason to think business cycles are becoming more highly synchronized. As of this writing, the U.S. is enjoying a robust expansion; Europe seems to be engineering a modest economic recovery; and Japan is in a recession.

Next, let's think about why the optimal foreign allocation went up so much when we currency-hedged the foreign bonds in the portfolios. Hedged bonds have interest-rate risk but no exchange-rate risk. In contrast, an unhedged foreign bond has interest-rate risk and also exchange-rate risk. In other words, the U.S. bond is the only asset that does not carry exchange-rate risk. Consequently, U.S. investors have a strong incentive to favor U.S. bonds in their portfolios. Currently, hedging the foreign bonds levels the playing field. U.S. investors no longer have reason to favor U.S. bonds. Consequently, it should not be surprising to see the optimal allocation to foreign bonds rise sharply. Going forward, we expect the optimal allocation to foreign bonds to remain much larger in a U.S. investor's portfolio if those foreign bonds are currency-hedged.

WHAT HAPPENS AFTER EMU?

On January 1, 1999, 11 countries in Europe fixed their exchange rates for all time. By mid-2002, their own national currencies will cease to be legal tender, and the new replacement currency, the Euro, will circulate instead. It is widely anticipated that within a few more years, at least four other European countries will join the Euro "club," with still other eastern European countries joining later. This will be one of the most significant financial events ever in Europe, with implications for economic policy, financial markets, and even the balance of world financial power.

The remainder of this chapter focuses on the implications of the introduction of the Euro from the perspective of one narrow group, U.S. bond investors. To this group, the introduction of the Euro will effectively reduce the universe of bond diversification opportunities. The major purpose of the analysis is to assess how important this reduction in diversification is likely to be. The basic methodology will be to simulate what European markets would have looked like as diversification outlets from a U.S. perspective if EMU had happened on January 1, 1986, rather than on January 1, 1999.

SOME POST-EMU CHANGES

Before investigating the specifics of EMU, lets look at what to expect as the Euro comes into being and subsequently, what the likely implications are for European bond markets.

From January 1999 on, all government debts will be issued in Euros, and existing national debt will be redenominated. Bond market conventions and practices will be harmonized, and as a result, the new market for Euro denominated bonds will become more transparent and efficient. At the same time, the relatively large volume of issuance will mean that the new market will be more liquid (recall that all governments will issue in Euros, and that corporate issuers will use the new currency, too, instead of issuing different tranches of bonds in myriad European currencies). Many observers expect the new euro bond market to resemble the U.S. market, with greater depth and diversity, as new kinds of fixed-income instruments such as asset-backed securities are issued.

SOME TECHNICAL ISSUES

One of the objectives of uniform market practices is to encourage increased transparency and efficiency. That is beneficial for U.S. investors. This section summarizes some of the characteristics of the new market.

First, money market instruments will all trade on an actual/ 360 basis, for T+2 settlement. Bonds will trade on an actual/ actual basis, and conventional settlement will be T+3. Prices will be quoted in decimals (admittedly, this will be a disadvantage to investors with 32 fingers).

It is expected that bid/ask spreads will be narrower than the norm today, simply because the average issue sizes will be larger and because there will be more cross-border competition among banks and brokers. Again, this is an advantage to the U.S. investor.

The 11 countries initially entering EMU will account for about one-third of the weight of the standard global benchmarks, the Salomon World Government Bond Index and the J.P. Morgan Global Bond indices. Accordingly, euro denominated sovereign bonds will represent about the same weight in global indices as U.S. bonds do.

To date, it is unclear which of the many European government futures will come to dominate trading in euro denominated bonds or how the basket of deliverable euro bonds will be designed. Since euro bonds issued by different governments are expected to trade at risk and liquidity spreads to each other, and since the spreads will change, this is not a trivial question. Nor is it clear which of the euro bonds will become the benchmark. Some issuers expect the euro swap to eventually play this role.

From the perspective of a U.S. investor, all of the changes detailed above are either positive or at worst neutral. However, there is one major negative factor. In effect, a U.S. investor will have fewer foreign bonds available for diversification. The remainder of the chapter deals with the practical significance of this problem.

EMU AND DIVERSIFICATION

EMU has one obvious consequence: From the perspective of a bond or currency investor, the menu of global diversification choices shrinks. With 11 countries entering EMU initially, the number of foreign bonds available to a U.S. investor will be reduced by nine.[1] One consolation is that for Euro denominated bonds, the remaining bond market is likely to be deeper and broader than many of the government bond markets it replaces. Many new opportunities will be available in euros, including considerably expanded markets for corporate and high-yield bonds, the opportunity to bet on sovereign spreads on Euro bonds issued by the various EMU members, and asset-backed securities. Liquidity will improve. But the conclusion that diversification opportunities will decline seems inescapable. If it is, then there are two implications: (1) the risks of global bond portfolios may rise, and (2) the benefits of global diversification may fall.

Fortunately, the diversification costs of EMU, seen from the perspective of a U.S. investor, may not be as great as one might think. For a start, many European bond markets have already become highly correlated in recent years, so the introduction of the euro may not really reduce the investment universe as much as simply counting the gross number of "lost" countries suggests. More careful study is needed. Moreover, as was mentioned above, many new spread trade opportunities may arise in European bonds with EMU. In addition there are many new European markets—new in the sense of having received little attention to date by most investors—in non-EMU countries such as Poland, Hungary, and the Czech Republic. Finally, a number of EU mem-

---

1. This reduction would ordinarily be 10, but Belgium and Luxemborg are already a monetary union.

bers, such as the UK, Sweden, Greece, and Denmark, are not (at least initially) EMU members, so their bond markets will still be available for diversification.

GLOBAL BOND PORTFOLIO VOLATILITY

All this said, one presumed effect of EMU may be to increase the volatility of global bond portfolios, because they are concentrated in fewer bond markets. To get a sense of how important this effect might be from a U.S. bond investor's perspective, let's consider how things might have been if EMU had occurred a decade ago.

First, we will consider the risk of a typical global portfolio during the past decade (1986–96). We chose a well-known global bond index widely used as a benchmark (the J.P. Morgan Hedged Index). Then we modified the index for the 1986–1996 period to reflect the current EMU of 11 countries. Specifically, we modified the J.P. Morgan index to eliminate the opportunity to diversify into all 11 EMU countries. Instead, we imagined that all 11 countries had been replaced in 1986 by a single monetary union. We chose Germany to play the role of EMU in the J.P. Morgan index because Germany is the most important of the European bond markets. With this modification, we measured what the J.P. Morgan's risk and return would have been from a U.S. investor's perspective, if monetary union had occured in 1986. This will help to show how much reduced diversification would have cost in terms of increased volatility had EMU-11 formed a monetary union in 1986. Note that we ignore the effect of any new spread trading opportunities within EMU, the potential for new markets to develop in European corporate or asset-backed securities, or the beneficial effect of increased liquidity. Moreover, we will also ignore new European bond markets, such as Poland, Hungary, and the Czech Republic. In this sense, the experiment is conservative; it overstates the volatility costs of EMU from lost diversification because it only tells one side of the story. It doesn't consider new opportunities that could enhance diversification opportunities following EMU.

The results are shown in Table 3–1. Notice that the effect of the current EMU of 11 members is negligible if euro volatility

T A B L E   3–1

Simulation of Global Bond Portfolio Volatility, January 1986
to December 1996

	U.S.	JPM	JPM/EMU11 (Adjusted)
Mean	8.3%	8.3%	8.1%
Volatility	4.6%	3.7%	3.8%

turns out to be similar to that of the German market. In fact, in
our experiment the J.P. Morgan hedged global portfolio recorded
a volatility of 3.7 percent from 1986 to 1996. Replacing the EU-11
elements by Germany alone resulted in volatility of 3.8 percent.[2]
In other words, for all practical purposes, the volatilities were
identical. If EMU had happened in 1986 and the resulting Euro
bond market had resembled the German market, then the volatility of the global index would have been unaffected.

   You may also notice that the return for the global index did
fall somewhat, from 8.3 percent to 8.1 percent. This is because
Germany was one of the least attractive European markets to hold
during this period, at least as measured by return alone. Most
European bond yields were converging to German levels, that is,
yield spreads to Germany were falling. As a result, non-German
European markets enjoyed more capital gains than the German
market did. So holding Germany instead of the EU-11 cost a
global investor modestly in terms of return.

GLOBAL DIVERSIFICATION FROM A U.S. INVESTOR'S PERSPECTIVE

All the above experiments show is that the volatility of a global
portfolio is not likely to increase much post-EMU. That does not
prove that the diversification benefits for a U.S. investor will not
decrease. To see how much the benefit of global diversification
could decline for a U.S. investor, we can extend this experiment in

---

2. The difference is not statistically significant.

the following way. Suppose we compare the historic risk and return performance of U.S.-only and globally diversified bond portfolios from 1986 to 1996. We let the foreign component of the portfolio increase from 0 percent (all U.S.) to 100 percent (all foreign) in 10 percent increments.[3] The results are shown in Figure 3–2. An all-U.S. portfolio had a volatility of 4.6 percent; the all-foreign portfolio recorded 3.7 percent (Figure 3–2).

The least risky portfolio contained about 70 percent U.S. bonds and 30 percent foreign bonds, and had volatility of 3.5 percent. Accordingly, by diversifying, a U.S. investor would have reduced his bond portfolio's risk (measured by volatility) by about 24 percent, from 4.5 percent to 3.5 percent.

Now suppose all the EU-11 countries had not been available. That is, we will again assume that the weight of all the EU-11 in the J.P. Morgan non-U.S. bond index is replaced by Germany alone. The result is also shown in Figure 3–2.

As you can see, negligible diversification benefit is lost when 11 European countries are replaced by Germany alone. The least risky portfolio contained about 70 percent U.S. bonds and 30 percentforeign bonds, and had volatility of 3.6 percent. That is, the minimum variance allocation to foreign investments did not change much, nor did the volatility of the resulting portfolio (from 3.5 percent to 3.6 percent).

The major conclusion: Even without much diversity within Europe (and remember that these experiments were conservative), the gains from foreign diversification remain considerable after EMU. In fact, the EMU-restricted set of European bond markets produced almost as much diversification opportunity as the entire J.P. Morgan global index did. Perhaps EMU will not be as important to U.S. bond investors as might have been thought, at least as measured by the reduction in diversification benefits.

What if EMU expands to include the UK, Denmark, Sweden, and Greece (the EMU-15)? Then the minimum risk portfolio would contain about 50 percent U.S. and 50 percent global

---

3. This analysis is presented in detail for earlier time periods in Lee Thomas, "The Performance of Currency Hedged Foreign Bonds," *Financial Analysts Journal*, 1989.

F I G U R E 3–3

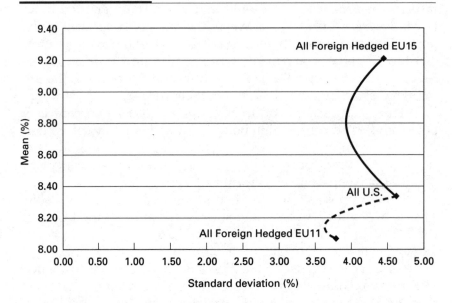

bonds. Its volatility would be 3.9 percent, down by 15 percent from the volatility of a U.S.-only portfolio. The gains from international bond diversification fall, but they remain economically significant. (Figure 3-3.)

CHAPTER 4

The Multiple Dimensions of Global Equity Risk Management—A Practitioner's Perspective

Steven A. Schoenfeld
Head of International Equity Strategies
Barclays Global Investors
San Francisco, California

INTRODUCTION: THE DYNAMIC REALITY OF GLOBAL EQUITY RISK

The last half of the 1990s has witnessed numerous examples of risk impacting the portfolios of global equity market investors. Extreme market volatility, political instability, changes in economic systems, and operational dislocations have all added to the risks that international markets have presented to investors during these turbulent last few years of the century. The Mexican peso crisis of 1994–1995, the sharp drop in the South African rand in 1996, the Asian currency and economic crisis of 1997, de-facto default on sovereign debt by Russia, and the imposition of capital controls by Malaysia in 1998 are all salient examples of some of the macro-level exogenous shocks that hit international equity investors. Yet micro-level changes can have an equally dramatic impact on portfolios, for example, the reduction of restrictions on foreign investors in Korea, Indonesia, the Philippines, and Singapore in 1997, or the treatment of major privatizations

The author gratefully acknowledges the research contribution to the development of this chapter of Binu George, Research Analyst in the International Equity Strategies Group at Barclays Global Investors, and Mark Sodergren, a summer research associate at Barclays in 1998 from the University of Chicago Graduate School of Business.

and cross-border mergers by benchmark index providers in the 1997–1999 period.

Despite these macro- and micro-level risks, cross-border equity investing continues to grow, largely due to the benefits of diversification and potential return enhancement. The simple fact that risks and returns in world markets are not perfectly correlated means that when appropriately diversified, market risk can actually benefit global equity investors. But this risk must be understood, measured, and effectively managed. And other types of risks, primarily operational in nature, are almost never a benefit to investors, and must be either avoided or mitigated.

This chapter provides an overview of the investment risks that a global equity manager must address. It provides numerous examples to illustrate key points, but it makes no attempt to comprehensively detail the myriad country- and security-specific risks present in the world's equity markets. The chapter is designed to be a general overview, from a practitioner's perspective, and is structured using current, real-world examples that large institutional fund managers (such as Barclays Global Investors) face when operating in this asset class. Subsequent chapters of this book address in more detail the various players in the marketplace, the techniques and instruments of risk management, and regional and country-specific risk factors.

The definition of *risk* in a standard dictionary is "the potential likelihood of a loss." This would seem to suggest that it is something to be avoided at all costs. In the world of equity investing, however, not all risks can or should be sidestepped. Risks that arise as a result of a poorly managed investment process should not be tolerated, since they increase the uncertainty of the final outcome without a commensurate improvement in expected return. Also eschewed should be all unsystematic or diversifiable risks, again because they bear no compensation. Systematic risks, however, can be accepted selectively based on their expected return and on their marginal effect on the investor's total portfolio risk.

Furthermore, certain international equity risks, such as currency risk, may in fact deliver a positive element of diversification to a predominantly domestic portfolio. This potential benefit means that, if a developed international equity allocation is not unduly large, it is usually not optimal for the investor to hedge currency exposure.

The various forms of equity market risk can be grouped under two general categories, operational risk and investment risk. Investment managers must identify, quantify, and manage each type of risk within these broad categories. Furthermore, fund management firms must have a dedicated risk management infrastructure designed to supervise the various functional areas' individual risk management efforts. An example of this type of "holistic approach" to risk management is illustrated in Figure 4–1. This diagram illustrates the extensive research and due diligence activity performed by a large global investment manager prior to entering a new emerging market.

OPERATIONAL RISK

Operational risk is the risk associated with the nuts and bolts of the investment process. Often neglected as the less-glamorous relative of investment risk, (which can be modelled quantitatively) it can surface with devastating results. Operational environment risk, trading risk, portfolio management, and systems risk are some of the manifestations of operational risk. Mitigating against operational risks can often help reduce investment performance risk. These are discussed in more detail below.

Operational Environment Risk

Cross-border investing, by definition, adds layers of complexity and risks for portfolio managers. A portfolio manager and an entire firm's infrastructure has to be cognizant of all the aspects of the investing environment in which they operate.

Awareness of all pertinent regulations, such as tax legislation, in nondomestic markets is essential so as not to run afoul of the law and thereby place funds in jeopardy. A close watch must be placed on issues such as dividends, mergers, and spinoffs. Lack of a quick and effective response to these occurences can result in a dilution of the investment value or other actions unfavorable to the investor.

F I G U R E 4–1

Emerging Market Risk Management Process

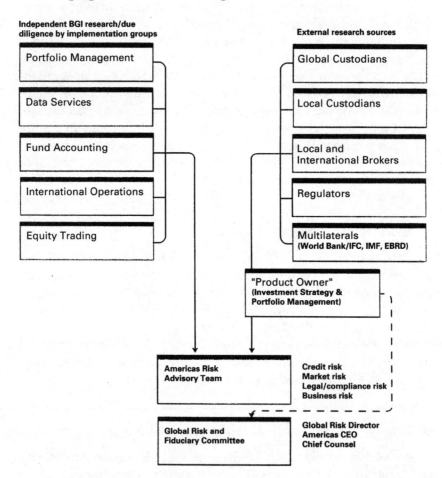

Actions of a more serious nature include loan defaults or unilateral restructuring of contracts by sovereigns. Exchange controls that limit or prevent repatriation are other forms of sovereign risks. The worst possible outcome is outright expropriation and forced nationalization of private assets by the government.

Other operational risk issues include those related to settlement complexity and the custody and safekeeping of assets. As investors have extended their portfolios into emerging markets, these "nuts and bolts" issues have gained prominence.

Operational environment risk can overlap with certain investment risks, such as economic, political, and regulatory risk. Investment managers should not attempt to rigidly separate risk management efforts between operational and investment categories—as the two are often intertwined—especially during extraordinary times, such as with the imposition of capital controls in Malaysia in September 1998. See the *sidebar* on Malaysia for a detailed look at how asset managers were forced to maneuver to adjust to a major change in capital market policy.

Trading Risk

The very first step in implementing the investment decision—the acquisition of the asset—is fraught with risk. The presence of several layers of people and processes between the portfolio manager and the trader on the exchange introduces the possibility of errors in the trade order. These errors can take various forms, such as trading the wrong security, getting the wrong number of shares, and making a purchase instead of a sale. They have to be dealt with by instituting a structure that encourages self-monitoring and includes cross-checks at each step of the process.

Aside from unintentional lapses, there is the very serious and well-known issue of a trader intentionally not achieving the best execution possible for the investor. One example of this is known as *front-running*, in which a trader or broker buys (sells) ahead of an investor's purchase (sale), thus making a profit at the investor's expense. Due to the size and depth of their trades, index fund managers need to be acutely aware of this risk. Another example is when the trader executes a trade without paying careful attention to the price. These problems can be remedied by redesigning the trade process so that the trader's incentives are aligned with those of the investor. One way to do this is to get several competitive bids before the trade and agree on the price beforehand.

A well-executed trade is not very useful if it is not successfully settled. There is always the risk of counterparty default, i.e., the failure to deliver securities purchased or cash for securities sold. This risk is minimized by a system that relies on thorough evaluation and continuous monitoring of counterparties. The evaluation process should assess their creditworthiness and establish maximum limits of exposure permissible for each counterparty. A less worrisome but more frequent issue is the delay in clearance and settlement because market mechanisms cannot keep pace with the volume of transactions. This can result in the asset being uninvested and therefore not earning the requisite return.

Portfolio Management Risk

Once the asset has been acquired, it has to be managed safely and efficiently. The separation of management and audit is a basic principle that is often ignored. In February 1995 the venerable British merchant bank Barings paid a high price for this. A bank that survived two world wars, a depression, a stagflation and countless business cycles was pushed to its collapse by a 28-year-old floor trader.[1] Nick Leeson was able to take positions that caused a loss in excess of a billion dollars because the necessary safeguards to segregate functions were inadequate. Simple, yet essential, parts of any well-managed portfolio management process are measures such as cross-checks on all investment functions, limits on individual exposure, and a clear segregation between fund management and portfolio accounting. In addition, a regularly convened and well-documented investment review committee, chaired by a senior manager in the firm, is essential for monitoring and oversight.

Systems Risk

In the information age, up-to-date systems and technology have become indispensable in managing investments. They have allowed the handling and processing of tens of thousands of securities and hundreds of billions of dollars in real-time. The flip side

---

1. A comprehensive analysis of the collapse of Barings is the Bank of England report, available in full at *http://www.numa.com/ref/barings/bar00.htm*

B O X 4–1

Y2K

During 1998 and 1999 the approach of the year 2000 focused much attention on what is colloquially known as the Y2K issue. The underlying problem is the inability of older computer systems, programmed with just two digits for the year code, to distinguish between 1900 and 2000. Firms have addressed this by instituting rigorous checks on the code underlying their systems and rectifying or weeding out the problem pieces. However, every firm interacts with several others electronically and is therefore vulnerable to the Y2K problem through its links. This interconnectedness has raised the specter of systemic risk because just a few infected systems could contaminate the entire network. In the U.S., the premium placed on the December 1999/2000 eurodollar futures trade (the contract covering the turn of the century) has spiked as high as 10% to 15%. This magnitude is a good indication of the financial market's concern about this event within the U.S. However, preparations for Y2K have lagged significantly in other countries, especially in emerging markets. Global investment managers have worked diligently to mitigate and minimize the linkage risks that could impact non-domestic portfolios.

of this is that at the current scale of operations, the option of falling back to a manual approach does not exist. The reliance on interlinked systems is complete. This means that firms have to continuously monitor the health and reliability of their systems. Factors such as the lack of a failsafe backup system or reliance on an expensive legacy hardware technology can cripple a business. This risk is best explained by focusing on a current issue which has been a major systems and technology project for every financial firms, the Year 2000 (Y2K) issue. Y2K systems and related issues are discussed in the *sidebar* on Y2K.

INVESTMENT RISK

Investment risk is specific to market performance and is substantially magnified in the international arena. The presence of

multiple economic, political, currency, and regulatory environments makes dealing with risk a major challenge for the international investor. The main areas of investment risk are
company-specific risk, market-level (or systematic) risk, economic
and political risk, corporate governance/regulatory risk, currency
risk, and correlation (or paradigm shift) risk.

Company Specific Risk

Financial statements and valuation measures are the basic tools
most investors use to evaluate a company. But a proper analysis is
not possible unless the investor understands the assumptions and
regulations underlying the numbers. For foreign investments, this
can be an arduous task; their statements are seldom in accordance
with the U.S. model of generally accepted accounting principles
(GAAP). In general, foreign regulations are not as rigorous and do
not require as much disclosure as in the U.S.[2] The discrepancies
may be relatively innocuous, such as differences in the treatment
of depreciation and goodwill. Or, the difference may entail something as harmful as laxity in the treatment of off-balance-sheet
items, for example, pending lawsuits or derivatives exposure. The
bottom line is that investors must fastidiously perform analysis
and research in order to minimize the possibilities of unpleasant
surprises at a later date.

Systematic (Market-Level) Risk

Beyond company-specific risk, global equity investors are faced
with overall market-level risk, which often translates into levels of
total market exposure relative to a benchmark. Much of this kind of
risk can be hedged using modern equity risk management instruments, such as stock index futures, index options, and index swaps.
For large institutional managers, the most efficient instruments for
managing this systemic risk are listed futures and options. The
sidebar on Global Equity Risk Management Instruments provides

---

2. Certain organizations, most notably the International Accounting Standards Committee
   (IASC), are working to achieve uniformity in the accounting principles used for
   financial reporting around the world.

B O X 4–2

Global Equity Risk Management Instruments:
Index Futures, Options, and Swaps

In the mid-1980s, only a few major stock markets had listed stock index derivatives available for the management of risk exposure in the underlying instruments. Even Japan, one of the largest markets, only started trading index futures in late 1986, and this activity began offshore—in Singapore—due to regulatory constraints (domestically listed Japanese stock index futures only began in September 1988). These instruments are now a common feature of global equity risk management, with all developed-market equities having standardized index futures or options contracts trading, with similar instruments increasingly available for the more advanced emerging markets.

The most successful contracts have developed with appropriate regulatory structures and have information-sharing agreements with the exchange where the underlying cash securities are traded (often this trading takes place in the same market). The U.S. Commodity Futures Trading Commission (CFTC) requires that such information-sharing agreements be in place before they will approve (via a "no-action letter") the use of non-U.S. equity index futures contracts for use by American investors. The following table lists the primary markets, instruments, and benchmarks for listed stock index derivatives. With the exception of the markets with an asterick (*), these contracts are CFTC-approved for use by American investors.

Market	Type of Instrument	Primary benchmark(s)
United States	Futures/Options/Futures Options	S&P 500, S&P 100, Nasdaq 100, DJIA
Euro-Bloc * Pan-European *	Futures/Options/Futures Options	DJ STOXX, DJ Euro STOXX, FTSE EuroTop 300, FTSE EuroBloc 100, MSCI Euro, MSCI Pan-Europe
United Kingdom	Futures /Options	FTSE 100, FTSE Mid 250

Continued

Box 4–2 Concluded

Japan	Futures/Options/Futures Options	Nikkei 225, Nikkei 300, TOPIX
Germany	Futures/Options	DAX
France	Futures/Options	CAC-40
Switzerland *	Futures/Options	SMI
Netherlands *	Futures/Options	EOE
Italy	Futures/Options	MIB-30
Sweden	Futures/Options	OMX
Finland *	Futures/Options	HEX
Denmark *	Futures/Options	KFX
Spain	Futures/Options	IBEX
Portugal *	Futures/Options	PSI
Norway *	Futures/Options	OBX
Belgium *	Futures/Options	BEL-20
Austria *	Futures/Options	ATX
South Africa *	Futures	JSE All Share Index
Canada	Futures/Options	S&P/TSE 60
Mexico	Futures/ Options	IPC
Brazil *	Futures	IBOVESPA
Australia	Futures/Options	All-Ordinaries
New Zealand	Futures	Top 40
Hong Kong	Futures/Options/Futures Options	Hang Seng, MSCI Hong Kong
Singapore *	Futures/Futures Options	MSCI Singapore
Taiwan	Futures/Futures Options	MSCI Taiwan
Korea *	Futures/Options	KOPSI 200
Thailand *	Futures/Futures Options/Options	DJGI Thailand, SET 50
Malaysia *	Futures	KLSI

In addition to these listed index contracts, a broad and deep market in OTC equity derivatives has developed in the world's major financial centers.

more information on the development and availability of such instruments.

Shifts in market structure can also introduce risks into a portfolio which cannot be hedged. For example, in a number of international markets with restrictions on foreign investors, particularly in Asia, certain shares and share classes are available to foreigners trade with a premium. This adds additional risk beyond that of the market and the specific security, since the premiums expand and shrink with the sentiment of international

F I G U R E   4–2

Singapore Foreign Premium

Average of OCBC, DBS, OUB, SPH, SIA, UOB.
Source: Banco Santander.

investors, and hold the risk of collapse if governments introduce
policies that open up the market. Figure 4–2 provides graphic evidence of what can happen to premiums (in this case, in Singapore
in July and August 1997) when restrictions are eased concurrent
with a shift in global investor sentiment. As a post-script, in early
1999, the Singapore government lifted restrictions on foreign
ownership of banks, leading banks to merge their foreign and
local share classes. While holders of foreign shares were offered
bonus shares, the foreign shares still dropped relative to local
shares, as the previously-existing premium was higher than the
value of the share bonus.

Economic and Political Risk

Perhaps the most difficult risk to quantify in international investing is broad economic and political risk. The information available is very subjective in nature and hard to obtain in a timely
manner. Unfortunately, the countries for which the information is

the least easily available are often the countries where the shift in successive regimes has important implications for the investor. Furthermore, even seemingly stable and credible regimes can radically shift policies, as was evident in the dramatic change of treatment of foreign investors in Malaysia in 1998. (See *sidebar* on Malaysian Capital Controls)

Political risk is the risk associated with the stability—or lack thereof—of the governing institutions of a country. The failure of a government to deliver higher standards of living in the long term will lead to popular discontent. This can be aggravated if the government did not have a widespread mandate to begin with. Any perception of corruption and favoritism will add more fuel to

B O X 4–3

Malaysian Capital Controls

Malaysia was greatly impacted by the Asian economic crisis of 1997–1998. Foreign investors, already affected by the stock market's sharp drop, were informed on September 1, 1998, that they would be subjected to a unilateral moratorium on the repatriation of funds. A one-year freeze was declared on most portfolio capital withdrawals from Malaysia.

This major political-economic event highlighted the need for maintaining close contact with operational counterparties (such as brokers and subcustodians) in each market where investment takes place. Nimble fund managers with strong operational capabilities were able to adapt to the new investment regime relatively quickly and develop solutions that assured compliance with fiduciary responsibilities and created options for their clients. Furthermore, Malaysia's imposition of controls created uncertainties which required continuous monitoring, since the rules imposed by the central bank and the central depository were fluid, both at initial implementation in Autumn 1998, and when controls were "eased" in February 1999. This loosening of the capital controls also established a system of "Exit Levies" for assets already in Malaysia and imposed a capital gains tax on any new money invested. A new series of operational challenges were created for investment managers, requiring intense risk management procedures.

the fires of resentment. A weak executive position is not disastrous if the country has a relatively efficient bureaucracy or a respected judiciary. But if all the branches of the government are discredited, a transition can easily get out of hand and result in considerable damage to lives and property.

Economic risk can be summarized as the risk of unexpected, adverse changes in the economic stability of a country. The most visible symptom of an economy in trouble is a rapidly accelerating inflation rate. This can ignite social unrest and lead ultimately to the downfall of the government. Signs of economic risk can sometimes be found in the fiscal and foreign account areas. A government that continuously spends more than it earns will eventually end up in a debt trap. Also of concern are economies that produce high growth rates but are financed by dependence on foreign capital. A sudden withdrawal of capital could and has caused serious disruption to firms and their stakeholders, as real assets do not cope very well with large fluctuations in capital. Similarly, markets where companies and banks have severe asset/liability mismatches, such as in many Asian emerging markets in the mid 1990s can create enormous instability when short-term borrowing can no longer cover the financing needs of long-term projects.

A more general investment risk is that of being exposed to just a few markets both because this weakens the diversification benefits of combining weakly correlated markets, and it also might translate into being exposed to an insufficient number of industries. This will make the portfolio very vulnerable to downturns in demand for those commodities or products.

Although economic and political risks can be difficult to measure and quantify, many financial firms use some of the variables mentioned above to build proprietary models of country risk.[3] While these models have not proven themselves to be precient during the latter part of the 1990s, it is inevitable that research will continue and that efforts to model the generally subjective areas of economic and political risk will continue.

---

3. Some of the better-known firms are Moody's, Standard & Poor's, Political Risk Services, and the Economist Intelligence Unit.

Corporate Governance and Regulatory Risk

In addition to the macroeconomic environment, the regulatory framework that a firm operates under plays a large role in determining the value of a firm. Especially in the international arena, the investor must be confident that she understands the regulations as well as the standards of enforcement on matters pertinent to her, such as property rights, protection for minority investors, and bankruptcy laws. Independent regulators armed with strong enforcement powers are the hallmark of a favorable investing environment. Independence usually means that the regulators have legally mandated roles and that budgets and are not beholden to politicians for either power or finances. An effective regulator also needs to maintain the proper balance between the sometimes conflicting roles of market protector and market promoter. A major conference on Risk in Emerging Markets sponsored by the World Bank and the Brookings Institution held in March 1999 highlighted corporate governance and regulatory risk as the top priority for improving the investment environment in develping economies. The influential Russell 20-20 Association also has a major focus on this area.

Currency Risk

Currency risk is clearly something specific to international investing. It is also a risk that can have a dramatic impact on a portfolio.[4] There are some good reasons why an investor might want to accept this risk. First, it can diversify domestic monetary policy uncertainty. Second, to the extent that the domestic consumers goods basket contains imports, exposure to the corresponding currencies can help immunize against price fluctuations of the basket. In most markets, the investor has the choice of almost eliminating this risk by the judicious use of hedging instruments, such as forwards and futures. However, there are some markets where it is either impossible or prohibitively expensive to hedge. In these situations, the investor either has to use

---

4. A rule of thumb for international assets is that currency risk is about one third of equity risk and about two thirds of bond risk.

other currencies to cross-hedge, or if that is not effective, to make a decision regarding whether the expected return on the asset is worth the risk.

The literature on currencies offers several models that claim to produce early warning signals on currency devaluation and capital controls.[5] The factors considered usually include FX reserves, public debt (especially short-term), capital flows, and current account balance.

Correlation (Paradigm Shift) Risk

While correlations of individual country price levels are far more stable than actual returns, they can and do fluctuate substantially. A prudent investor realizes that correlation estimates, no matter how econometrically precise the technique, are essentially based on the limited draws that the basket of history has to offer. A paradigm shift, for example major change in risk appetite and credit by global investors, can alter correlations and cause securities to exhibit relationships that have rarely been seen in the past. Long Term Capital Management (LTCM), a huge, highly regarded, hedge fund, paid a high price for this discovery. LTCM's errors were compounded by the high leverage used in their positions.[6] Stress-testing the portfolio under extreme conditions is the best way of preparing for the risks associated with paradigm shift, such as a complete change in the way that markets price credit risk.

It is the presence of correlations substantially below 1.0 in international equity markets (which is the measure of perfect correlation) that allows investors to partake of the benefits of diversification. The arrival of the European Monetary Union (EMU) raised concern about the fall in these benefits because of the expected rise in correlations within the euro-zone countries.

5. Two good papers on this topic are B. Eichengreen, A. Rose, and C. Wyplosz, "Exchange Market Mayhem: the Antecedents and Aftermath of Speculative Attacks," *Economic Policy*, vol. 21, 1995, pp. 249–312; and Paul Krugman, "Currency Crises," NBER Conference, October 1997.
6. An excellent analysis of this is "Meriwether's Meltdown," by Nicholas Dunbar, *RISK Magazine*, October 1998, pp. 33–36.

B O X 4–4

EMU

On January 1, 1999, eleven countries (Austria, Belgium, Finland, France, Germany, Ireland, Italy, Luxembourg, Netherlands, Portugal, and Spain) adopted the euro as their currency. All national legacy currencies have become merely denominations of the euro. This epochal move required changes to the trading, settlement, and reporting of many securities. Most firms adopted a "big bang" approach to this change. This meant that from January 1st, all transactions began to be settled in euros. To avoid confusion on "E-day," firms needed to ensure that their counterparties, such as brokers and custodians, were in agreement on the date and mode of the switch. For example, for EuroZone stock exchanges that continued to quote equity prices in legacy currencies, a clear understanding needed to be established on the timing for the conversion to euro to occur. While the transition to the euro went extraordinarily smoothly, the planning and effort that enabled this process to occur "glitch-free" was immense and provided very useful experience for the international financial community to prepare for many Y2K issues (see Y2K Box).

While a common monetary policy and a closely aligned fiscal policy did bring the equity markets of the 11 founder nations closer together, there still remain many differences between the countries. This is most evident in the varied composition of the markets. In Germany, for example, the two largest sectors are banking and insurance, while in Finland, the top two sectors are electrical & electronics and forest products.[7]

Ultimately, the best way to counter the potential reduction in diversification is to introduce new assets that have improved risk diversification properties. Emerging markets, for example, continue to be a good diversifier for developed markets, despite the enormous volatility this asset class experienced in the mid to late 1990s. Figure 4–3, which depicts the average volatility of a portfolio of developed international (non-U.S.) and emerging markets,

---

7. MSCI data, as of September 30, 1997.

F I G U R E 4–3

Diversification Benefits of Emerging Markets:
January 1988 to September 1998

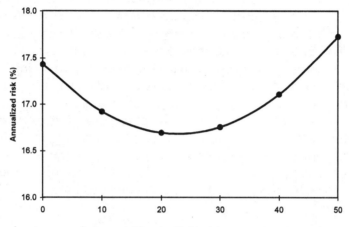

Percentage of Emerging Markets in International Portfolio

shows that the addition of a certain percentage of emerging markets exposure to a global equity portfolio has historically reduced
total portfolio risk. In fact, one result of European market integration has been an acceleration of the trend of U.S. plan sponsors
adapting broader, integrated benchmarks/strategies which seam-
lessly combine developed and emerging markets, such as mandates based on the MSCI ACWI ex-U.S. Index.

Index (Data Vendor) Risk

While the rise of indexing has dramatically mitigated the investment risks inherent in traditional active management
approaches, it has also been responsible for the creation of a new
risk, data vendor risk.[8] This is the risk that index vendors—such
as Morgan Stanley Capital International (MSCI), the Financial

---

8. According to a study by Price Waterhouse Coopers, indexing accounted for 15% of
   U.S. tax-exempt institutional assets in 1997. In the UK and Netherlands, it
   commands a similar proportion and is growing in popularity in the rest of Europe
   and Japan.

Times/Standard and Poor's-Actuaries, (FT/S&P-A), Dow Jones STOXX, and the International Finance Corporation—might make suboptimal index-construction decisions that are unquestioningly adopted by index fund managers. There are also the very common data transmission errors and delays that can affect the investment process. Calculation errors can also be frequent occurances. This risk can be mitigated by a process that "goes beyond passive" in approaching index-based investing. Firms which take this approach seek to maximize value for their clients by not taking any index information as a given. Data is always cross-checked, and the index is "proven" by performing calculations from the bottom up. Often, index fund managers are the first to discover index calculation errors, and then provide feedback to index vendors. All major index decisions are carefully studied to be sure that the best interests of the clients are being served. This might involve visits by portfolio managers to the region or country in question to ascertain information firsthand. It certainly includes consultations with index calculators to ensure that major changes to the index, such as large additions or deletions are not made without incorporating all pertinent information, that reflect real world constraints that portfolio managers confront when implementing the changes.

Portfolio Transition Risk

Another major area of risk involves the various risks that occur when large multi-market equity portfolios are transitioned to new strategies or new managers, or both. During complex transitions, a variety of factors and tradeoffs must be measured and determined, usually in consultation with the client. Figure 4–4 provides a "roadmap" of one such transition, completed in 1998, in which the client was shifting from separate developed market (EAFE) and emerging markets (IFCI) portfolios to an integrated international index strategy (tracking the MSCI All Country World Index ex-U.S. benchmark), while retaining a smaller stand-alone emerging markets strategy. Throughout the benchmark/strategy transition process, a variety of tracking and operational risks must be measured and minimized. A consultative role might also be played by the manager, since the tradeoffs between transaction cost savings

FIGURE 4–4

Transitioning a Strategy—Managing Costs and Risks

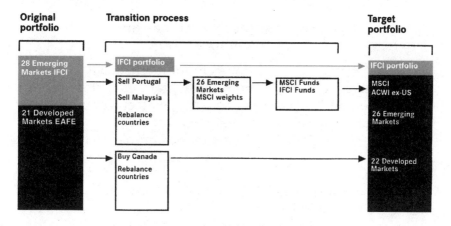

and accepting higher tracking error are not always clear-cut and require decisions by the owner of the assets. Such transitions can be even more complex when assets are being transferred between managers.

Oversight of the Investment Process

Most investment management firms devote substantial resources and effort toward oversight of day-to-day portfolio management and investment strategy implementation. This usually takes the form of multiple layers of investment committees, starting at the local offices and often divided up by asset class. For example, a global fund manager might have U.S.-based investment review committees (IRC) for domestic and international equities, or a combined IRC for all index equity strategies. These "local" committees should report to broader, "global" investment committees, and information/guidance for investment innovation and performance should follow in both directions. The ultimate objective is to have a seamless web of oversight and information flowing among senior managers and day-to-day portfolio managers.

In addition, the general principle of a clear separation of functions should be viewed as the basic building block of equity risk management. Among these functions are portfolio management, fund accounting, custody/trust services, and risk oversight.

Overall Portfolio Commitment/
Risk Measurement

Ultimately, the myriad risks inherent in international stocks are only a small component of an investor's total risk. It is vital for the owner of the assets (plan sponsor, endowment, or individual) to understand how non-domestic equities fit into the entire investment plan. The ultimate contribution of this allocation is to reduce overall portfolio risk through the addition of weakly correlated assets.

There are a number of commercially available analytical tools to measure the risk components of adding asset classes to a total portfolio. A set of rigorous investment guidelines (which establishes overall allocation to different asset classes) should then be established and closely monitored. End-investors also need to establish an appropriate time frame for monitoring their portfolio and investment managers. Usually, monthly reporting is sufficient, with a more detailed analysis each quarter. However, each investor must work with his managers to establish the appropriate template of performance data and time frame for analysis and delivery to the investor.

For pension plan sponsors, the establishment of appropriate performance benchmarks is also essential. These would include the appropriate standard or custom asset-class benchmarks, manager-universe performance benchmarks, and peer group performance measures.

DEVELOPING A RISK MANAGEMENT "CULTURE" WITHIN THE EQUITY PORTFOLIO MANAGEMENT PROCESS

Although most world-class investment management firms and financial institutions appropriately maintain a separate, independent risk management function, the day-to-day implementation of risk management principles must occur within the operational line accountabilities of the investment management process. It is therefore essential that a proactive approach to risk management be engineered into the portfolio management function. Such an effective internal culture would need to be intently focused on the fiduciary responsibility entrusted to asset managers and to hold each portfolio management team accountable for its actions or inactions. Such a culture, with a dedication to risk minimization, cannot and should not completely suppress appropriate risk-taking in the portfolio management process. It is ultimately this balance between risk awareness and the pursuit of reward in global equity markets that best serves investors.

CHAPTER 5

Currency Observations: Hedging Currency Risk

Raymond T. Dalio
Chief Investment Officer
Bridgewater Associates, Inc.
Wilton, Connecticut

Investing internationally is a package deal. One gets two exposures wrapped together, the underlying asset and the currency. However, these exposures are separable through currency hedging. International investors can and should decide how much of each exposure to have, and how to have these exposures independently managed. Making these decisions, creating a currency hedging plan, is prudent when the international exposure reaches 15 to 20 percent of the total portfolio. Failing to do so leaves a large, inadvertently acquired, and unmanaged risk in the portfolio. The purpose of this article is to provide a basic overview of the key issues that investors should address in developing such a hedging strategy.

A general rule when creating your hedging strategy is to follow the same steps you would in deciding on the other exposures in your portfolio. Most important, you should decide on the appropriate *strategic exposure* to foreign currency and whether this exposure should be *actively* or *passively managed*.

WHAT SHOULD THE STRATEGIC EXPOSURE BE?

Said differently, assuming no market view, how much foreign currency exposure should you have in your portfolio? The process you use to answer this question is the same one you use when deciding on your asset allocation mix. Your exposure should be based on the expected returns, risks, and correlations of currencies. Then, once the amount you want to keep in the portfolio is decided, the hedge ratio you set should be the amount that leaves you with that net currency exposure. For example, if you determine that you would like to have 10 percent of your portfolio exposed to foreign currency, and you have 20 percent, you would set a benchmark of 50 percent hedged. In other words, rather than determining the appropriate percentage to be hedged, one should determine a desired strategic currency exposure and hedge to achieve it. That hedged amount will be your benchmark.

So what is the right strategic exposure to have? That depends on one's assessment of the expected returns and risks of currencies, as well as the expected correlations with the other exposures in the portfolio. Because currency movements are zero sum, i.e., for one currency to go up, another must go down, it is probably best to assume that the expected return is 0 percent although the actual return might be quite different. This simply means the expected return is zero. The standard deviation of a typical portfolio has been about 11 percent over the past 25 years, which is also a reasonable assumption going forward. The correlations with the other assets in the portfolio depend on the assets, but in general, they are quite close to 0 percent.

Where will plugging these numbers into your portfolio optimizer take you? While there is a wide range of possible outcomes depending on such factors as what assets are in your total portfolio, there are some general outcomes. Generally speaking, such an analysis will lead investors to choose to hedge away currency risks so that the amount left is not greater than 10 to 15 percent of the portfolio. If one's international investments equal 20 to 30 percent that might normally lead to being 50 percent hedged. If one's international investments total only 10 to 15 percent of the portfolio, that might normally result in being unhedged.

There are only two characteristics unique to currencies that you need to understand to solve for the right strategic exposure: (1) it costs money to hedge, and (2) currency exposures are in addition to other exposures, not instead of them. I'll explain.

Concerning the first point, the expected return from being hedged is slightly less than that of being unhedged because of the transaction costs of hedging. As these are typically about 15 basis points (if done passively), it should be assumed that a hedged portfolio will have a return about 15 basis points lower than an unhedged portfolio. Given this, one needs to assess incremental benefits. For example, what is it worth to reduce or eliminate an exposure that has a standard deviation of 11 percent and no expected return? It should be added that one typically sees that risk reduction from hedging typically occurs in a nonlinear way. Said differently, the benefits of the first 25 or 50 percent of hedging are much greater than those coming from next 25 or 50 percent. For this reason, it is rarely the case that being 100 percent hedged is appropriate.

Regarding the second point, because currency exposures are in addition to one's other exposures, not instead of, lower risk is acheived by having less currency exposure rather than more. Currencies have little or no correlation with other assets in the portfolio. One might think that this is a reason to keep them, i.e., to be unhedged, because they would diversify and hence reduce the portfolio's risk. In fact, the reverse is the case. Having significant currency exposure in the portfolio increases the risk, even though currencies are uncorrelated with the other assets. That is because the currency exposure is *in addition* to the other exposures. The reason that replacing a higher-correlation asset with a lower-correlation asset normally reduces risk is that there is a substitution which keeps the total exposure unchanged. When one increases the total exposure, e.g., buying gold futures as an overlay on one's portfolio, one is likely to increase the portfolio's risk, even if the correlation is negative. Similarly, when reducing your currency exposure, you will almost certainly reduce your portfolio risk, despite currency's low correlations.

There is only one other point that should be made before concluding the discussion of strategic exposure: *The time horizon is relevant.* The longer one's time horizon, the less risky currency will appear. That is because over a long enough time horizon, its effect on the return will approach 0 percent i.e., the expected return. However, if this is a consideration, it is important to understand how long a time horizon one has to have in order to be unconcerned about the currency risk. Based on past currency movements, in order to be 90 percent confident that currencies will have an annual return of not more than –1 percent to +1 percent, one would have to wait 325 years.[1]

Once the desired strategic exposure is determined, the benchmark exposure should be that hedge ratio that gets you there. *There are four possible benchmarks, 100 percent unhedged, 100 percent hedged, partially hedged (e.g., 50 percent) and option hedged. All four can be obtained passively.* Option hedged benchmarks, e.g., buying puts to hedge the currency exposure, are sometimes used instead of a partially hedged benchmark when the investor is more inclined to have his currency losses come in smaller, more frequent doses than larger, infrequent amounts. They should not be used as an alternative to fully hedged or fully unhedged benchmarks because they will systematically deliver either more or less currency exposure than has been determined to be consistent with your strategic objective.

If you choose an option benchmark, it is essential that the one you pick is consistent with your strategic objectives. For example, some options are consistent with a 50 percent hedged objective, while others are not. Their deltas (sensitivity to price changes) will be broadly equivalent to desired hedged ratios. When choosing an option hedge instead of a corresponding partially hedged benchmark (e.g., 50 percent), it is also essential to measure the actual performance in relation to the passive option hedge, not the partially hedged alternative. That is because options have different systematic risks than their corresponding partial hedges. For example, options will do better when the markets move a long way directionally. If an active manager is operating to an option mandate but is being measured against a 50 percent hedged benchmark, the differences in returns of the manager and the benchmark will be the systematic risk and the manager's alpha combined. As a result, one cannot distinguish how well the manager is performing from how well options are doing relative to the 50 percent hedged. For example, a manager could outperform the fixed hedge ratio (e.g., 50 percent hedged)

---

1. This assumes that each year's returns are independent. If one assumed serial correlation to exist similar to the past, one would have to wait 20 years to be 90 percent confident that the returns would fall between +/- 1 percent.

but underperform the option hedge alternative, giving the mistaken impression that the manager added value when in reality he did not. That is why the benchmark should always be the investor's passive alternative.

ACTIVE OR PASSIVE?

The only purpose of active management is to add value to the strategic exposure's return, i.e., a position which can be obtained passively. Said differently, the active versus passive decision is made for currency in the same way it is made for other markets, based on one's expectations for value-added. This statement is true for *all* managers, whether managing to a fixed benchmark (100 percent hedged, 100 percent unhedged, or partially hedged) or an option hedged benchmark. As a result, the investor should specify the benchmark and study the manager's performance relative to it.

The investor should also understand and assess how the manager attempts to add value. There are only two ways to add value, fundamentally and technically. While the tactical deviations from the benchmark the manager chooses to make in order to add value might differ (e.g., price direction, interest rate carries, volatility, etc.), one's approach to making this bet will be fundamental, technical, or some mixture of the two. Fundamental analysis is based on the belief that there are cause-and-effect relationships which need to be understood in order for pricing anomalies to be sensibly identified and "value-added" to be created. Technical analysis is based on the assumption that past price relationships are indicative of future price relationships. Whether betting on price, volatility, or anything else, managers follow one or both approaches. In assessing currency manager, like any other manager, you should decide on which approach is more consistent with your own investment philosophy.

Since the only reason to hire an active manager is because you expect that they are likely to add value, it is worth noting what sort of added value has been created in the past. The most comprehensive study of currency manager performance was conducted by Brian Strange of Currency Performance Analytics. He studied the performance of 158 currency overlay mandates

F I G U R E 5–1

	Active (value adding)	*Passive* (indexing)
Fixed hedge benchmark (e.g., 50% hedged)		
Option hedge benchmark		

managed over the last 10 years and determined that "currency overlay managers have added considerable value—about 1.9 percent per year on average."

When examining individual managers, it is often difficult to compare their value-added (alpha) because virtually no two client mandates are the same. Judging performance against hedged and unhedged mandates is made additionally difficult by the effect that the market's direction has on the alpha. For example, managers who are operating to an unhedged benchmark will find it easy to add value when foreign currencies are falling, while managers who are operating to a fully hedged benchmark will find it tough. To achieve the best perspective concerning the managers ability to add value, you should examine performance across mandates.

SUMMARY

In summary, the alternatives an investor must decide between are expressed in Figure 5–1. An investor's benchmark can be either a fixed hedge ratio (e.g., 50 percent hedged) or an option hedge. Active managers can be hired to beat the benchmark or passive managers can be used to match it. When you are able to check the box which best suits your objectives, you will have moved most of the way toward having a currency hedging plan. Getting to this point is what most investors find most difficult. Of course, selecting specific managers and deciding on other aspects of the mandate (e.g., Is cross-hedging appropriate?) will be required. But these choices will be vastly easier to make once you have made the core strategic decisions.

Asset Allocation and the Rewards of Multiple-Asset-Class Investing

Roger C. Gibson CFA, CFP
President
Gibson Capital Management, Ltd.
Pittsburgh, Pennsylvania

Let every man divide his money into three parts, and invest a third in land, a third in business, and a third let him keep in reserve.

—*Talmud* (circa 1200 B.C.–500 A.D.)

Source: © Roger Gibson, 1998; Morgan Stanley Capital International: Used with permission. © 1998 Ibbotson Associates, Inc. All rights reserved. (Certain portions of this work were derived from copyrighted works of Roger G. Ibbotson and Rex Sinquefield); Data from NAREIT® copyright © (1998) by National Association of Real Estate Investment Trusts®. NAREIT® data is reprinted with permission. Statements, calculations, or charts made by the author which use NAREIT® data have not been approved, verified, or endorsed by NAREIT®; *GSCI® performance data used with permission of Goldman, Sachs & Co.; GSCI is a registered service mark of Goldman, Sachs & Co.*

Asset allocation is not a new idea! The Talmud quote is approximately 2000 years old. Whoever said it knew something about risk. He also knew something about return. He may have been the world's first proponent of asset allocation. Today, we talk about asset allocation rather than diversification, but it is really just a new name for a very old and time-tested investment strategy. A more contemporary translation of the advice might read: "Let every investor create a diversified portfolio that allocates one-third to real estate investments, one-third to common stocks, with the remaining one-third allocated to cash equivalents and bonds."

Is it still good advice today? Let's examine the recommendation in more detail.

The overall portfolio balance is one-third fixed-income investments and two-thirds equity investments. The one-third allocated to fixed-income mitigates the volatility risk inherent in the two-thirds allocated to equity investments. Diversification across two major forms of equity investing with dissimilar patterns of returns further reduces the equity risk. The result is a balanced portfolio, tilted toward equities, appropriate for an investor with a longer investment time horizon who is simultaneously concerned about both risk and return. It is a remarkably elegant and powerful asset allocation strategy. Imagine trying to develop a one-sentence investment strategy, knowing that a wide variety of investors, most of whom are not yet born, will follow the advice for the next 2000 years! You would be hard-pressed to come up with something better!

The unknown author of the Talmud quote could not possibly have envisioned today's investment world. Over the past decade, democracies and free enterprise have replaced many of the world's dictatorships and centrally directed economies. New capital markets are forming, and investment alternatives have proliferated. People from around the world can exchange volumes of information instantaneously via the Internet, virtually without cost. The world has truly gotten smaller and increasingly interconnected as economic events in one part of the world impact markets on the other side of the globe.

In spite of all of this change, investors are not that different today from what they were a hundred years ago. They want high returns, and they do not want to incur risk in securing those returns. Diversification is a time-honored investment principle. In this chapter, let's explore the role of multiple-asset-class diversification in giving investors the returns they long for while mitigating the risks they face.

INTEREST-GENERATING VS. EQUITY INVESTMENTS

The world of investment alternatives can be broadly divided into two groups, interest-generating investments and equity investments. With the former, you are a lender of money, and your return comes in the form of interest payments. With the latter, you go into business with your money, and your return takes the form of dividends and capital appreciation. The return and volatility characteristics of these two forms of investing are very different.

Figure 6–1 shows the long-term performance of a $1 investment in several different U. S. capital market investment alternatives. Clearly, the interest-generating investments, Treasury bills and long-term government bonds, have followed a lower growth path than the equity investments, large and small company stocks. You can find the compound returns for each of these investment alternatives in Figure 6–2 under the column Geometric Mean. The interest-generating alternatives have historically provided single-digit returns ranging from 3.8 percent to 5.7 percent. These returns have been only modestly above the underlying long-term inflation rate of 3.1 percent. The equity alternatives, by comparison, have generated double-digit compound annual total returns of 11.0 percent and 12.7 percent. These returns significantly outpaced inflation, thus providing investors with the opportunity to build the purchasing power of their capital. Investors pay a price, however, in earning the double-digit returns available from equity investments: a high level of volatility.

INFLATION VS. VOLATILITY

Although investors face a wide variety of risks in managing their money, the two biggest risks are inflation and volatility. Within a portfolio context, actions taken to reduce one of these risks tend

FIGURE 6–1

Wealth Indices of Investments in the U.S. Capital Markets, 1925–1997

Wealth Indices of Investments in the U.S. Capital Markets   Year-End 1925 = $1.00

From 1925 to 1997

to increase exposure to the other. It is therefore important for an investor to understand both risks and the tradeoff between them.

F I G U R E   6–2

Basic Series: Summary Statistics of Annual Total Returns, 1926–1997

From 1926 to 1997

Series	Geometric Mean	Arithmetic Mean	Standard Deviation	Distribution
Large Company Stocks	11.0%	13.0%	20.3%	
Small Company Stocks	12.7	17.7·	33.9	
Long-Term Corporate Bonds	5.7	6.1	8.7	
Long-Term Government	5.2	5.6	9.2	
Intermediate-Term Government	5.3	5.4	5.7	
U.S. Treasury Bills	3.8	3.8	3.2	
Inflation	3.1	3.2	4.5	

−90%   0%   90%

* The 1933 Small Company Stock Total Return was 142.9 percent.

To simplify the discussion of these risks, we will use Treasury bills as a proxy for interest-generating investments and large company stocks as a proxy for equity investments. Later, we will consider an investor whose task it is to balance his portfolio between interest-generating investments and equity investments in a strategically advantageous manner, taking into consideration the risks of both inflation and volatility.

Let us first consider the risk of inflation. Figure 6–3 shows the loss of purchasing power caused by various rates of inflation. Throughout the 1990s, the inflation rate averaged approximately

FIGURE 6–3

Inflation Risk

	Purchasing Power of $1000				
	Inflation Rate				
	2%	**3%**	**4%**	**5%**	**6%**
10 Years	$ 820	$ 744	$ 676	$ 614	$ 558
20 Years	$ 673	$ 554	$ 456	$ 377	$ 312
30 Years	$ 552	$ 412	$ 308	$ 231	$ 174
	Purchasing Power Loss				
	Inflation Rate				
	2%	**3%**	**4%**	**5%**	**6%**
10 Years	18%	26%	32%	39%	44%
20 Years	33%	45%	54%	62%	69%
30 Years	45%	59%	69%	77%	83%

3 percent. Even at a modest 3 percent rate, inflation will reduce the purchasing power of $1000 to $744 over a decade, a purchasing power loss of 26 percent! Over two and three decades, the purchasing power losses are 45 percent and 59 percent respectively. Inflation takes its toll insidiously, but with a progressively greater impact over time. It is therefore more of a long-term risk than a short-term risk. Of the two investment alternatives under discussion, Treasury bills are much more susceptible to inflation than large company stocks, since, historically, the rate of return on T-bills has been only marginally in excess of the underlying inflation rate.

Keep in mind that the interest from Treasury bills is subject to federal income taxes. With an assumed 30 percent marginal tax rate, Treasury bills' long-term compound return of 3.8 percent becomes 2.7 percent after taxes, in a 3.1 percent inflationary environment. Thus, even with full reinvestment of after-tax income, a Treasury bill investor would not have been able to preserve the purchasing power of her capital. Although other interest-generating investments, such as government and corporate bonds, had higher returns than Treasury bills, they are likewise very susceptible to the damaging impact of inflation.

Volatility is the other major risk, and it is most pronounced with various forms of equity investing. The standard deviation statistic in Figure 6–2 measures this volatility and verifies that very high volatility levels have accompanied the high returns generated by equity investments. By comparison, the low returns from interest-generating investments have been much less volatile, as evidenced by their low standard deviation statistics. The distribution graph on the righthand side of Figure 6–2 gives a visual picture of the comparative volatility of the investment alternatives. The height of the "skylines," or histograms, shows the relative frequency of returns across the range indicated on the bottom of the table.

Although you can see the ups and downs of common stock investing on Figure 6–1, the logarithmic scale used for the vertical axis masks the visual impression of that volatility.[1] Figure 6–4, which shows the year-by-year pattern of total returns for large company stocks versus Treasury bills, provides a much better picture of common stock volatility. The solid line traces the wildly fluctuating annual returns (dividend income plus capital appreciation) for large company stocks.

A solid horizontal line drawn through the graph at 13 percent indicates the arithmetic mean (simple average) return of large company stocks. The standard deviation statistic of 20.3 percent defines a range around the simple average return, within which approximately two-thirds of large company stocks' return observations fall.[2] This range is indicated by the dashed horizontal lines drawn at 33.3 percent and –7.3 percent, derived by adding and subtracting the 20.3 percent standard deviation from large company stocks' simple average return of 13 percent. As you can see, most of the returns are indeed within the range between the dashed lines. Returns fall outside the range on either the high or low side, approximately one year out of three.

---

1. With a logarithmic scale, the same vertical distance represents the same percentage change on the graph, regardless of where it is measured. As a result, the rate of return for any investment alternative can be inferred directly from the slope of its growth path.

2 . Statistically, common stock returns are approximately normally distributed. With a normal distribution, roughly two-thirds of the observations fall within one standard deviation of the mean.

F I G U R E   6–4

Volatility Risk

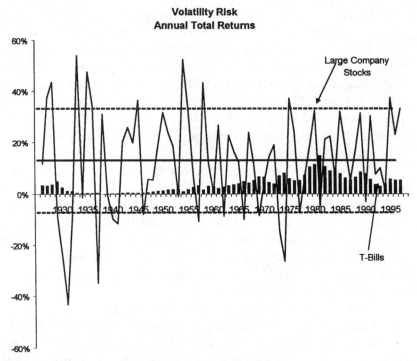

Volatility Risk
Annual Total Returns

The vertical bars show the pattern of annual Treasury bill returns. Although on average, Treasury bills have a low rate of return, they have the advantages of stable principal values and a consistently positive pattern of returns. Note that over the entire 72-year period, Treasury bills had only one year when their return exceeded the 13 percent simple average return of large company stocks!

Although large company stock returns are very volatile, investors have been rewarded for bearing this risk by earning a long-term compound rate of return that has been 7.2 percent higher than that available from Treasury bills. Whereas inflation tends to be a longer-term risk, volatility is a shorter-term risk causing equity investors to periodically suffer negative returns. Over the time period covered in these charts, large company stocks lost money roughly three years out of ten with an average annual loss of –12.33 percent. If, however, the common stock investor patiently waited through the bad years, good years prevailed to offset the losses. Time, therefore, tends to solve the problem of volatility.

Returning to Figure 6–4, it is easy to identify the bad one- or two-year periods to be a common stock investor. It is more difficult, however, to identify bad 10- or 20-year periods to be in large company stocks, since longer time periods have good years mixed in with the bad years. The longer the time frame, the more likely it is that the realized compound return from large company stocks will dominate the performance of Treasury bills, as is illustrated in Figure 6–5. If you compare the holding period returns of large company stocks against government and corporate bonds, you would see the same pattern of increasing equity dominance.

THE BROAD PORTFOLIO BALANCE DECISION

The most important portfolio decision the investor makes is choosing the balance between interest-generating and equity investments. This decision simultaneously determines the growth path the portfolio is likely to follow over time and the general

FIGURE 6–5

Large Company Stock Returns' Dominance over Treasury Bill Returns, (1926–1997)

Length of Holding Period	Number of Holding Periods	Periods When Large Company Stock Returns Exceeded T-Bill Returns	
		No.	%
1 Year	72	46	64
5 Years	68	55	80
10 Years	63	53	84
15 Years	58	54	93
20 Years	53	53	100

FIGURE 6–6

Interest-Generating vs. Equity Investments

	Interest-Generating Investments	Equity Investments
Advantage	Less volatility	Long-term, real capital growth
Disadvantage	Inflation susceptibility	High volatility
Appropriate for	Short time horizons	Long time horizons

level of volatility in returns. Risk is time horizon dependent. If an investor's time-horizon is short, volatility is a bigger risk than inflation, and the portfolio should be oriented primarily toward stable principal-value, interest-generating investments. If an investor's time horizon is long, inflation is a bigger risk than volatility, and the portfolio should be oriented primarily toward equity investments. Figure 6–6 summarizes these observations.

Obviously, a continuum of interest-generating and equity allocation possibilities exists. The greater the equity commitment, the higher the expected return and the greater the portfolio volatility associated with reaching for that return. With their lower volatility, the interest-generating investments in the portfolio, act as ballast, dampening portfolio volatility as well as expected return.

THE POWER OF DIVERSIFICATION

An old adage advises us to "not put all of our eggs in one basket." Although there are obvious advantages to using more than one basket to carry our eggs, the benefits of diversification are more powerful and subtle than this adage suggests.

When you construct an investment portfolio using multiple asset classes, you discover that portfolio volatility is less than the weighted average of the volatility levels of its components.[3] This occurs as a result of the dissimilarity in patterns of returns among

---

3. The only exception to this is the rare situation of perfect positive correlation of returns among the investments in the portfolio.

FIGURE 6–7

The Diversification Effect

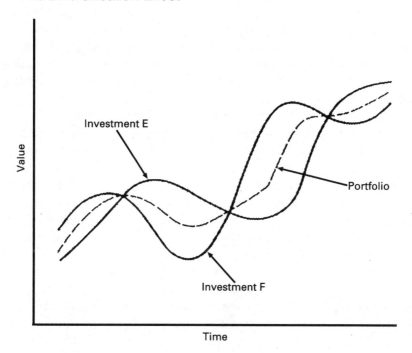

Source: Roger C. Gibson, *Asset Allocation: Balancing Financial Risk,* 2d ed., McGraw-Hill, New York, 1996.

the components of the portfolio. This advantageous reduction in portfolio volatility can be called the *diversification effect.*

Figure 6–7 shows the performance of two investments, E and F, both of which have similar levels of return and volatility. A portfolio composed of both investments would perform as indicated by the dotted line. Note that the patterns of returns for investments E and F are dissimilar. They do not always move up and down together. This dissimilarity produces the diversification effect that causes the portfolio's volatility to be less than the average of the volatility levels of its two components. You can see this easily on the graph. The portfolio still has ups and downs, but it is a less volatile pattern than for either investment E or F.

The *cross-correlation of returns* (or simply correlation) is a statistical measure of the dissimilarity in patterns of returns. Correlation statistics range between –1.0, for investments that move countercyclically to one another, and +1.0, for investments that move up and down in lockstep. All other things being equal, negative correlations are better than positive correlations because countercyclical patterns create a more pronounced smoothing impact on portfolio returns.

Let's take a look at how this works in the real world. Consider the portfolio possibilities created by various combinations of large company stocks and long-term government bonds. To map out the volatility and return characteristics of different stock and bond portfolio allocations, we need estimates of the expected return and standard deviation for both large company stocks and long-term government bonds, as well as the correlation statistic that measures the degree of dissimilarity in the patterns of returns between the two. For simplicity, we will presume that the future performance of stocks and bonds will be similar to what it has been on average over the past seven decades. Figure 6–2 provides the information we need for the expected return and standard deviation statistics. The arithmetic mean, rather than the geometric mean, is used to estimate the expected return statistic.[4] The correlation coefficient for large company stocks and long-term government bonds has been +.19.

Using this information, the curved solid line on Figure 6–8 shows the performance characteristics of all the different portfolios created by different allocations of stocks and bonds. Point B corresponds to a portfolio allocated entirely to long-term government bonds. Point S corresponds to a portfolio allocated entirely to large company stocks. The straight dashed line connecting B and S shows the performance of the portfolio possibilities if stocks and bonds are perfectly positively correlated. In this situation, there is no diversification effect as we have defined it. The portfolio's volatility is equal to the weighted average of the volatility levels of its components.

---

4. The expected return is an estimate for a single-period return. The arithmetic mean is its best estimate. The standard deviation statistic is also measured relative to the arithmetic mean, not the geometric mean.

FIGURE 6-8

Long-Term Government Bond/Large Company Stock Portfolio Possiblities

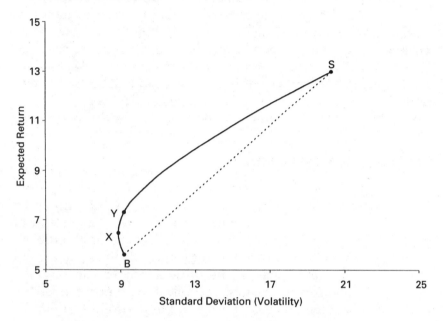

Source: Illustration produced with data generated using Vestek Systems, Inc., software.

Because stocks and bonds are not perfectly positively correlated, however, each stock and bond portfolio allocation has less
volatility than the weighted-average volatility of its components.
As a result, the set of portfolio possibilities is described by the
solid line that bows out from the straight dotted line. The horizontal distance between the dotted and solid lines measures the
beneficial diversification effect for any portfolio.

Somewhat surprisingly, the minimum volatility portfolio is
not composed entirely of long-term government bonds. Point X
on the graph corresponds to the minimum volatility portfolio. Its
allocation is 88 percent bonds and 12 percent stocks. It has a standard deviation of 8.9 percent, which is lower than the 9.2 percent
standard deviation of long-term government bonds, and its
expected return of 6.5 percent is nearly a full percentage point
higher. Ultraconservative investors, lacking an understanding of

the power of diversification, often hold portfolios allocated entirely to bonds. This illustration indicates that such investors have an opportunity to simultaneously improve expected returns while lowering their volatility risk by modest diversification into equity investments. If they are already comfortable with the volatility level of an all-bond portfolio, they can choose portfolio Y, allocated 77 percent to bonds and 23 percent to stocks. Its standard deviation of 9.2 percent is equivalent to that of an all-bond portfolio, but its expected return is 7.3 percent, 1.7 percent higher than bonds. This is an example of the power of the diversification.

THE EFFICIENT FRONTIER

An *efficient portfolio* is defined as one that maximizes expected return for a given level of volatility. Alternatively, it can be defined as a portfolio that minimizes volatility for a given level of expected return. The *efficient frontier* is the locus of all efficient portfolios, from the minimum volatility portfolio to the maximum return portfolio. On Figure 6–8, the efficient frontier extends along the curved solid line connecting portfolio X with portfolio S. The portfolios along the line from portfolio B to portfolio X are inefficient in that alternative portfolio structures exist that produce higher expected returns for each level of volatility.

This simple bond and stock diversification example considers only two investment alternatives. Adding additional choices to the menu of portfolio building blocks available creates new opportunities that may further capitalize on the diversification effect and lead to portfolio allocations that generate higher expected returns along the volatility range. When this occurs, the efficient frontier can shift into a higher position, as shown in Figure 6–9.

INTERNATIONAL DIVERSIFICATION

Figure 6–10 is a pie chart depicting the distribution of the total investable capital market as of December 31, 1997. Why not take diversification to its logical conclusion and design portfolios that use all of these major world asset classes? This would generate more opportunities for the ups and downs of one asset class to

Three- vs. Four-Investment-Alternative Efficient Frontiers

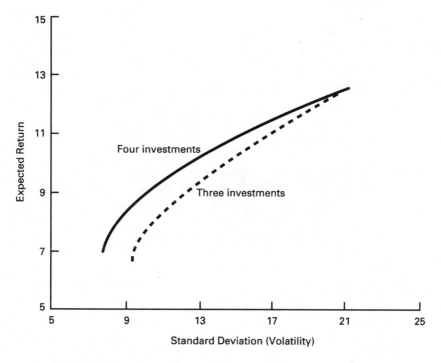

Source: Roger C. Gibson, *Asset Allocation: Balancing Financial Risk,* 2d ed., McGraw-Hill, New York, 1996.

partially offset the ups and downs of another. Multiple-asset-class portfolios should give investors a better relationship between the returns they want and the volatility they wish to mitigate.

Let's begin with interest-generating investments and examine the impact of international diversification on a domestic bond portfolio. Figure 6–11 graphs the comparative performance over rolling 20-year periods of a 100 percent U. S. long-term corporate bond portfolio versus portfolios with 10 percent, 20 percent and 30 percent international bond allocations. There are six lines on the chart, one for each 20-year rolling period ending 1992 through 1997. In each case, the bond portfolio volatility decreased and return increased as the allocation to international bonds increased from 10 percent to 30 percent.

F I G U R E   6–10

Total Investable Capital Market, December 31, 1997
(Preliminary)

$ 49.1 Trillion

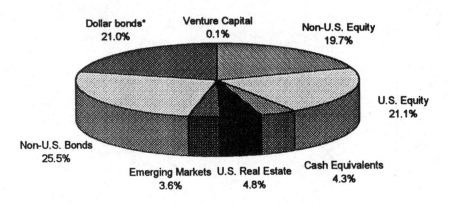

Dollar bonds*
21.0%

Venture Capital
0.1%

Non-U.S. Equity
19.7%

U.S. Equity
21.1%

Non-U.S. Bonds
25.5%

Emerging Markets
3.6%

U.S. Real Estate
4.8%

Cash Equivalents
4.3%

* Includes High-Yield Bonds
Source: Brinson Partners, Inc.

Figure 6–12 examines the impact of international diversification on a domestic common stock portfolio. The data for international common stock returns begins three years earlier than for
international bonds, and we therefore have nine rolling 20-year
periods to examine. In all but one 20-year period, the international diversification steadily improved the portfolio returns as
the commitment increased from 0 percent to 30 percent. The
notable exception was the 20-year period ending 1997. Over this
time period, domestic stock returns were sufficiently higher than
international stock returns, so as to slightly impair the portfolio
returns as we added international stocks to the domestic stock
portfolio.[5] This is not an argument against international diversifi-

---

5. Diversification into an asset class with lower returns does not necessarily result in a
   lower portfolio return. Depending on the magnitude of the difference in returns
   and the correlations among the portfolio components, diversification into a lower-
   returning asset class may actually result in an increase in portfolio return. The
   section of this chapter entitled Multiple-Asset-Class Investing contains several
   examples of this.

FIGURE 6–11

International Diversification of a Bond Portfolio
(Rolling 20-Year Periods Ending December 1992 Through
December 1997)

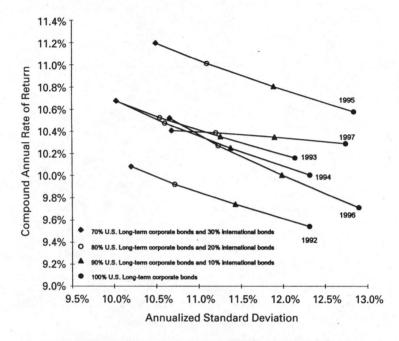

Source: Roger C. Gibson, *Asset Allocation: Balancing Financial Risk,* 2d ed., McGraw-Hill,
New York, 1996. Updated by author, Roger C. Gibson; Based on data from Salomon Brothers, Inc.;
Used with permission. ©1998 Ibbotson Associates, Inc. All rights reserved. (Certain portions of
this work were derived from copyrighted works by Roger G. Ibbotson and Rex A. Sinquefield.)

cation. Rather, this exception highlights the fact that there will be
time periods when domestic stocks generate higher returns than
international stocks. But, unless you possess the market-timing
skills to predict which asset class will be superior, a diversified
approach remains the best strategy. Over every 20-year period,
portfolio volatility was lower with a 10 percent or 20 percent
international commitment. And in almost every period, volatility
remained lower with a 30 percent international commitment, as
compared to an all-domestic common stock portfolio.

F I G U R E   6–12

International Diversification of a Stock Portfolio
(Rolling 20-Year Periods Ending December 1989 Through
December 1997)

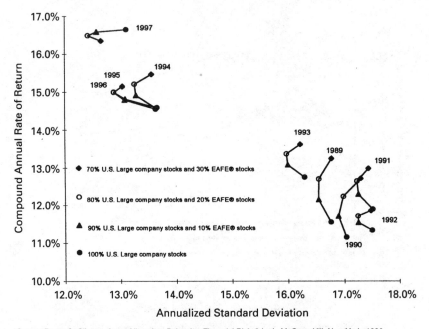

Source: Roger C. Gibson, *Asset Allocation: Balancing Financial Risk*, 2d ed., McGraw-Hill, New York, 1996.
Updated by author, Roger C. Gibson; Morgan Stanley Capital International; Used with permission. ©1998
Ibbotson Associates, Inc. All rights reserved. (Certain portions of this work were derived from copyrighted
works by Roger G. Ibbotson and Rex A. Sinquefield.)

MULTIPLE-ASSET-CLASS INVESTING

So let's now examine multiple-asset-class investing in a broader
equity context. The equity side of the portfolio is usually responsible for great portfolio returns when they occur. The equity side of
the portfolio is also most often responsible for significant losses.
Figure 6–13 shows the performance of 15 different equity portfolios over the period from 1972 through 1997. The portfolios are
intentionally unlabeled in order to conduct a "blindfolded" exercise. Of these 15 portfolios, four are identified by squares, six are
triangles, four are diamonds, and one is a circle. As you move to
the right along the chart, portfolio volatility increases. Likewise,

FIGURE 6–13

Fifteen Equity Portfolios (1972–1997)

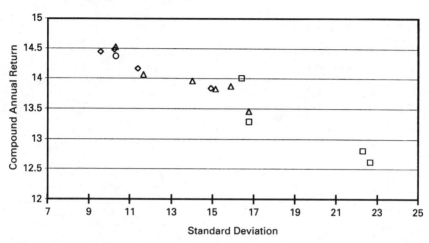

Source: © Roger C. Gibson, "Asset Allocation and the Rewards of Multiple-Asset-Class Investing", 1998.

returns increase as you move from bottom to top. Assume that you have a reliable crystal ball and know with certainty that each one of these portfolios will have the same performance over the next 26 years that it had over the period from 1972 through 1997. Now answer these questions:

- If you had to choose between owning a randomly chosen portfolio identified by a square or one identified by a triangle, which would you choose?
- If you had to choose between owning a randomly chosen portfolio identified by a triangle or one identified by a diamond, which would you choose?
- If you had to choose between owning a randomly chosen portfolio identified by a diamond or simply owning the circle, which would you choose?

I have posed this series of questions to my clients and to audiences at speaking engagements. The answers are consistent. When given the choice, people prefer the triangles to the squares, the diamonds to the triangles, and the circle to the diamonds.

F I G U R E   6–14

The Rewards of Multiple-Asset-Class Investing (1972–1997)

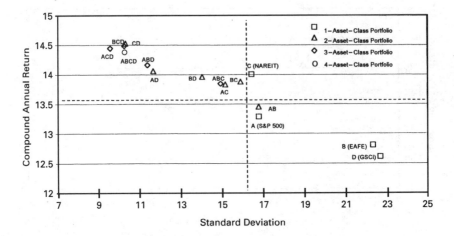

A	S&P	Domestic Stocks
B	EAFE®	International Stocks
C	Equity REITS	National Association of Real Estate Investment Trusts, Inc.
D	GSCI	Goldman Sachs Commodity Index

AB	Equal Allocation of S&P 500 and EAFE®	ABC	Equal Allocation of S&P 500, EAFE®, and Equity REITS
AC	Equal Allocation of S&P 500 and Equity REITS	ABD	Equal Allocation of S&P 500, EAFE®, and GSCI
AD	Equal Allocation of S&P 500 and GSCI	ACC	Equal Allocation of S&P 500, Equity REITS, and GSCI
BC	Equal Allocation of EAFE® and Equity REITS	BCD	Equal Allocation of EAFE®, Equity REITS, and GSCI
BD	Equal Allocation of EAFE® and GSCI	ABCD	Equal Allocation of S&P 500, EAFE®, and Equity
CD	Equal Allocation of Equity REITS and GSCI		REITS, and GSCI

Source: © Roger Gibson, 1998; Morgan Stanley Capital International: Used with permission. © 1998 Ibbotson Associates, Inc. All rights reserved. (Certain portions of this work were derived from copyrighted works of Roger G. Ibbotson and Rex Sinquefield); Copyright © (1998) by National Association of Real Estate Investment Trusts®. NAREIT® data is reprinted with permission. Statements, calculations, or charts made by the author which use NAREIT® data have not been approved, verified, or endorsed by NAREIT®; *GSCI® performance data used with permission of Goldman, Sachs & Co.*

Now turn to Figure 6–14.
Each square is a single-asset-class portfolio.

- "A" is the Standard & Poor's 500 Composite Index (S&P 500). The S&P 500 presently includes 500 of the largest U. S. stocks, as measured in terms of the total market value of shares outstanding. The index measures the total return of a capitalization-weighted basket of these stocks and, for our purposes, represents the domestic common stock asset class.

- "B" is the EAFE Index (Europe, Australia, and Far East), which measures the total return of a sample of common stocks of companies representative of the market structure of 20 European and Pacific Basin countries. It represents the international common stock asset class.
- "C" is the National Association of Real Estate Investment Trusts (NAREIT) Equity Index, which measures the total return of equity real estate investment trusts. Equity REITs are similar to closed-end funds of real estate properties. The NAREIT Equity Index is a proxy for the real estate asset class.
- "D" is the Goldman Sachs Commodity Index (GSCI). This index measures the total return of a collateralized position in the Goldman Sachs Commodity Index futures contract. The GSCI represents a diversified cross section of the major raw and semifinished goods used by producers and consumers. The major components of the index are energy, agricultural products, livestock, industrial metals, and precious metals.

The triangles represent every possible two-asset-class portfolio that investors can construct using the four single-asset classes (A, B, C, and D) as building blocks. Each portfolio is rebalanced annually to maintain an equal-weighted allocation among the asset classes. For example, the triangle AB represents the performance of a portfolio weighted equally between the S&P 500 (domestic stocks) and EAFE (international stocks).

The diamonds represent every possible three-asset-class portfolio that investors can construct with the four single-asset classes. The circle is an equally balanced portfolio using all four asset classes.

When an investor chooses a triangle portfolio over a square, he is indicating a preference for a two-asset-class portfolio over a single-asset-class portfolio. This decision is a rational one, since two-asset-class portfolios, in general, have less volatility and more return than the single-asset-class portfolios. Likewise, the three-asset-class portfolios (diamonds) have better volatility and return characteristics than the two-asset-class portfolios (triangles). The four-asset-class portfolio (circle) is a better choice than a random placement in one of the three-asset class portfolios (diamonds). The order of preference moves to the left, in the direction of less volatility, and upward, toward higher returns.

The reduction in volatility observed as we progress from one- to four-asset-class portfolios is not unanticipated. This is to be expected due to the dissimilarity in returns among the portfolio components. The generally rising pattern of returns, however, is surprising. The GSCI, for example, had lower returns with considerably more volatility than the S&P 500; yet a portfolio allocated equally between the two had a higher return with much less volatility than either of its components. Indeed, all six of the two-asset-class portfolios had higher returns with less volatility than three out of four of the single-asset classes used to build them.

When comparing the returns of these 15 equity portfolios, single-asset-class portfolios generated the three lowest returns, whereas the highest returning portfolios were all multiple-asset-class structures. When we compare the volatility levels of these portfolios, we find that four out of the five most volatile portfolios were single-asset-class structures. The low volatility alternatives are all multiple-asset-class portfolios.

In Figure 6-14, dashed lines divide the graph into four quadrants. The best-performing portfolios occupy the upper-left quadrant. These portfolios generated the highest returns with the least volatility. Each is a multiple-asset-class portfolio. The worst performing portfolios occupy the lower-right quadrant. Four portfolios occupy this space. Three are single-asset-class portfolios (S&P 500, EAFE, and GSCI), and one is a two-asset-class portfolio (S&P 500 with EAFE).

Return for a moment to the four single-asset classes. If we offer investors the opportunity to choose how they would invest their money, given complete certainty that each asset class would perform as indicated on the graph, they would likely pick portfolio C, equity REITs. The choice seems obvious. Equity REITs had both a higher return and less volatility than any of the other asset classes. Yet a portfolio allocated equally among the other three asset classes generated a higher return than REITs, with approximately 30 percent less volatility. Compare the position of C versus ABD in Figure 6–14. This amazing result occurred despite the fact that each of the other three asset classes had lower returns with more volatility than REITs!

If we asked an investor to eliminate one of the four asset classes as a building block for the multiple-asset-class portfolios, he would probably choose D, the Goldman Sachs Commodity Index. Of all 15 portfolios on the graph, GSCI has the lowest return with the most volatility. Yet the five highest-returning portfolios have D as an equal component. And the seven least-volatile portfolios have D as an equal component. Obviously, there is more going on here than is captured by the return and volatility statistics on Figure 6–14. We are missing the crucial information about how each asset class's pattern of returns correlates with the others. The GSCI, for example, has a pattern of returns that is the most dissimilar to the other asset classes. Accordingly, it produces the strongest diversification effect when combined with other asset classes.

Figure 6–15 shows the performance statistics for the 15 equity portfolios. The data in this exhibit makes a very strong case for multiple-asset-class investing. For investors concerned primarily with maximizing portfolio returns, you can see that multiple-asset-class strategies have dominated single-asset-class strategies. For investors who are more concerned about volatility, again multiple-asset-class strategies are dominant. The Sharpe ratios displayed provide a risk-adjusted performance measurement for each portfolio.[6] Again, we find multiple-asset-class strategies delivering much higher rates of risk-adjusted returns than single-asset-class strategies.

At the bottom of Figure 6–15 there are summary comparisons for four-, three-, two- and one-asset-class approaches. This summary provides perhaps the most compelling argument for multiple-asset-class investing. As we move toward broader diversification, rates of return increase, volatility levels decrease, and

---

6. The Sharpe ratio is a measure of reward relative to total volatility. The statistic is a ratio of a portfolio's excess return above that of a Treasury bill divided by the portfolio's standard deviation. The Sharpe ratio affirms the notion that a portfolio should generate some incremental reward for the assumption of volatility. Otherwise, it would be better to simply own Treasury bills.

F I G U R E 6–15

The Rewards of Multiple-Asset-Class Investing
(1972 through 1997)

Performance Statistics for the Fifteen Equity Portfolios

Compound Annual Returns and Future Values of $1.00 Ranked High to Low			Standard Deviations (Volatility) Ranked Low to High		Sharpe Ratios Ranked High to Low	
	%	$		%		
CD	14.53	34.00	ACD	9.59	ACD	0.79
BCD	14.48	33.67	BCD	10.26	BCD	0.74
ACD	14.44	33.36	ABCD	10.30	CD	0.74
ABCD	14.38	32.89	CD	10.32	ABCD	0.73
ABD	14.16	31.31	ABD	11.40	ABD	0.64
AD	14.06	30.59	AD	11.68	AD	0.61
C	14.01	30.21	BD	14.05	BD	0.50
BD	13.96	29.88	ABC	14.95	ABC	0.46
BC	13.87	29.31	AC	15.18	AC	0.46
ABC	13.84	29.07	BC	15.92	BC	0.44
AC	13.83	29.00	C	16.44	C	0.43
AB	13.45	26.62	AB	16.79	AB	0.39
A	13.28	25.61	A	16.79	A	0.38
B	12.81	22.94	B	22.30	B	0.26
D	12.61	21.95	D	22.66	D	0.25

Average Performance Statistics: Four-, Three-, Two-, and One-Asset-Class Portfolios

Compound Annual Returns and Future Values of $1.00 Ranked High to Low			Standard Deviations (Volatility) Ranked Low to High		Sharpe Ratios Ranked High to Low	
	%	$		%		
Four	14.38	32.89	Four	10.30	Four	0.73
Three	14.23	31.85	Three	11.55	Three	0.66
Two	13.95	29.90	Two	13.99	Two	0.52
One	13.18	25.18	One	19.55	One	0.33

F I G U R E   6–16

The Five Worst Years (1972 through 1997)

Portfolios Structures

A S&P 500		B EAFE®		C NAREIT		D GSCI		E Equal Allocation	
Year	Return	Year	Return	Year	Return	Year	Return	Year	Return
1974	−26.47	1990	−23.19	1974	−21.40	1981	−23.01	1974	−7.63
1973	−14.66	1974	−22.15	1973	−15.52	1975	−17.22	1981	−5.74
1977	−7.18	1973	−14.17	1990	−15.35	1997	−14.07	1990	−3.16
1981	−4.91	1992	−11.85	1987	−3.64	1993	−12.33	1992	3.71
1990	−3.17	1981	−1.03	1994	3.17	1976	−11.92	1994	4.46

Sharpe ratios improve. The four-asset-class portfolio has a compound rate of return 1.2 percent higher than the average compound returns of it components. That is, a $1 investment in a continuously rebalanced portfolio of all four components has a future value of $32.89, compared with an average future value of $25.18 for the four components standing alone. The four-asset-class portfolio has 47 percent less volatility than the average volatility levels of its components. And the Sharpe ratio of the four-asset-class portfolio shows that it has generated over twice as much risk-adjusted return as the average of its components.

Figure 6–16 gives another picture of the risk reduction achieved by the breadth of diversification. Here we list the five worst years, from 1972 through 1997, generated by each of the single-asset classes as compared with the four-asset-class portfolio. Most of the improvement in downside risk is due to the tendency of the Goldman Sachs Commodity Index to perform counter-cyclically to the other asset classes, an attribute that was of great value during the worldwide bear market for common stocks during 1973 and 1974. But even with the elimination of the GSCI as a building block, the analysis supports a multiple-asset-class approach with the remaining three asset classes.

It is often difficult to see the beneficial impact on return created by broader diversification because diversification examples mix fixed-income investments with equity investments. In this situation, the large difference between the returns of fixed-income and equity investments obscures the increase in portfolio return attributable to the diversification effect. Because the longer-term rates of return of the four equity asset classes used in this analysis were fairly similar, you can see the positive impact diversification has on both dampening volatility and increasing return.

WHY ISN'T EVERYONE DOING MULTIPLE-ASSET-CLASS INVESTING?

If multiple-asset-class investing is so wonderful, why isn't everyone doing it? There are three primary reasons. First, investors lack an awareness of the power of diversification. The typical investor understands that diversification may reduce volatility but suspects that it simultaneously impairs returns. As we have demonstrated, diversification tends to improve returns, not diminish them. Investors need to be educated about this dual benefit.

Second, the question of market timing arises. Investors naturally want to believe that there must be some way to predict which asset class will come in first place. And some money managers suggest that they in fact can make such market-timing predictions accurately. Let's assume that we have a market timer with whom we consult annually for his prediction of the following year's best-performing asset class among the S&P 500, EAFE, NAREIT, and GSCI. Had he successfully predicted the winning asset class over the past 15 years, from 1983 through 1997, an investor following his recommendations would have earned a compound rate of return of 32.33 percent. If such market-timing skill exists, there should be evidence of money managers earning these rates of return. A check of Morningstar's database, reveals that there is a universe of nearly 600 mutual funds with at least 15 years of performance history. Included is the full variety of professionally managed domestic and international funds, equity and fixed-income funds, as well as various specialty funds. How many of these funds had compound rates of return in excess of 32.33 percent? None! Not one got remotely close.

Maybe we are asking too much proficiency from our market timer. Let's assume that his prediction for the winning asset class each year never finished first but instead came in second place among the four asset classes. This does not seem like a particularly impressive achievement. Yet it would have generated a 15-year compound annual return of 19.59 percent. Out of nearly 600 funds, only three had better investment performance. This is only one-half of one percent of all professionally managed mutual funds. And none of the three funds relied on market timing to deliver their impressive returns.

Perhaps this is still asking too much of the market timer. What if we ask him to simply recognize the long periods of dominance of one asset class over another? For example, our market timer might instruct us to invest our funds in EAFE during the portion of the 15-year period that fell in the 1980s and then switch to the S&P 500 for the 1990s. This strategy would have generated a compound return of 22.81 percent. Again, not one mutual fund manager among 638 funds achieved that rate of return. Apparently, predicting the performance of asset classes is hard to do successfully.

The third reason involves investor psychology. Investors use their domestic market as a frame of reference for evaluating their investment results. For example, a United States-based investor will compare her equity returns to a market index like the S&P 500. This frame of reference is not a problem in years when the domestic market underperforms other asset classes, since diversification into better-performing markets rewards a multiple-asset-class investor. When the domestic market comes out on top, however, the investor perceives that diversification has impaired her returns. This sense of winning or losing arises primarily from the investor's immediate frame of reference. For example, the four-asset-class portfolio we have been discussing had a 10.4 percent return in 1997. Given either an EAFE or GSCI frame of reference, investors perceive this as a "winning" return, since these asset classes had returns of 2.05 percent and −14.07 percent respectively in 1997. This return is lousy from either an S&P 500 or NAREIT perspective, since these asset classes had returns of 33.36 percent and 20.26 percent respectively.

Each year, the multiple-asset-class strategy loses relative to some of its component asset classes and wins relative to others. That is the nature of diversification. As of the date of this writing, the S&P 500 is everyone's favorite asset class, despite the fact that its return ranked 13th and its volatility was third highest out of the 15 equity portfolios in the example. The S&P 500's current popularity is a result of its remarkable performance from 1995 through 1997. Yet over the 26-year period of our analysis, the S&P 500 came in first place only four times. This is fewer first place finishes than EAFE, NAREIT, or GSCI. The frame-of-reference problem is particularly acute because two of these first-place finishes happened quite recently, in 1995 and 1997. This three-year period of S&P 500 dominance seems like an eternity to investors and fuels dissatisfaction with the lower returns generated over the same time period by a multiple-asset-class strategy. As a friend in the business observed, the problem with diversification is that it works whether you want it to or not!

This frame-of-reference problem should not be underestimated. Investors compare their investment results with their friends while playing golf or at cocktail parties. The true multiple-asset-class investor is still in the minority. During periods when the U.S. market prevails, this person will feel particularly vulnerable talking with friends who own a more traditional domestic stock and bond portfolio. Recently, a client told me that he would rather follow a strategy where he loses when his friends are losing than follow a superior long-term strategy that at times loses while his friends are winning. There is pain in being different.

Equity investing is a long-term endeavor, and investors should devise and implement strategies with the long term in mind. Investors naturally attach more significance to recent investment experience than to longer-term performance, but they should resist the temptation to abandon more diversified strategies in favor of chasing yesterday's winner.

The multiple-asset-class investing analysis presented here is a pedagogical illustration which, for simplicity, utilizes equal-weighted strategies of various combinations of the S&P 500, EAFE, NAREIT, and GSCI. Although I am a strong proponent of multiple-asset-class investing, I do not recommend an equal-weighted strategy for my clients. My reasoning is partially rooted in the psychological concerns of this frame-of-reference issue. A more suitable alternative would be to allocate the four-asset-class portfolio 40 percent to the S&P 500, 30 percent to EAFE, 20 percent to NAREIT, and 10 percent to GSCI. This allocation weights the portfolio in favor of more familiar asset classes and would have given its investor a 16.6 percent return in 1997. This return still lags the first place S&P 500 asset class, but the performance is closer to the investor's frame of reference. Interestingly, this alternative would still have a greater return and less volatility than any of its components had over the 26-year period of our analysis. But its performance relative to an equal-weighted strategy would be inferior. The compound return of this 40/30/20/10 allocation was 14.04 percent, compared with 14.38 percent from the equal-weighted strategy. Its standard deviation of 12.96 percent was also worse than the 10.3 percent standard deviation of the equal-weighted strategy. Although its performance is not as favorable, the alternative portfolio structure may still be the better choice, given the psychological issues involved.

Occasionally, a client follows this analysis and questions its merit because it relies on historical data that may be irrelevant when looking into the future. His or her argument rests on the notion that the world is very different today than it was during the time period covered by my multiple-asset-class investing analysis; risks and opportunities exist now that have no historical precedent. Although that may be true, investor behavior is much the same as it has always been. Investors prefer predictability to uncertainty, and they face a menu of investment alternatives differentiated according to their levels of volatility. The buying and selling activity of investors establishes security prices that bring supply and demand into equilibrium. For this to occur, more-volatile asset classes must have higher expected returns than less-volatile asset classes. This leads to competitive, risk-adjusted returns across investment alternatives. The diversification benefits of a multiple-asset-class approach rest on dissimilarity in patterns of returns across investment alternatives in the short run, and competitive asset pricing in the long run. These conditions should hold in the future, even in the face of risks and opportunities that are unique to our times. But for the sake of argument, let's assume with the critics that the future is simply unknowable.

If there is no basis upon which to make predictions about the future, the wisest investment strategy is to broadly diversify portfolios in order to mitigate the risks of unknowable markets. Their criticism, in fact, supports the argument in favor of multiple-asset-class investing.

INVESTMENT PORTFOLIO DESIGN FORMAT

Figure 6–17 provides a format for designing a portfolio according to the principles discussed in this chapter. We begin at the left with the total value of the investor's portfolio. Investors naturally tend to prefer to retain their current investment holdings. This inertia inhibits clear investment decision-making. To overcome this problem, it is helpful if the investor hypothetically converts all of his current investments to cash before proceeding with the portfolio design. This process creates an opportunity for the investor to make fresh decisions based on her present and future needs, unencumbered by past investment decisions.

The most general level of decision-making is labeled Investment Policy. At this level, the investor determines her allocation among short-term debt investments, long-term debt investments, and equity investments. As was discussed previously, this is the most important decision the investor makes, because it determines the portfolio's growth path through time and the general volatility level. Subject to the investment policy decisions, the investor proceeds to the Asset Allocation level. Here, I advocate a globally diversified, multiple-asset-allocation approach. In order to obtain the diversification benefits described in Figure 6–11, we allocate the long-term debt investments between domestic and international bonds. The equity investments are allocated across four asset classes. The 15-equity portfolio analysis previously discussed uses an index representing each of these equity asset classes. By globally diversifying the portfolio in this manner, the investor creates the maximum opportunity for the diversification effect to work its magic. The final level of decision-making involves the choice of specific investment positions to execute the strategy.

FIGURE 6–17

Investment Portfolio Design Format

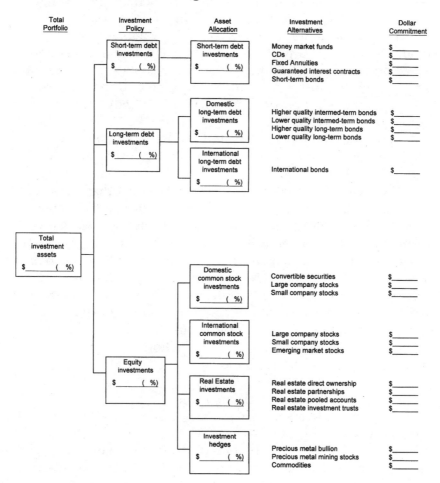

Source: Roger C. Gibson, *Asset Allocation: Balancing Financial Risk,* 2d ed., McGraw-Hill, New York, 1996.

CONCLUSION

Asset allocation is vitally important. The benefits of diversification are powerful and robust, not just in terms of volatility reduction, but also for return enhancement. To evaluate the desirability of an asset class as a portfolio building block, it is not enough to know only its return and volatility characteristics. One must also know how its pattern of returns correlates to the patterns of returns of the other portfolio components. All other things being equal, the more dissimilarity there is among the asset classes within a portfolio, the stronger the diversification effect, providing investors with not only less volatility but also greater returns in the long run.

The beauty of diversification lies in the fact that its benefits are not dependent on the exercise of superior skill. They arise from the policy decision to follow a multiple-asset-class investment approach. Imagine for a moment that each of the portfolios in Figure 6–13 represented the performance of a different common stock manager, each actively engaged in trying to outperform his competitors through superior skill in security selection. We would want to know what the managers in the upper-left quadrant are doing to generate returns that are on average over 1 percent higher, with more than a one-third reduction in volatility, as compared to the managers in the lower-right quadrant. Amazingly, these marked performance advantages did not rely on skill, but rather on a simple policy decision: diversify!

The multiple-asset-class strategy resembles a tortoise-and-hare story. Over any one-year, three-year, or ten-year period, the race will probably be led by one of the component single-asset classes. The leader will, of course, attract the attention. The tortoise never runs as fast as many of the hares around it. But it does run faster on average than the majority of its competitors, a fact that becomes lost due to the attention-getting pace of different lead rabbits during various legs of the race. It is noteworthy that the time period for the multiple-asset-class analysis presented in this chapter is 26 years.[7] The length of a marathon is 26 miles.

---

7. Twenty-six years is the longest period of time for which performance data were
   available for all four indices representing the equity asset classes.

Think of this 26-year, multiple-asset-class illustration as a marathon. The GSCI rabbit led the first third of the race during the 1970s. The second third of the race was run in the 1980s, when the EAFE rabbit ran the fastest. During the final third of the race , the 1990s, the S&P 500 rabbit was out-pacing all others. There is always a hare running faster than the multiple-asset-class tortoise, and depending on the leg of the race, it is usually a different hare that takes the lead. Yet the tortoise, in the long run, leaves the pack behind. We know the moral of the story: slow and steady wins the race. In the end, patience and discipline are rewarded. To secure the reward, we need to relinquish our domestic frame of reference and invest as citizens of the world.

ACKNOWLEDGMENTS

This chapter would have been impossible without the assistance of many companies who graciously provided research support and capital market data. Accordingly, I would like to thank Ibbotson Associates; Brinson Partners, Inc.; Salomon Smith Barney; Morgan Stanley & Co. Inc.; National Association of Real Estate Investment Trusts, Inc.; and Goldman Sachs & Co. I also want to thank several people on my staff at Gibson Capital Management, Ltd., for their assistance in research support, exhibit preparation, text layout, and copy editing: Brenda Berczik, Michael Reinert, Mona Higgins, and Keith Goldner.

CHAPTER 7

Asset Allocation and Portfolio Strategies

Vinod Chandrashekaran, Ph.D.
Senior Consultant, Research
BARRA Inc.
Berkeley, California

INTRODUCTION

The decade of the 1990s marked the advent of globalization both at the macroeconomic level (as measured by indicators such as international trade) and at the financial level (as indicated by international capital flows, increased interest in international investment, and so forth). Among the events that have propelled the world economy in this direction are the dismantling of the communist regimes in the former Soviet Union and eastern European nations; the coordination of monetary policies by western European nations under the European Monetary System; the formation of the European Monetary Union of 11 nations on January 1, 1999; the dramatic growth rate in many Asian economies, such as China, Thailand, Malaysia, and Indonesia, over much of this decade; and the much-heralded arrival of the Information Age. The world economy also faced a number of crises over this time period, including the Mexican peso devaluation in 1994; the crisis in southeast Asia that began in late 1997; the decline in property values in Japan, leading to a severe banking crisis and extreme sluggishness in the Japanese economy; and several spectacular bankruptcies, such as Barings Bank in the U.K. and Orange County in the U.S. Over much of the nineties, large multinational companies that are well-positioned to take advantage of the global marketplace have been rewarded with high earnings growth rates and rich stock market valuations.

Along with this greater opportunity in the global economy have come greater risks, since financial systems—indeed, entire economies—are now interlinked as never before. In this economic environment, it is quite important for the global investor to fully understand the risks of international investment strategies and be prepared to carefully manage them.

This chapter deals with two main themes; the *measurement* of risk and the *management* of risk. The next section presents a recent historical perspective on the volatility and correlations across selected world equity markets. In that section, I show that correlations across these markets appear to have increased, in some instances quite dramatically, since the southeast Asian crisis of July 1997. That is followed by a discussion of ways to attribute the total risk of an internationally diversified equity portfolio into its main constituents, namely, currency risk and local market risk. The analysis presented in this section suggests a useful way to formulate the currency-hedging decision. Finally, there is an examination of the use of portfolio optimization in international asset allocation. Given inputs on means, variances, and covariances of asset returns, optimal portfolios efficiently trade off risks and returns at the aggregate level and produce portfolios that dominate other possible asset combinations, at least on paper. Portfolio optimization offers an efficient and disciplined way to optimally utilize all available information in the portfolio construction process. One final note: Throughout this discussion, I employ examples involving diversified international equity portfolios. The general concepts carry over to fixed-income investments as well. In instances where there might be significant differences, I indicate this with brief comments.

RECENT HISTORICAL PERSPECTIVE

In this section, I examine the volatilities and correlations of international equity markets over the two-year period from July 1996 through June 1998. From an asset allocation perspective, *forecasts* of volatilities and correlations are important. Therefore, I will give brief attention to statistical techniques that can be employed to obtain good forecasts of these quantities.

Global Market Volatility

Undeniably, world financial markets have undergone a sea change since the crisis in southeast Asia began in July 1997. Table 7–1 presents the volatility of selected world equity markets from a local-currency perspective over the 12-month period prior to July 1997 and the 12-month period following July 1997. It should come as no surprise that volatilities have increased across-the-board in all the financial markets studied in Table 7–1. Since the second period includes the crash of October 1997, it is natural to conjecture that the events around October 1997 might be responsible for the higher second-period volatilities observed in the table. Figure 7–1 provides another perspective on this question by plotting rolling volatilities of local-currency returns estimated over 180-day periods for a subset of the markets depicted in Table 7–1. The figure shows that for some markets (e.g., Brazil and Mexico),

TABLE 7–1

Annualized Standard Deviation of Daily Returns for Various International Equity Markets

Country	7/1996 to 6/1997	7/1997 to 6/1998
Developed Markets		
U.S.	13.5%	16.9%
U.K.	9.9%	15.8%
Germany	13.8%	23.5%
Japan	15.5%	22.8%
Emerging Markets, Southeast Asia		
Singapore	14.3%	34.8%
Thailand	30.8%	57.7%
Emerging Markets, Latin America		
Argentina	20.6%	33.3%
Brazil	16.1%	39.1%
Mexico	14.9%	27.8%

Measured in local currency.

FIGURE 7–1

Rolling 180-Day Annualized Standard Deviation of Daily
Returns (in Dollar Terms) on Selected Countries

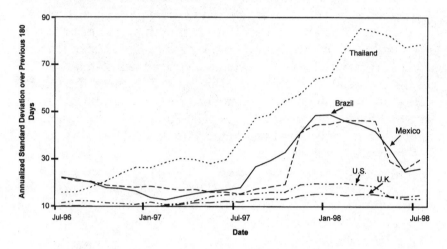

rolling volatilities over very recent periods did indeed drop
sharply when the 180-day window excluded the period around
October 1997. In spite of this, there is strong evidence in Figure
7–1 to suggest that volatilities have not returned to their pre-July
1997 levels. For example, even relatively less volatile markets
such as the U.S. and the U.K. have seen increases in standard
deviation on the order of at least 2 percent per annum.

Global Market Correlations

An important determinant of the risk of an internationally diversified equity portfolio is the correlation structure across global markets. Table 7–2 shows market correlations from a local-currency
perspective over the same two periods considered in Table 7–1. A
number of inferences are possible from the table. First, not surprisingly, correlations within southeast Asian markets have increased
over the 12-month period since the crash. Second, perhaps driven
by the global financial crisis, correlations within developed markets (such as the U.S., U.K., and Germany) have also increased
since the crash. Third, correlations of Latin American markets
with the U.S. market show dramatic increases since the crash.

T A B L E 7–2

Correlation Matrices for Various International
Equity Markets

Country	Period	U.S.	U.K.	Germany	Japan	Singapore	Thailand	Argentina	Brazil
U.K	1	0.29							
	2	0.48							
Germany	1	0.17	0.50						
	2	0.32	0.62						
Japan	1	0.06	0.27	0.26					
	2	0.11	0.29	0.32					
Singapore	1	0.08	0.15	0.24	0.23				
	2	0.10	0.35	0.35	0.31				
Thailand	1	−0.05	−0.00	0.05	0.02	0.24			
	2	0.12	0.26	0.22	0.25	0.47			
Argentina	1	0.44	0.17	0.14	0.02	0.07	0.00		
	2	0.70	0.39	0.26	0.18	0.22	0.17		
Brazil	1	0.32	0.28	0.25	0.08	0.09	−0.03	0.42	
	2	0.57	0.40	0.30	0.18	0.16	0.18	0.70	
Mexico	1	0.34	0.20	0.21	0.03	0.22	0.18	0.34	0.29
	2	0.68	0.40	0.28	0.17	0.18	0.14	0.75	0.62

Correlations are computed using daily returns over two time periods. Period 1 runs from July 1996 through June 1997, and period 2 runs from July 1997 through June 1998.

Figure 7–2 shows rolling 180-day correlations in local-currency terms between selected markets and the U.S. The figure confirms that the increased correlations in Table 7–2 do not appear to be unduly influenced by the market behavior around October 1997.

Forecasting Market Volatility and Correlations

Academic research over the past 15 years suggests that while a historical perspective of global market volatilities and correlations is useful to the extent that it offers valuable clues to market participants on the likely future structure of these parameters,

F I G U R E 7–2

Rolling 180-Day Correlations of Daily Returns (in Dollar Terms) on Selected Countries with the U.S. Stock Market

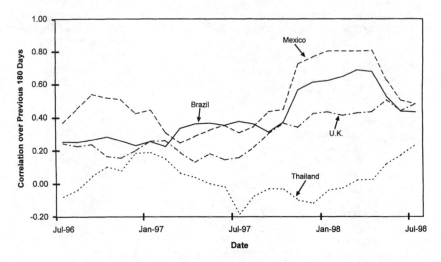

sophisticated statistical models can improve upon naïve forecasts that are based simply on extrapolations of the past into the future. With regard to volatility prediction, the ARCH-family of models, pioneered by Engle (1982), is widely used. Since Engle's work, numerous variants of the ARCH model have been proposed in an attempt to improve volatility forecasts. One extremely popular variant of the ARCH model, called the GARCH(1,1) model, was proposed by Bollerslev (1986). This model postulates that variances evolve according to the following equation:

$$\sigma_t^2 = \omega + \alpha \varepsilon_{t-1}^2 + \beta \sigma_{t-1}^2 \qquad (1)$$

In equation 1, σ_t^2 is the forecast made at the start of time period t for the variance of return over time t; σ_{t-1}^2 is a similar forecast one period earlier; ε_{t-1} is the return in period t-1 over its mean value; and ω, α, and β are parameters. Table 7–3 shows the parameters for a GARCH(1,1) model, fitted to various international equity markets using daily local-currency returns over the period July 1997 through June 1998. By simply iterating equation 1 as many times as needed, the GARCH model can be used to

TABLE 7–3

Estimates of GARCH(1,1) Model Parameters for Selected Countries, July 1997 Through June 1998*

Country	ω (x 10^{-5})	α	β	GARCH Forecast Standard Deviation for July 1, 1998 (% per annum)	Forecast Standard Deviation for July 1998,Using Daily GARCH model (% per annum)	Long-Run Forecast Standard Deviation, Using GARCH model (% per annum)
U.S.	0.665	0.0542	0.8724	14.95	15.00	15.05
U.K.	2.254	0.0509	0.7112	15.37	15.38	15.39
Germany	3.669	0.1163	0.6928	19.54	21.41	21.92
Japan	1.553	0.1055	0.8155	27.32	24.71	22.17
Singapore	9.388	0.1812	0.5738	28.08	30.47	30.95
Thailand	5.969	0.2241	0.7576	60.14	66.51	90.32
Argentina	2.838	0.1439	0.7732	32.41	30.73	29.27
Brazil	5.699	0.2486	0.6524	27.77	34.24	37.93
Mexico	3.816	0.1834	0.6536	31.47	26.29	24.19

* Using local market daily returns.

produce forecasts over any desired horizon. For example, Table 7–3 shows GARCH forecasts for volatilities for July 1, 1998 (short-term forecast), over the month of July 1998 (medium-term forecast), and the long-run forecast. In the GARCH model, the sum of the coefficients α and β is a measure of the persistence of shocks to the volatility process. Generally speaking, shocks to volatility are most important over the short-term, and their influence gradually dissipates over time. However, the rate at which the impact of these shocks dies out depends on the value of $\alpha + \beta$. Another feature of GARCH is that as the forecast horizon lengthens, you would expect volatility forecasts to approach the long-run forecast. An examination of the table reveals instances where shocks die out very slowly (e.g., Thailand) and instances where the forecast for the month of July 1998 is close to the long-run forecast (e.g., Germany).

Many researchers have observed that volatilities tend to increase following down moves in the market and tend to decrease following up moves. Nelson (1991) proposed the EGARCH model to capture this asymmetric response of volatility to movements in the market. Glosten, Jagannathan, and Runkle (1993) performed a comprehensive assessment of the performance of various types of GARCH models and found that a specification that is similar to EGARCH is quite accurate in volatility prediction. Other extensions of GARCH models have addressed the forecastability of correlations across different markets. For example, Bollerslev, Engle, and Wooldridge (1988) proposed the multivariate GARCH-M model to capture time-varying covariances across asset classes. One drawback of many of these extensions is that the resulting models are quite cumbersome to estimate.

ATTRIBUTING THE RISK OF AN INTERNATIONALLY DIVERSIFIED PORTFOLIO

Marginal Contribution to Total Risk

Marginal contribution analysis is a useful way to attribute the risk of a portfolio to the various positions held in the portfolio. Let h denote the vector of asset holdings in the portfolio and let V denote the predicted covariance matrix of these assets. The predicted standard deviation of this portfolio is given by:

$$\sigma_p = \sqrt{h'Vh}$$

The marginal contribution of a given asset to the total risk of the portfolio is defined as the increase in portfolio standard deviation due to a 1 percent increase in the position of the asset financed by a 1 percent decrease in cash. The vector of marginal contributions is given by:

$$\text{MCTR} = \frac{d\sigma_p}{dh} = \frac{Vh}{\sigma_p}$$

The weighted sum of asset marginal contributions, using asset holdings as weights, is equal to the portfolio standard deviation. This means that the weight of each asset in the portfolio times its marginal contribution can be interpreted as the propor-

T A B L E 7–4

Marginal Contribution to Total Risk

Developed Markets Portfolio				
Country	Portfolio Weight	Marginal Contribution to Total Risk (% per annum)	Portfolio Weight times MCTR (% per annum)	Proportional Contribution to Risk
U.S.	0.35	11.32	3.96	0.29
U.K.	0.25	11.33	2.83	0.21
Germany	0.20	15.86	3.17	0.23
Japan	0.20	18.71	3.74	0.27
Total	1.00	—	13.71	1.00
Emerging Markets Portfolio				
Country	Portfolio Weight	Marginal Contribution to Total Risk (% per annum)	Portfolio Weight times MCTR (% per annum)	Proportional Contribution to Risk
U.K.	0.10	6.71	0.67	0.02
Germany	0.05	8.39	0.42	0.01
Japan	0.05	10.80	0.54	0.02
Argentina	0.25	21.68	5.42	0.17
Brazil	0.25	26.02	6.50	0.21
Thailand	0.30	59.10	17.73	0.57
Total	1.00	—	31.28	1.00

Measured in dollar terms.

tion of the portfolio standard deviation attributable to the asset. We should note here that marginal contribution analysis requires a forecast of the variances and covariances of various markets. Since our purpose here is primarily pedagogical, we use realized variances and covariances over the period July 1997 through June 1998 as our forecasts in all our marginal contribution analysis.

Table 7–4 shows an example of this technique applied to two internationally diversified equity portfolios, one invested in developed markets and the other invested primarily in emerging markets. From the table, it is clear that proportional contribution to risk using marginal contribution analysis can be quite different from the actual asset weight in the portfolio. Examples of this are Japan in the developed markets portfolio (27 percent contribution to risk versus 20 percent by weight of portfolio) and Thailand in the emerging markets portfolio (57 percent contribution to risk versus 30 percent by weight).

Currency Risk and Local Market Risk

In the context of an international portfolio, it is useful to extend marginal contribution analysis to examine separately the contributions of currency risk and local market risk. It should be noted that this analysis is far more important for internationally diversified bond portfolios than for equity portfolios. The reason is that currency risk comprises a substantial fraction of the risk of a bond portfolio, whereas it is typically less important for equity portfolios. This claim is predicated on the assumption of relatively stable currency exchange rates, and as will be shown below, currency risk can be quite important for equity portfolios under certain scenarios. Table 7–5 reports the volatility of selected world equity markets from a dollar perspective over the 12-month period prior to July 1997 and the 12-month period following July 1997. Comparing Table 7–5 with Table 7–1, you can see some instances (e.g., Singapore, Thailand, and Mexico) in which currency risk is quite substantial even for equity portfolios. Table 7–6 presents a marginal contribution analysis to show separately the components due to currency risk and local-market risk. Consistent with the relatively stable exchange rates across developed markets, the portfolio in Panel A of this table shows that the marginal contribution to risk due to currency exposure is fairly small. There are two ways to see this. First, the annualized standard deviation of the fully hedged developed markets portfolio is 13.64 percent compared to 13.71 percent for the unhedged portfolio. Second, this panel shows that at the margin, currency exposure contributes about 7 percent to the risk of this portfolio. In contrast, Panel B shows that currency exposure to emerging markets can contribute significantly to portfolio risk. The annualized standard

T A B L E 7–5

Annualized Standard Deviation of Daily Returns (in dollars)

Country	7/1996 to 6/1997	7/1997 to 6/1998
Developed Markets		
U.S.	13.5%	16.9%
U.K.	11.0%	15.1%
Germany	13.4%	22.0%
Japan	17.9%	29.0%
Emerging Markets, Southeast Asia		
Singapore	14.4%	41.2%
Thailand	32.4%	72.0%
Emerging Markets, Latin America		
Argentina	20.6%	33.2%
Brazil	16.1%	39.4%
Mexico	17.1%	38.4%

deviation of the fully hedged emerging markets portfolio is 27.86 percent compared to 31.28 percent for the unhedged portfolio, which shows that currency hedging can reduce risk quite significantly. Panel B also shows that at the margin, currency exposure contributes about 15 percent to the risk of this portfolio.

Currency Hedging

In Table 7–6, the column labeled Marginal Contribution to Total Risk of Currency shows the marginal effect on portfolio risk of increasing currency exposure. Simply reversing the sign of the entries in this column yields the marginal benefit to hedging the corresponding currency exposure. For the developed markets portfolio, it is clear that a manager wishing to reduce the currency risk of this portfolio should consider hedging the exposure to Japanese yen. Table 7–7 shows that if the Japanese yen exposure is

T A B L E 7–6

Marginal Contribution to Total Risk Decomposed into
Currency and Local-Market Components

Panel A: Developed Markets Portfolio

Country	Weight in Portfolio	Marginal Contribution to Total Risk of Local Market (% per annum)	Proportional Contribution to Total Risk of Local Market	Marginal Contribution to Total Risk of Currency (% per annum)	Proportional Contribution to Total Risk of Currency
U.S.	0.35	11.32	0.29	0.00	0.00
U.K.	0.25	11.29	0.20	0.03	0.00
Germany	0.20	16.34	0.24	–0.48	0.00
Japan	0.20	13.83	0.20	4.87	0.07
Total	1.00	—	0.93	—	0.07
Singapore (currency only)	0.00	—	0.00	3.46	0.00

Panel B: Emerging Markets Portfolio

Country	Weight in Portfolio	Marginal Contribution to Total Risk of Local Market (% per annum)	Proportional Contribution to Total Risk of Local Market	Marginal Contribution to Total Risk of Currency (% per annum)	Proportional Contribution to Total Risk of Currency
U.K.	0.10	7.42	0.02	–0.71	–0.00
Germany	0.05	8.96	0.01	–0.57	–0.00
Japan	0.05	7.99	0.01	2.80	0.00
Argentina	0.25	21.68	0.17	–0.01	–0.00
Brazil	0.25	25.78	0.21	0.23	0.00
Thailand	0.30	44.47	0.43	14.63	0.14
Total	1.00	—	0.85	—	0.15
Singapore (currency only)	0.00	—	0.00	5.04	0.00

T A B L E 7-7

Effect of Currency Hedging on Portfolio Standard Deviation

Portfolio	Unhedged	Fully Hedged	Hedge Currency with Highest Marginal Contribution	Proxy Hedge Currency with Highest Marginal Contribution
Developed markets portfolio	13.71	13.64	12.96% (hedge Japanese yen)	13.25% (hedge with Singapore dollar, correlation with yen is 0.51)
Emerging markets portfolio	31.28	27.86	27.88% (hedge Thai baht)	29.98% (hedge with Singapore dollar, correlation with baht is 0.50)

fully hedged, the risk of this portfolio falls to 12.96 percent compared to 13.71 percent in the unhedged case. For the emerging markets portfolio, Table 7–6 shows that hedging the Thai baht exposure will lead to reduction of currency risk. From Table 7–7, you can see that if the Thai baht exposure is fully hedged, the risk of this portfolio drops from 31.28 percent to 27.88 percent.

Proxy Hedging

On some occasions, based on cost of hedging considerations or because of certain expectations of currency movements, a manager might consider hedging a given currency with another closely related proxy. This is referred to as *proxy hedging*. To illustrate this idea, let's examine the effect of hedging the risk of the Japanese yen exposure in the developed markets portfolio and the Thai baht exposure in the emerging markets portfolio, using the Singapore dollar as the proxy currency in both cases. The Singapore dollar has a correlation of approximately 0.5 with both the Japanese yen and the Thai baht. The last rows of Panels A and B of Table 7–6 confirm that a (marginal) long position in the

Singapore dollar has marginal contribution to total risk compara-
ble to that of the Japanese yen in the developed markets portfolio
and to that of the Thai baht in the emerging markets portfolio.
This implies that a short position in the Singapore dollar is likely
to offer some reduction in risk. The last column in Table 7–7,
which computes the risk to the two portfolios of taking "full
proxy-hedged" short positions in Singapore dollars, confirms that
there is indeed a reduction in risk.

Extensions of Marginal Contribution Analysis

In the discussion above, I have focused almost entirely on ways to
use marginal contribution analysis to study the risk of an internationally diversified portfolio and to aid in currency-hedging decisions. This type of analysis is directly applicable to passive portfolio management. Active managers are typically focused on
risk and expected returns. The marginal contribution analysis presented above can be extended in a straightforward way to the
active management problem by defining the notion of *value added*,
or *certainty equivalent return*, as follows:

$$VA = h'\mu - \lambda h'Vh$$

In this equation, μ is the expected return vector of the assets
in the portfolio and λ is the coefficient of risk aversion for the
active manager. The vector h may contain total holdings or active
positions relative to the benchmark. Essentially, this analysis turns
the risk of the portfolio into a penalty on the expected return of
the portfolio. The marginal contribution to value added is defined
as follows:

$$MCVA = \frac{d(VA)}{dh} = \mu - 2\lambda Vh$$

The analysis in the previous sections can be extended to this
case with minor modifications.

CONSTRUCTING MEAN-VARIANCE OPTIMAL PORTFOLIOS

Overview of Mean-Variance Optimization

Mean variance optimization offers managers a disciplined and efficient way to make asset allocation decisions. The process is *disciplined* in the sense that it requires managers to turn their insights about various markets into quantitative forecasts of means, variances, and covariances. They may also arrive at their views by an iterated process of specifying a portfolio that is currently being held, using these holdings to compute implied views about various markets, refining their views and constructing a new candidate portfolio, and so on. It is *efficient* because it results in a portfolio that optimally trades off risk and return. For a target risk level, it identifies the portfolio that has the highest expected return, and for a target mean return, it can compute the portfolio with the lowest risk.

One major drawback of the mean-variance approach is that it is susceptible to the "error maximization" phenomenon. Since mean-variance investing relies on the inputs provided by the manager to form optimal portfolios, it is likely to pick assets that have low *predicted* variances and low *predicted* covariances with other assets, and it is likely to favor assets with high *expected* returns. In short, it is likely to pick assets with extremely favorable forecasts. Statistically, such forecasts are very likely to be biased, since they are likely to be contaminated with "high model error." As a result, the realized performance of these portfolios may not measure up to the predicted performance. Researchers have suggested a number of ways to mitigate the error-maximization property of mean-variance optimizers. See, for example, Jorion (1986) and Ledoit (1997) and the references cited therein for suggestions to mitigate the impact of extreme errors on mean-variance portfolios.

Risk Reduction via Optimization

Table 7–8 examines the results of a simple mean-variance optimization exercise. The expected returns in the table are purely

T A B L E 7–8

Mean-Variance Optimized Portfolios

Country	Expected Excess Return (over U.S. Treasury bills) (% per annum)	Forecast Standard Deviation of Excess Return (% per annum)	Weights in Portfolio That Has Maximum Sharpe Ratio (%)	Optimal Portfolio That Has Same Expected Return as U.S. Market (%)
U.S.	15	16.9	28.4	45.3
U.K.	18	15.1	64.5	23.4
Germany	12	22.0	0.0	19.6
Japan	14	29.0	7.1	11.7
Total			100.0	100.0
Expected excess return of portfolio			16.9%	15.0%
Forecast standard deviation of portfolio			13.3%	13.4%
Expected Sharpe ratio			1.27	1.12

hypothetical numbers, meant only for use in this exercise. The expected excess returns and forecast standard deviations in the table are assumed to be from a dollar perspective. Table 7–8 shows that mean-variance optimization can result in significant risk reductions. As the last column in the table shows, an investor with these views can achieve the same expected return as the U.S. market (15 percent per annum in the example) at far lower risk (13.4 percent for the mean-variance optimal portfolio, versus 16.9 percent for the U.S. market). The table also shows the composition of the portfolio with the highest *ex ante* Sharpe ratio, i.e., the highest ratio of expected excess return to risk. Combinations of this portfolio with cash will generate the mean-variance efficient set of portfolios. Figure 7–3 plots the risky asset mean-variance frontier

F I G U R E   7–3

Mean Variance Frontier for Asset Allocation

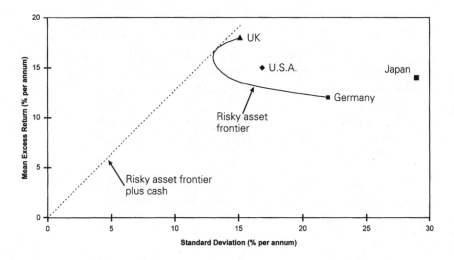

(excluding cash) and the risky asset frontier plus cash. The figure clearly shows the substantial diversification benefits from building mean-variance portfolios.

SUMMARY

Recent events in world financial markets highlight the need to have a systematic approach to portfolio construction in general, and risk management in particular. The complex interplay of various effects on the risk of internationally diversified portfolios demands the use of rigorous analytical models to manage and forecast risk. This chapter offers two analytical tools, marginal contribution analysis and optimal portfolio construction, that aid in quantitative risk management, as well as a brief discussion of GARCH models and their use in forecasting risk.

REFERENCES

Bollerslev, Tim: "Generalized Autoregressive Conditional Heteroskedasticity," *Journal of Econometrics*, vol. 31, 1986, pp. 307–327.

Bollerslev, Tim, Robert F. Engle, and Jeffrey M. Wooldridge: "A Capital Asset Pricing Model with Time-Varying Covariances," *Journal of Political Economy*, vol. 96, 1988, pp. 116–131.

Engle, Robert F.: "Autoregressive Conditional Heteroskedasticity with Estimates of the Variance of United Kingdom Inflation," *Econometrica*, vol. 50, 1982, pp. 987–1007.

Glosten, Lawrence R., Ravi Jagannathan, and David E. Runkle: "On the Relation between the Expected Value and the Volatility of the Nominal Excess Return on Stocks," *Journal of Finance*, vol. 48, 1993, pp. 1779–1801.

Jorion, Philippe, "Bayes-Stein Estimation for Portfolio Analysis," *Journal of Financial and Quantitative Analysis*, vol. 21, 1986, pp. 279–292.

Ledoit, Olivier: "Improved Estimation of the Covariance Matrix of Stock Returns with an Application to Portfolio Selection," working paper, University of California, Los Angeles, 1997.

Nelson, Daniel B.: "Conditional Heteroskedasticity in Asset Returns: A New Approach," *Econometrica*, vol. 59, 1991, pp. 347–370.

CHAPTER 8

Management of Currency Fluctuations Associated with International Investments

Ranga Nathan
Senior Vice President
Global Risk Management
Sakura Dellsher, Inc.
Chicago, Illinois

INTRODUCTION

Returns on investments which are denominated in a foreign currency are dependent on two factors: returns in the local currency and the exchange rate fluctuations between the foreign currency and the investor's domestic currency. This chapter deals with the impact that currency fluctuations have had on overall returns, examines the circumstances under which active overlay programs are feasible, and shows how to measure the effectiveness of active overlay programs.

IMPACT OF FOREIGN CURRENCY FLUCTUATIONS

Table 8–1 summarizes the impact of foreign currency fluctuations on four equity investments denominated in foreign currencies over the 10-year period from 1988 through 1997. In all cases, the investor's domestic currency is U.S. dollars.

The impact of each component (index in local currency and exchange rate fluctuation) for a year is measured as the *absolute* value of the change in that component. *Average impact* is the average of such absolute values for each component over the 10 years.

TABLE 8-1

Impact of Foreign Currency Fluctuations*

Year	FTA Index in GBP	FTA FX GBP/USD	DAX Index in DMK	DAX FX DMK/USD	Tokyo Index in JPY	Tokyo FX JPY/USD	EAFE Index Local CY	EAFE FX FX/USD
1988	11.2	-4.2	32.8	-12.3	37.1	-3.2	33.0	-3.3
1989	34.3	-10.8	34.8	6.0	22.7	-13.1	21.9	-9.1
1990	-8.8	19.6	-21.9	12.7	-39.3	5.9	-29.7	9.2
1991	20.1	-3.2	12.9	-1.5	-0.5	8.9	8.4	3.8
1992	19.2	-18.9	-2.1	-6.1	-22.9	0.0	-5.7	-6.5
1993	26.7	-2.5	46.7	-6.9	10.9	11.8	29.3	2.8
1994	-5.5	6.1	-7.1	12.2	9.0	12.2	-2.2	10.5
1995	22.3	-1.0	7.0	7.8	2.0	-3.8	9.4	1.9
1996	15.5	10.4	28.2	-6.8	-6.1	-10.8	11.7	-4.8
1997	22.9	-3.6	47.1	-14.3	-19.0	-11.1	14.6	-11.0
Total impact	18.6	8.0	24.1	8.7	16.9	8.1	16.6	6.3
% impact	70%	30%	74%	26%	68%	32%	73%	27%

*FTA is London FTA All Share Price Index, total return (with dividends). *Source:* Chase Global Data & Research.
DAX is DAX General Index (without dividends). *Source:* Chase Global Data & Research.
Tokyo is Tokyo Stock Price Index, total return (with dividends). *Source:* Chase Global Data & Research.
EAFE is Morgan Stanley EAFE Index. *Source for values in U.S. dollars:* Chase Global Data & Research.
GBP/USD is the exchange rate between pound sterling and U.S. dollars. *Source:* Chase Global Data & Research.
DMK/USD is the exchange rate between deutschemark and U.S. dollars. *Source:* Chase Global Data & Research.
JPYUSD is the exchange rate between Japanese yen and U.S. dollars. *Source:* Chase Global Data & Research.
FX/USD under EAFE is the weighted average exchange rate between the several currencies associated with EAFE and U.S. dollars. *Source:* A.G. Bisset & Co.

Relative impact is the average impact of a component divided by the total of the average impacts of the two components.

In the case of an investment in the FTA, the sterling/U.S. dollar fluctuations had an average relative impact of 30 percent on the overall returns realized by an investor. The currency impact is 26 percent in the case of an investment in DAX, whereas it is 32 percent in the case of the Tokyo stock price index. For EAFE, the currency impact is 27 percent.

Any component which has such a large impact on overall returns deserves to be analyzed and, if possible, managed.

PASSIVE METHODS OF MANAGING CURRENCY FLUCTUATIONS

The two passive methods of dealing with exchange rate fluctuations are no hedge and full hedge (see Figure 8–1).

1. No hedge entails doing nothing at all.
   a. A foreign currency appreciation (P1) against U.S. dollars (USD) either enhances positive local currency

FIGURE 8–1

Foreign Currency Fluctuation (FX)

Passive management
No hedge
• Benefit: (P1) full translation gain
• Risk: (P2) full translation loss

Full hedge (Futures/Forwards/Swaps)
• Benefit: (Q2) total protection against adverse FX
• Risk: (Q1) no benefit fron favorable FX

Active management
Steps
• Hedge during adverse FX
• No-hedge during favorable FX

Benefits (correct FX directional forecast)
• (P1) accrue favorable FX
• (Q2) protect against adverse FX

Risks (incorrect FX directional forecast)
• (P1) no protection during adverse FX
• (Q1) loss of benefit of favorable FX

Foreign Currency Fluctuation (FX)

	Favorable		Adverse	
No hedge	**P1**		**P2**	
	Exposure	Gain	Exposure	Loss
	Hedge	0	Hedge	0
	Net	Gain	Net	Loss
Hedge	**Q1**		**Q2**	
	Exposure	Gain	Exposure	Loss
	Hedge	Loss	Hedge	Gain
	Net ≈ For. Diff.*		Net ≈ For. Diff.*	

*For. Diff. = forward differential

returns or mitigates negative local currency returns.
At times, a negative local currency return is turned
into a positive USD return.

   b. Conversely, a foreign currency depreciation (P2)
      against USD either worsens negative local currency
      returns or reduces positive local currency returns.
      At times, a positive local currency return is turned into
      a negative USD return.

2. Full hedge entails hedging the exchange rate risk
   throughout each year (Q1,Q2). Exchange rate
   fluctuations have no effect on the amount invested.[1]
   However, the local currency returns are

   a. Enhanced if the forward rate differential is favorable
      (interest rate in the currency of denomination is lower
      than that in USD).

   b. Reduced if the forward rate differential is unfavorable
      (interest rate in the currency of denomination is higher
      than that in USD).

The results of the above passive methods applied to the four
equity investments are summarized in Table 8–2. For ease of comparison, we use probability of loss as a measure of risk. Probability of loss is defined by the area to the left of the zero return
vertical of a normal distribution curve whose mean and standard
deviation are the same as those of a given stream of annual
returns.

A review of Table 8–2 suggests that neither of the passive
methods is consistently better than the other for this ten-year
period. Any pattern that may be discerned is unique to this specific period and may not apply to other periods.

In summary, no clear pattern emerges as to which of the two
passive methods is clearly preferable over the other.

---

1. Of course, the gain or loss from the investment during the year is affected; but ignoring
   this effect in this context does not detract from the principles being illustrated here.

TABLE 8-2

Portfolio Returns Under Various Treatments of Foreign Currency Fluctuations*

	FTA				DAX				Tokyo				EAFE			
	No Hedge	Full Hedge	100% Efficient	Zero % Efficient	No Hedge	Full Hedge	100% Efficient	Zero % Efficient	No Hedge	Full Hedge	100% Efficient	Zero % Efficient	No Hedge	Full Hedge	100% Efficient	Zero % Efficient
1988	6.5	8.7	8.7	6.5	16.5	37.2	37.2	16.5	32.7	41.5	41.5	32.7	28.6	34.1	34.1	28.6
1989	19.7	29.4	29.4	19.7	42.9	38.5	42.9	38.5	6.6	27.9	27.9	6.6	10.8	23.5	23.5	10.8
1990	9.1	-15.0	9.1	-15.0	-12.0	-21.9	-12.0	-21.9	-35.8	-38.9	-35.8	-38.9	-23.2	-30.9	-23.2	-30.9
1991	16.3	14.0	16.3	14.0	11.2	9.9	11.2	9.9	8.4	-1.8	8.4	-1.8	12.5	4.5	12.5	4.5
1992	-3.3	12.5	12.5	-3.3	-8.0	-7.3	-7.3	-8.0	-22.9	-23.5	-22.9	-23.5	-11.9	-10.0	-10.0	-11.9
1993	23.5	23.1	23.5	23.1	36.6	40.2	40.2	36.6	24.0	11.1	24.0	11.1	32.9	26.1	32.9	26.1
1994	0.2	-6.5	0.2	-6.5	4.3	-8.1	4.3	-8.1	22.3	11.4	22.3	11.4	8.1	-2.1	8.1	-2.1
1995	21.1	21.9	21.9	21.1	15.4	8.8	15.4	8.8	-1.8	7.6	7.6	-1.8	11.6	11.1	11.6	11.1
1996	27.5	14.9	27.5	14.9	19.4	30.9	30.9	19.4	-16.2	-1.3	-1.3	-16.2	6.4	13.8	13.8	6.4
1997	18.6	21.7	21.7	18.6	26.1	50.5	50.5	26.1	-28.0	-14.8	-14.8	-28.0	2.1	17.2	17.2	2.1
Mean	13.9	12.5	17.1	9.3	15.2	17.9	21.3	11.8	-1.1	1.9	5.7	-4.9	7.8	8.7	12.1	4.5
Standard deviation	10.3	13.8	9.4	13.3	17.6	24.9	22.0	19.9	23.8	23.7	24.5	21.7	16.6	19.2	17.7	17.3
Probability of loss	11.1	20.1	5.1	25.8	20.7	24.5	17.8	28.7	51.7	46.9	41.2	58.4	33.0	33.3	26.1	40.4

* No hedge derived from local currency index values and currency fluctuation. See Table 8-1 for sources.
Full hedge derived from local currency index values and fully hedged results. *Source* for fully hedged results: A.G. Bisset & Co.

ACTIVE MANAGEMENT OF CURRENCY FLUCTUATIONS

An active currency overlay program involves a periodic decision by the manager (daily, weekly, etc.) as to whether or not a hedge is required. Given no specific constraints, the manager initiates a hedge when the foreign currency is projected to depreciate and removes the hedge when an appreciation is projected. Some managers (for example those using option replication methods) do not explicitly form market views as to currency appreciation or depreciation. For purposes of this discussion, we can assume implicit market projections reflected by the hedge/no-hedge actions they take. The quality of the research underlying such projections determines the outcome over a period. The objective of the manager during each sub-period is protection or enhancement, depending on whether the currency movement is adverse or favorable.

To study the efficacy of such management, let's start with two hypothetical active programs:

1. *Efficiency of 100 percent.*[2] This hypothetical program assumes the availability, at the beginning of each year, of a perfect directional forecast of exchange rate movement during that year. Given a forecast of a depreciation of a currency against USD, the exchange rate risk is fully hedged for the year (Q2). With a forecast of an appreciation of the currency, the risk is accepted with no hedge during the year (P1). Therefore, the result in each year is the better of the two results from the no-hedge and full-hedge methods.

2. *Efficiency of zero percent.* This hypothetical program assumes that the manager is consistently wrong in making directional forecasts. Hedges are established in years during which a currency appreciates (Q1). No hedges are in place during years of currency depreciation (P2). The result in each year is therefore the worse of the two results from no-hedge and full-hedge methods.

---

2. For a more detailed description of efficiency, see "Performance Measurement of Active Overlay Programs," *Derivatives Quarterly*, Fall 1997.

The results of the 100 percent efficient and zero percent efficient programs are shown in Table 8–2, for each of the four equity investments studied.

Next, let's consider various levels of efficiency between zero and 100 percent at intervals of 10 percent. For example, a program with an efficiency of 70 percent can be described as follows:

1. During a year of currency appreciation against USD, the program wrongly hedges 30 percent of the net appreciation (Q1) and accrues correctly 70 percent of the net appreciation to the investor (P1).
2. During a year of currency depreciation against USD, the program correctly hedges 70 percent of the net depreciation (Q2) and accrues 30 percent of the net depreciation to the investor (P2).
3. The result in each year from this program equals 0.7 times the result from the hypothetical 100 percent efficient program, plus 0.3 times the result from the hypothetical 0 percent efficient program.

The analyses are summarized in Figures 8–2 through 8–5. The figures have probability of loss as the X axis and return as the Y axis. Thus, the southeast quadrant combines low return and high risk; and the northwest quadrant combines high return and low risk. The following general observations can be made from these charts.

1. The program with 100 percent efficiency produces a higher return *and* a lower risk than both of the passive methods.
2. The program with 0 percent efficiency generates a lower return *and* a higher risk than both of the passive methods.
3. One needs an active program with an efficiency of over 50 percent to perform better than *both* passive methods, on *both* counts: higher returns and lower risk.

FEASIBILITY OF ACTIVE MANAGEMENT PROGRAMS

The charts show that when the efficiency of a program is in excess of 50 percent, i.e., if the underlying analyses outperform the toss

FIGURE 8–2

FTA

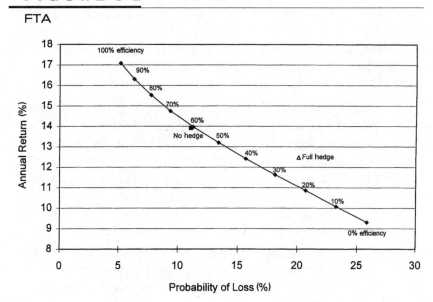

FIGURE 8–3

DAX

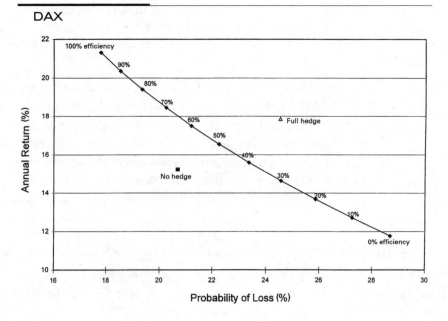

FIGURE 8-4

Tokyo

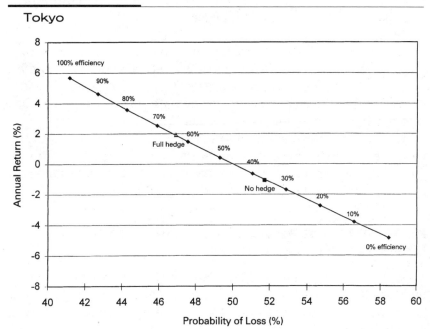

FIGURE 8-5

EAFE

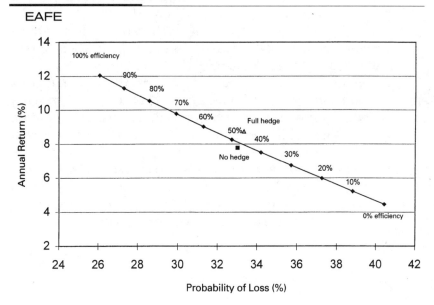

of a coin, improvements can be achieved in terms of both return and risk. This, therefore, is the primary requirement of any active currency management program.

A review of the performance of 10 overlay managers shows that efficiencies within the 60 percent to 90 percent range can be achieved. Not every manager exceeds 50 percent efficiency results in every year in each currency. But the data strongly suggests that it is feasible to judiciously construct "portfolios of managers," which can, over a reasonable period, increase returns and/or reduce risk. This is indirectly supported by an empirical study of the actual performance of 11 active currency-overlay managers managing 152 overlay accounts in the last 10 years.[3]

PERFORMANCE BENCHMARK FOR ACTIVE MANAGEMENT PROGRAMS

This analysis also suggests that a fair benchmark against which to measure the performance of active programs is the result from a 50 percent efficient program. Note that this is the same as a 50 percent hedge benchmark.

Of course, the benchmark should be adjusted when constraints are imposed. For example, if investment guidelines call for a minimum hedge at all times of, say, 60 percent, then the benchmark should apply to only the portion of the fluctuations being actively managed (40 percent). In this case, the benchmark will be adjusted to 80 percent hedge.

A standard overlay program, as described above, suggests either (a) no hedge (when the currency is expected to appreciate) or (b) a hedge in the form of a short position in the currency, the face value of the hedge being the same as the face value of the exposure (when the currency is expected to depreciate). Some programs seek to add value to these standard results by (a) buying a currency long when appreciation is expected and/or (b) implementing short hedges which are larger than the exposure. Other programs even create market positions in currencies which

---

3. See Brian Strange, "Currency Overlay Managers Show Consistency," *Pensions & Investments,* June 15, 1998.

are not exposed. The investor should be careful in using the suggested benchmark when utilizing such overlay programs, by properly separating exposure management results and trading results.

SUMMARY

The impact of currency fluctuations on overall returns from international investments is high enough to warrant a consideration to manage such fluctuations. Neither of the two passive management methods is decidedly superior to the other. An active management program requires an efficiency of at least 50 percent before it can improve on the results of passive programs. Since good currency-overlay managers have efficiencies in excess of 50 percent, and since none of them is the best at all times and for all currencies, a "portfolio" of active management programs can be constructed that should outperform both passive methods over a period, with potentially lower overall risk. "Half hedge" is a logical benchmark against which to measure the performance of active currency-overlay management programs.

CHAPTER 9

Sovereign Credit Ratings: A Primer

David Beers
Managing Director
Standard & Poor's Sovereign Ratings Group
London, England

Standard & Poor's sovereign credit ratings, which now cover local and foreign currency debt issued by governments in 77 countries and territories (Table 9–1), are an assessment of each government's capacity and willingness to repay debt according to its terms.

Sovereign ratings are not "country ratings," an important but often misunderstood distinction. Sovereign ratings address the credit risks of national governments but not the specific default risks of other issuers. Ratings assigned to other public- and private-sector entities in each country can, and frequently do, vary. Ratings of some issuers may be the same as the sovereign's, while others will be lower. In rare instances, the ratings of some issuers may even be higher. In all instances, however, the sovereign's ratings set the benchmark for the ratings assigned to other issuers under its jurisdiction.

The frequency of defaults by sovereign issuers of bank and bond debt—the risk the ratings address—has declined in recent years, at least until 1998. In fact, since 1975 (and even earlier), no sovereign issuer has defaulted on local or foreign currency debt rated by Standard & Poor's. Will such defaults occur in the future? Judging from the volume of bond issuance in the 1990s by emerging market sovereigns, and the number ratings in the

T A B L E 9–1

Standard & Poor's Sovereign Credit Ratings*

Issuer	Local Currency	Foreign Currency	Issuer	Local Currency	Foreign Currency
Austria	AAA	AAA	Columbia	A	BBB–
France	AAA	AAA	Slovak Rep.	A	BBB–
Germany	AAA	AAA	Tunisia	A	BBB–
Japan	AAA	AAA	Egypt	A–	BBB–
Liechtenstein	AAA	AAA	Greece	A–	BBB–
Luxembourg	AAA	AAA	Hungary	A–	BBB–
Netherlands	AAA	AAA	Malaysia	A–	BBB–
Norway	AAA	AAA	Poland	A–	BBB–
Singapore	AAA	AAA	Thailand	A–	BBB–
Switzerland	AAA	AAA	Croatia	BBB+	BBB–
United Kingdom	AAA	AAA	Lithuania	BBB+	BBB–
United States	AAA	AAA	Uruguay	BBB+	BBB–
			Oman	N.R.	BBB–
Canada	AAA	AA+			
Denmark	AAA	AA+	India	BBB+	BB+
New Zealand	AAA	AA+	Korea	BBB+	BB+
Sweden	AAA	AA+	Philippines	BBB+	BB+
Belgium	AA+	AA+	South Africa	BBB+	BB+
Ireland	AA+	AA+	Trinidad &		
			Tobago	BBB+	BB+
Taiwan	AA+	AA+	Panama	BB+	BB+
Australia	AAA	AA	El Salvador	BBB+	BB
Finland	AA	AA	Mexico	BBB+	BB
Italy	AA	AA	Morocco	BBB	BB
Spain	AA	AA	Argentina	BBB–	BB
Bermuda	N.R.	AA	Peru	BBB–	BB
Cyprus	AA+	AA–	Costa Rica	BB+	BB
Portugal	AA-	AA–			
			Jordan	BBB–	BB–
Iceland	AA+	A+	Paraguay	BBB–	BB–
Malta	AA+	A+	Bolivia	BB+	BB–
Slovenia	AA	A	Brazil	BB+	BB–
Hong Kong	A+	A	Lebanon	BB	BB–
Kuwait	A+	A			
Czech Republic	AA	A	Romania	BB	B+
Chile	AA	A–	Dominican	BB	B+
Israel	AA–	A–	Republic		
			Kazakhstan	BB–	B+
Estonia	A–	BBB+	Venezuela	N.R.	B+
China	N.R.	BBB+	Turkey	N.R.	B
Latvia	A–	BBB	Cook Islands	B–	B–
Qatar	N.R.	BBB			
			Indonesia	B–	CCC+
			Pakistan	N.R.	CCC–
			Russia	N.R.	CCC–

* Ratings as of October 15, 1998. N.R. = not rated.

speculative-grade category (BB+ or lower) (see Table 9–1), Standard & Poor's seems to believe they will. The default rates for sovereign issuers, over time, should broadly parallel the default rates for similarly rated corporate issuers.

If defaults occur more frequently in the sovereign sector, as we expect, this will not be an unprecedented development. Defaults on foreign currency bonds took place repeatedly, and on a substantial scale, throughout the 19th century and as recently as the 1940s. Sovereign default rates fell to low levels only in the first three decades after World War II (see Figures 9–1, 9–2, and 9–3), when cross-border sovereign bond issuance also was minimal. Past defaults reflected a variety of factors, including wars, revolutions, lax fiscal and monetary polices, and external economic shocks. As the 1990s draw to a close, fiscal discipline, debt management, and the contingent liabilities arising from weak banking systems, in particular, represent significant policy challenges for many sovereigns. The associated credit risks, which for a time

F I G U R E   9–1

Sovereign Foreign Currency Bond Defaults, 1820–1997

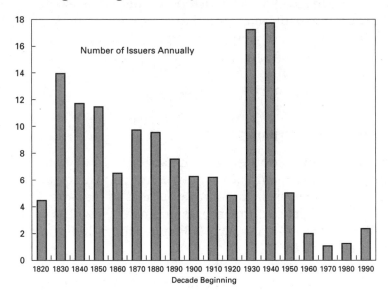

Source: Debt Cycles in the World Economy, Westview Press, 1992; and Standard & Poor's.

F I G U R E 9–2

Sovereign Default Rates, 1820–1997

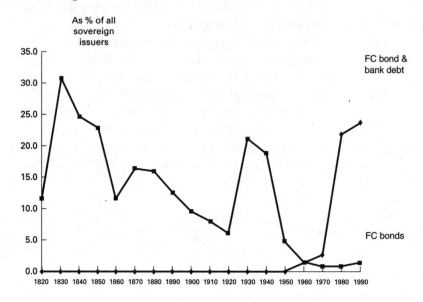

may seem manageable, can mushroom quickly, as events since 1997 in a number of emerging market countries have shown. Given these factors, it would be surprising if a new sovereign default cycle did not emerge over the next decade. Therefore, understanding sovereign ratings, what they mean, and the criteria behind them is more relevant than ever.

BEHIND THE RATINGS

Standard & Poor's appraisal of each sovereign's overall creditworthiness is both quantitative and qualitative. The quantitative aspects of the analysis incorporate a number of measures of economic and financial performance, as outlined below. The analysis is qualitative because Standard & Poor's ratings indicate future debt service capacity.

The ratings service uses both a "top-down" and a "bottom-up" analysis to determine sovereign ratings. Top-down analyses consider global systemic factors, which past experience suggests

F I G U R E 9–3

Sovereign Governments, 1800–1997

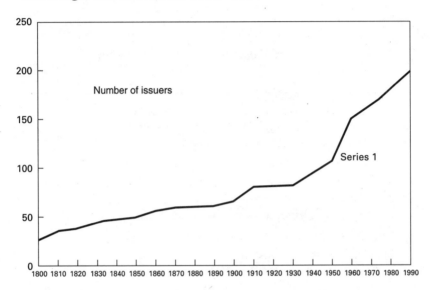

influence both the timing and the magnitude of sovereign defaults. Examples include quarterly analysis of default trends throughout the sector[1] and regular examination of global financial sector risks.[2]

The bottom-up analysis focuses on the credit fundamentals affecting each government. It divides the analytical framework into eight categories so that all important factors contributing to sovereign default are considered in turn (see Box 9–1). Each category relates to two key aspects of credit risk, economic risk and political risk. Economic risk addresses the government's ability to repay its obligations on time and is a function of both quantitative and qualitative factors. Political risk addresses the sovereign's willingness to repay debt.

---

1. *Sovereign Defaults in 1998: A Turning Point?*, Sovereign Ratings Service, November 1998
2. *Global Financial System Stress: Leading Indicators Signal Pressure in 16 Countries*, Sovereign Ratings Service, September 1998.

B O X   9 — 1

Sovereign Ratings Methodology Profile

POLITICAL RISK
- Form of government and adaptability of political institutions

EXTENT OF POPULAR PARTICIPATION
- Orderliness of leadership succession
- Degree of consensus on economic policy objectives
- Integration in global trade and financial system
- Internal and external security risks

INCOME AND ECONOMIC STRUCTURE
- Living standards, income, and wealth distribution
- Market, nonmarket economy
- Resource endowments, degree of diversification

ECONOMIC GROWTH PROSPECTS
- Size, composition of savings and investment
- Rate, pattern of economic growth

FISCAL FLEXIBILITY
- General government operating and total budget balances
- Tax competitiveness and tax-raising flexibility
- Spending pressures

PUBLIC DEBT BURDEN
- General government financial assets
- Public debt and interest burden
- Currency composition, structure of public debt
- Pension liabilities
- Banking, corporate, other contingent liabilities

PRICE STABILITY
- Trends in price inflation
- Rates of money and credit growth
- Exchange rate policy
- Degree of central bank autonomy

BALANCE OF PAYMENTS FLEXIBILITY
- Impact on external accounts of fiscal and monetary policies
- Structure of the current account
- Composition of capital flows

Continued

Box 9–1 Concluded

EXTERNAL DEBT AND LIQUIDITY
- Size and currency composition of public external debt
- Importance of banks and other public and private entities as contingent liabilities of the sovereign
- Maturity structure and debt service burden
- Level, composition of reserves and other public external assets
- Debt service track record

Willingness to pay is a qualitative issue, and it distinguishes sovereigns from most other types of issuers. Partly because creditors have only limited legal redress, a government can (and sometimes does) default selectively on its obligations, even when it possesses the financial capacity for timely debt service. In practice, of course, political and economic risks are related. A government that is unwilling to repay debt usually is pursuing economic policies that weaken its ability to do so. Willingness to pay, therefore, encompasses the range of economic and political factors influencing government policy.

As part of the committee process Standard & Poor's uses to assign credit ratings, each government is ranked on a scale of one (representing the highest score) to six (the lowest) for each analytical category in relation to the universe of rated and unrated sovereigns. There is, however, no exact formula combining the scores to determine ratings. The analytical variables are interrelated, and the emphasis can change, for example, when differentiating the degree of credit risk between a sovereign's local and foreign currency debt.

Because the default frequency of sovereign local currency debt differs significantly from foreign currency debt, both types of debt are analyzed. The same political, social and economic factors affect the government's ability and willingness to honor local and foreign currency debt, though in varying degrees. A sovereign government's ability and willingness to service local currency debt is supported by its taxing power and control of the domestic financial system, which gives it potentially unlimited access to local currency resources.

To service foreign currency debt, however, the sovereign also must secure foreign exchange, usually by purchasing it in the currency markets. This can be a binding constraint, as reflected in the higher frequency of foreign than local currency debt default.[3] The primary focus of Standard & Poor's local currency credit analysis is on the fiscal, monetary, and inflation outcomes of government policies that support or erode incentives for timely debt service. When assessing a sovereign's capacity and willingness to honor foreign currency debt, Standard & Poor's places more weight on the interaction between fiscal and monetary policies and the balance of payments, their impact on the growth of public and private external debt, external debt management, and the degree of each country's integration into the global financial system.

LOCAL CURRENCY DEBT RATING FACTORS

Key economic and political risks Standard & Poor's considers when rating sovereign debt include:

- The stability of political institutions and degree of popular participation in the political process
- Income and economic structure
- Fiscal policy and budgetary flexibility
- Monetary policy and inflation pressures
- Public debt burden and debt service track record

These factors, more than any others, directly affect the ability and willingness of governments to ensure timely local currency debt service. Further, because fiscal and monetary policies ultimately influence the country's external balance sheet, they also affect the ability and willingness of governments to service foreign currency debt.

The stability and perceived legitimacy of a country's form of government are important considerations. They set the parameters for economic policy-making, including how quickly policy

---

3. *Sovereign Defaults Continue to Decline in 1998,* Sovereign Ratings Service, September 1998.

errors are identified and corrected. France's AAA credit standing, for instance, in part reflects the country's democratic political framework. Policy-making is transparent, and the response by government to policy errors is predictable over time as a result. Romania's evolving political institutions, by contrast, constrain its B+ foreign currency and BB+ local currency ratings. The future direction of economic policy is less predictable for this reason.

A country's economic structure also comes into play. The decentralized decisionmaking of a market economy, with legally enforceable property rights, is less prone to policy error and more respectful of the interests of creditors than one where the state dominates. If market reforms succeed in the transition economies of central and eastern Europe, the credit standing of at least some of the region's sovereigns ultimately could converge with those of western Europe, where market economies are well entrenched.[4]

A government in a country with a growing standard of living and income distributions regarded as broadly equitable can more readily support even high public debt levels and withstand unexpected economic and political shocks than one with a poor or stagnant economy. But a sovereign with a recent history of default generally must manage with lower levels of leverage to rebuild credibility than one that has maintained an unblemished debt record. The United Kingdom, rated AAA, has a track record of honoring its obligations over centuries punctuated by war and financial distress. Argentina's ratings (BB foreign currency and BBB- local currency) still reflect the legacy of many years of economic mismanagement, including default. Its credit standing, while improving, is by no means as strong as Britain's, even though the Argentine government now has less debt in relation to national income.

These factors, in turn, influence the conduct of fiscal and monetary policies and their impact on future changes in the public debt burden. When evaluating fiscal policy, Standard & Poor's focuses on three related issues:

- The purpose of public sector borrowing

---

4. See *Rating the Transition Economies*, Sovereign Ratings Service, February 1997.

- Its impact on the growth of public debt
- Its implications for inflation

Deficit financing can be an appropriate policy tool for any government. Public sector infrastructure projects, for example, are prudently financed by borrowing when they generate revenues sufficient to cover future debt service. Singapore, rated AAA, has transformed itself into a prosperous, manufacturing- and service-based economy over the past 40 years, partly by astute investment in its public infrastructure.

More typically, governments borrow to finance combinations of consumption and investment that raise public debt. Still, analysis of public finance is complicated by the fact that the taxing and monetary powers unique to sovereigns can permit them to manage widely varying debt levels over time. Depending on their political support, policy-makers can raise taxes to meet their obligations. But a growing tax burden can adversely affect the economy's growth prospects. Moreover, public opinion often favors the lowest possible tax burden, so much so that proposals to raise tax rates occasionally drive governments from office. Efforts to cut spending can be stymied by powerful interests that benefit from government programs. Absent a political consensus favoring conservative fiscal principles, sovereigns thus can succumb to the temptation to print money, given their monopoly over the currency and control of the banking system.

INFLATION AND PUBLIC DEBT

Significant monetization of budget deficits fuels price inflation, which can undermine popular support for governments. As a result, policy-makers usually respond with measures to contain it. If they do not, and price increases accelerate, serious economic damage and an erosion of public trust in political institutions can result. Such conditions are fertile ground for a sovereign default. For these reasons, Standard & Poor's regards the rate of inflation as the single most important leading indicator of sovereign local currency credit trends. Inflation benchmarks and their relationship to different local currency rating categories are shown in Table 9–2.

T A B L E 9–2

Sovereigns: Inflation and Debt Ranges

LC Rating Category	Annual Inflation (%)
BB	25–100
BBB	10–50
A	7–25
AA	4–15
AAA	0–10

In evaluating price pressures in each country, Standard & Poor's considers their behavior in past economic cycles. The analysis is based in part on the level and maturity structure of the public debt burden—total borrowings of central, regional, and local governments in relation to GDP—together with the likely extent of future borrowing. Off balance sheet items, public sector pensions, and contingent liability items, such as banks and other enterprises, are scrutinized for their possible contribution to inflation. Related indicators include rates of money and credit expansion. Taking all these factors into account, the rating service makes a conservative assessment of average inflation over the next cycle, as measured by the consumer price index.

In addition, Standard & Poor's looks at institutional factors affecting inflation. For instance, an autonomous central bank with a public mandate to ensure price stability can be a strong check on fiscal imbalances, less so a central bank tied closely to the government. Among industrial countries, AAA rated Germany and the U.S. provide excellent examples of central banks where strong traditions of independence have evolved over the years. Similar examples among emerging market issuers include the central banks of Chile (A– foreign currency and AA local currency) and Israel (A– foreign currency and AA– local currency). On the other hand, Mexico's credit standing (BB foreign currency and BBB+ local currency) does not particularly benefit from the Banco de Mexico's formal autonomy, given the federal government's continued influence over the institution.

The depth and breadth of a country's capital markets also can act as an important discipline. The sovereign has fewer incentives to default on local currency obligations when they are held by a broad cross section of investors rather than concentrated in the hands of local banks. For this reason, the establishment of mandatory, privately funded pension funds in a number of countries—Chile and Argentina, among others—helps bolster their credit standing by creating an influential new class of bondholders. The experience of many OECD countries suggests that even when public debt is high, creditworthiness can be sustained over long periods when policy-makers are responsive to constituencies with vested interests in safeguarding the value of money.

FOREIGN CURRENCY DEBT-RATING FACTORS

Of course, the same economic and political factors affecting a sovereign's local currency credit standing also impact its ability and willingness to honor foreign currency debt, often to a greater degree because of the binding constraints the balance of payments can impose. As a result, Standard & Poor's analysis of foreign currency debt focuses on how government economic policies influence trends in public and private external debt levels over time.

In addition, from a political risk perspective, the extent of each country's integration in the global trade and financial systems must be considered. A high degree of integration generally gives the government strong incentives to meet its external obligations because of the correspondingly high political as well as economic costs of default.

Sudan (not rated), in default on its foreign currency bank loans since 1979, has struggled almost continuously in recent years with civil insurrection and the breakdown of effective administration. Its political and economic links with the outside world are at a low ebb. AAA rated Luxembourg, by contrast, is a small country highly integrated with Europe and the rest of the world. As a result, it has very strong incentives to play by the international financial rules of game. All sovereigns fall somewhere between these two extremes in terms of their integration in the global economy.

At the same time, relations with neighboring countries must be examined with an eye for potential security risks. National security is a concern when military threats place significant burdens on fiscal policy, reduce the flow of potential investment and put the balance of payments under stress. As Iraq's 1990 invasion of Kuwait (A foreign currency and A+ local currency) demonstrated, the very existence of the sovereign itself can sometimes come into question. Lebanon (BB– foreign currency and BB local currency) and Qatar (BBB foreign currency) are two other examples of sovereigns whose credit standing is constrained by their vulnerable geopolitical positions.

BALANCE OF PAYMENTS FLEXIBILITY

Standard & Poor's balance of payments analysis focuses on the impact of economic policy on the external sector as well as its structural characteristics. In the short run, the ability of policymakers to manage financial pressures from abroad depends partly on the structure of merchandise trade, services, transfers, and the like. Yet balance of payments pressures do not appear spontaneously or reach large magnitudes for structural reasons alone. In most cases, they can be traced back to flawed economic policies. The ratings service's approach reflects the premise that the macro- and microeconomic policies discussed earlier affect balance of payments behavior.

For this reason, the size of a country's current account deficit, even when very large, may not by itself be an important rating consideration. The tendency for some countries to run current account surpluses, while others run current account deficits, is well documented historically. It is the product of many factors, not all of them negative and not all related to government policies. Singapore ran very large current account deficits for much of its modern history, ones readily financed because they were not the byproduct of fiscal mismanagement. However, Thailand's (BBB– foreign currency and A– local currency) foreign exchange crisis in 1997 is a sharp reminder that large current account deficits can also be a symptom of serious underlying weaknesses, in this case a financial sector whose asset quality had weakened dramatically after years of rapid domestic credit growth. And as

Mexico's debt-servicing crisis in 1995 illustrated, current account deficits are a concern when government policies result in a public external debt structure vulnerable to sudden changes in investor sentiment.

EXTERNAL FINANCIAL POSITION

Consequently, Standard & Poor's examines each sovereign's external balance sheet alongside its analysis of balance of payments flows. The main focus is on trends in the public external debt position, the magnitude of contingent liabilities of the government, and the adequacy of foreign exchange reserves to service its and—especially in a crisis—the private sector's foreign currency debt. To complete the picture, Standard & Poor's calculates an international investment position. This is the broadest measure of a country's external financial position. It adds the value of the private sector's debt and equity liabilities to the public sector's external indebtedness denominated in local and foreign currencies.

Four important variables are:

- Net public external debt
- Net external debt of financial institutions
- Net external debt of the nonbank private sector
- Total debt service

Public external debt includes the direct and guaranteed debt of the central government, obligations of regional and local governments, and the nonguaranteed debt of other public sector entities. Net public external debt equals total public sector debt less public financial assets, including central bank reserves. Debt of other levels of government are analyzed and generally are consolidated with those of the national government if legal and political circumstances expose the sovereign to internal and external financial risks from this source.

To measure the magnitude of public debt, Standard & Poor's compares it with annual export flows of goods and services (along with net public and private transfers where they are positive). For the 77 sovereigns with public ratings in October 1998, the median net public external debt-to-export ratio was 60 percent. Sovereigns with this degree of leverage currently include Denmark (AA+ foreign currency and AAA' local currency), Israel (A– foreign currency and AA– local currency), and Egypt (BBB– foreign currency and A– local currency).

Other sectors' external debt also is measured in this way. Financial institutions' net debt equals their total external liabilities less total external assets. Net debt of the nonfinancial private sector equals their total debt less loans abroad. Debt of the private sector is examined because in some circumstances it can become a liability of the state.

Problems in the financial sector, in particular, can impair the sovereign's credit standing when they lead to official rescues of failing banks. Korea (BB+ foreign currency) and Thailand are sovereigns whose foreign and local currency ratings were sharply downgraded in 1997–1998 in part because of the escalating cost of supporting their banking sectors. Currently, Malaysia's banks weigh on the sovereign's credit standing (BBB– foreign currency and A– local currency). Asset quality is rapidly deteriorating, and the system already relies on substantial official financial support. By contrast, New Zealand's banking sector poses relatively little risk to the sovereign's credit standing. Asset quality is generally sound, and significantly, the system's largest institutions are owned by creditworthy foreign banks.

Sovereign external debt also is evaluated in terms of its maturity profile, currency composition, and sensitivity to changing interest rates. Along with new borrowings, these factors influence the size of future interest and amortization payments. Therefore, debt service, including interest and principal on both short- and long-term debt, is compared to projected exports. To some extent, debt contracted on concessional terms can offset a high public debt burden. Poland, for instance, has relatively high public external debt, around 82 percent of exports in 1998, but with favorable terms on restructured foreign currency debt, debt service is low, 10 percent of exports.

INTERNATIONAL LIQUIDITY

Central bank reserves are another external indicator, one whose importance varies across the ratings spectrum. Reserves usually act as a financial buffer for the government during periods of balance of payments stress. They include foreign currency and gold holdings, with the latter valued at market prices. Reserve adequacy is measured in relation to imports as well as projected current account deficits and total debt service. Whether or not a given level of reserves is adequate is judged in relation to the government's financial and exchange-rate policies and, consequently, to their vulnerability to changes in trade and capital flows.

Access to funding from the IMF and other multilateral and bilateral official sources is a related factor to consider. However, the mixed experience of recent Fund-led programs in Asia and Russia underscore the limited availability of official resources in relation to the funds deployed by banks and cross-border investors. As a result, reserve levels deserve particular scrutiny during periods of global financial volatility, such as the latter part of 1998, when bond markets effectively closed their doors to emerging market issuers.

The United States (AAA) maintains very low reserves. It can do so because the U.S. dollar generally has been floating against other currencies since 1971. The dollar's unique status as the key currency financing global trade and investment also reduces the need for gold and foreign exchange. Most other high-investment-grade sovereigns with floating currencies and little foreign currency debt also require relatively modest reserves.

At lower rating levels, though, international liquidity is more critical when, as is often the case, government debt is denominated in foreign currencies and significant amounts of local currency debt are held by cross-border investors. Public finance setbacks and other economic or political shocks could impair financial market access. Most Latin American sovereigns fall into this category and generally maintain above-average reserves for this reason. Argentina and Hong Kong (foreign currency A and local currency A+) require above-average levels of international liquidity because their currency boards issue notes backed by foreign exchange. Lebanon, which maintains reserves equal to nearly a year's worth of imports, is something of a special case. It does so because the economy's highly dollarized nature is intertwined with the its vulnerable geopolitical position, and this creates the need for an especially large financial cushion to maintain investor confidence.

LOCAL AND FOREIGN CURRENCY RATING DISTINCTIONS

Any divergence between a sovereign's local and foreign currency ratings reflects the distinctive credit risks of each type of debt. For example, longstanding political stability, fiscal and monetary policies resulting in relatively low inflation, and a high degree of international economic integration are characteristics of sovereign issuers of AAA rated local currency debt. The manageable public external debt burdens of these issuers, in turn, result in foreign currency debt ratings at the upper end of the investment-grade spectrum.

Differences between local and foreign currency debt ratings can widen to some degree further down the ratings scale. Such sovereigns typically fall into one of two categories. Sovereigns in the first category have long records of timely service on both local currency and foreign currency debt. Inflationary pressures are moderate, public finances are relatively sound, but foreign currency indebtedness may be relatively high or likely to become so over time. Sovereigns in the second category also have unblemished local currency debt servicing track records but relatively recent histories of foreign currency default. The local and foreign currency debt ratings assigned to them balance often substantial improvements in inflation and public finances with the risks inherent to still-heavy foreign currency debt burdens.

At the lower end of the rating scale, however, such rating differences sometimes narrow. A number of sovereigns in this category have emerged from local or foreign currency debt default quite recently and still carry the risk of policy reversals that can result in renewed default. Other sovereigns in this category may not have defaulted, but they face high inflation and other forms of social and political stress that carry a material risk of local currency default after payment of foreign currency debt can no longer be assured.

Canada (AA+ foreign currency and AAA local currency) is a good example of a government shouldering a public debt burden on the order of 90 percent of GDP—well above the OECD country average—but the political commitment to low or moderate rates of inflation seems well entrenched. Conversely, when public finances are weak and inflation is left unchecked, the stage can be set for an accelerating spiral that leads to default. Government-inspired indexation of debt and other contracts to price inflation often abets the process, as in the defaults of Brazil (BB local currency and BB– foreign currency) earlier this decade. But not all countries that have experimented with indexation suffer hyperinflation and default. Chile and Israel are sovereigns with long records of timely local currency debt service. Relatively conservative fiscal policies have underpinned their general credit standing in recent years by helping to unwind inflation and to contain the external debt burden.

Ratings of EU states joining the European Monetary Union (EMU) present a special case. Governments entering EMU, which started in January 1999, cede monetary and exchange rate responsibilities to the new European Central Bank. As a result, Standard & Poor's now rates each government's local currency debt (including euro-denominated) and foreign currency debt the same. Going forward, economic and fiscal factors, already important, will be the dominant criteria for differentiating the credit quality of sovereigns inside EMU.[5] Local and foreign currency ratings for Liechtenstein (AAA), Panama (BB+), and the Cook Islands (B-) are the same because these countries, too, are part of monetary unions.

As these examples illustrate, a number of factors must be examined when considering whether distinctions between local and foreign currency ratings are appropriate. The default frequency of sovereign local currency debt generally is much lower than for foreign currency debt, but local currency defaults do occur. Russia's August 1998 default on its rouble debt is a particularly instructive case. Ironically, its experience shows why

---

5. See *Local and Foreign Currency Ratings Converge for EMU Issuers,* Sovereign Ratings
   Service, June 1998.

most sovereigns resist the temptation to take such a drastic step. Governments rarely default on local currency debt because control over the domestic banking system gives them access to some finance, even when foreign currency debt is in default. By defaulting on its rouble debt, however, Russia suddenly cut itself off from *all* financial markets, both domestic and external. The government thus crippled the real economy, generated intense inflationary pressures, and sharply raised the default risk on its foreign currency debt.

SOVEREIGN RATING CHANGES

Until relatively recently, rated sovereigns formed an exclusive club of the world's most creditworthy governments. In 1980, Standard & Poor's rated debt of just a dozen sovereigns, all at the AAA level. Rating downgrades were relatively rare over the remainder of that decade and when they occurred, usually were of modest dimensions. Today, the sovereign sector is far more heterogeneous. The 77 sovereigns Standard & Poor's monitors carry ratings between AAA and CCC–. Given this range of credit quality, rating changes occur more frequently.

Current economic and financial indicators alone do not determine ratings. Sovereign ratings measure future debt service capacity, and the future, of course, is uncertain. As a result, Standard & Poor's rating committees consider reasonable "worst-case" scenarios over a three-to-five-year time horizon to gain a better understanding of future downside risks. A government's medium-term financial program, when available, is scrutinized, along with independent forecasts. The ratings service then looks at the interaction between public finances; external debt and other variables, such as real export growth; asset quality trends affecting the local banking system; and changes in overseas interest rates.

Rating changes occur whenever new information significantly alters Standard & Poor's view of likely future developments. (Analysts generally meet with government officials at least once annually, but the timing of on-site meetings itself is not a factor determining when the agency raises or lowers ratings or changes rating outooks.) For example, Ireland's foreign currency rating was upgraded to AA+ (and converged with its local currency rating) from AA in May 1998 to reflect its improved fiscal performance and declining public debt burden. By contrast, Kazakhstan's foreign and local currency ratings were downgraded to B+ and BB– from BB– and BB+ respectively, in September 1998. These actions stemmed from the government's ineffective response to mounting fiscal and current account deficits at a time when access to capital flows had greatly diminished for a number of emerging market issuers.

As these examples illustrate, the impact of public finances on external debt usually is a key factor driving changes in foreign currency credit ratings. Similarly, significant changes in the inflation outlook figure in local currency rating changes. However, the implications of rating changes can vary across the credit spectrum. Fiscal pressures were behind the loss of New Zealand's AAA foreign currency rating in 1983 and subsequent downgrades to AA– through 1991. Still, the erosion in its credit quality was neither sudden nor very great. This reflects an important characteristic of most high-investment-grade sovereigns, namely their ability to correct financial imbalances and even to bounce back in credit terms over time. Following a sustained tightening of budgetary policy, New Zealand's foreign currency rating was upgraded to AA in December 1994 and to AA+ in January 1996. Renewed fiscal weakness, however, resulted in a rating outlook change from stable to negative, in September 1998.

Again, Russia tells a rather different story. Currently, Standard & Poor's considers its foreign currency debt to have the highest default risk in the sovereign sector. The government's credit standing has fallen steeply since it was first assigned a BB– foreign currency rating in October 1996. Subsequently, the rating was further lowered in four steps to CCC–, and the outlook remains negative. If anything, since the onset of Russia's crisis in the summer of 1998, policy-makers have embraced heterodox policies which suggest that its economic troubles will persist for a long time to come. Often in such cases, a number of crises may be required to generate renewed support for genuine economic stabilization and reform.

SOVEREIGN RATINGS AND CORPORATE CREDIT RISK

Sovereign credit risk is always a key consideration in the assessment of the credit standing of banks and corporates. Sovereign risk comes into play because the unique, wide-ranging powers and resources of each national government affect the financial and operating environments of entities under its jurisdiction. Past experience has shown time and again that defaults by otherwise creditworthy borrowers can stem directly from the imposition of exchange controls, often, though not always, linked to a sovereign default.

In the case of foreign currency debt, the sovereign has first claim on available foreign exchange, and it controls the ability of any resident to obtain funds to repay creditors. To service debt denominated in local currency, the sovereign can exercise its powers to tax, to control the domestic financial system, and even to issue local currency in potentially unlimited amounts. Given these considerations, the debt ratings of international borrowers most often are at or below the ratings of the relevant sovereign. When obligations of issuers are rated higher than the sovereign's, this reflects both their stand-alone credit characteristics and other factors mitigating sovereign credit risk.[6]

---

6. See *Understanding Sovereign Risk* , Sovereign Ratings Service, January 1997 and *Less Credit Risk for Borrowers in Dollarized Economies*, May 1997.

CHAPTER 10

Hedging the Currency Exposure of a Nondollar Portfolio*

Ira G. Kawaller
President
Kawaller & Company, LLC
Brooklyn, New York.

With the availability of currency hedging instruments, including futures, forward, and options contracts, foreign exchange risk can be isolated and managed independently of the noncurrency risk associated with international investments. Managers can thus choose to regulate this currency exposure as conditions dictate. At one extreme, they may choose to maintain their exchange exposure intact; at the other, they may eliminate it entirely.

This discussion of currency risk management is especially timely now, given the transition of European currencies to the single euro currency. As a consequence of this structural change in the financial landscape, some of the benefits of diversification across currencies may be lost. With the resulting increased concentration of risk associated with a single currency, the euro, many managers may feel it appropriate to reconsider their risk management posture with respect to this exposure.

U.S. investors dealing in nondollar securities face two risks: the market risk of the investment in its home currency and the dollar to nondollar exchange rate risk. When the nondollar

---

* This chapter updates and revises an earlier version, "Managing the Currency Risk of Nondollar Portfolios," *Financial Analysts Journal*, May/June 1991. (Reprinted as a CME Strategy Paper, "Managing the Currency Risk of Nondollar Portfolios.")

currency is strengthening relative to the dollar, this may add to the desirability of the nondollar investment. But suppose the nondollar currency starts to weaken. What does the investor do then? Of course, he or she can sell the investment(s) and repatriate the currency back to dollars. However, depending on the bid/ask spreads on the individual instruments and the currency itself, as well as the commissions involved, such an adjustment might be expensive, especially if the shift back into dollars ends up being re-versed in the near future.

Before addressing the specific ways that an investor might deal with this risk, it will be useful to clarify some language related to pricing conventions. For some currencies, the convention in the marketplace is to quote the price of the currency in dollars (i.e., *American-terms pricing*). For others, the price of the dollar is quoted in nondollar currency units *(European-terms pricing)*. The terminology gets tricky when attention turns to options. It is helpful to understand, therefore, that a *call on dollars* (i.e., the right to buy dollars with nondollar currency units) is identical to a *put on nondollars* (i.e., the right to sell nondollars for dollars).

The vast majority of exchange-traded currency futures and options are designed using the American-terms pricing convention. As a consequence, the sizes of these contracts are specified as some fixed number of nondollar currency units, and prices are expressed in dollars per nondollar unit—for example, dollars per yen or dollars per peso. Given this article's focus on exchange-traded tools, the remainder of the discussion assumes American-terms pricing.

While risk management tools have evolved to include a host of esoteric and exotic alternatives to liquidating the portfolio when the nondollar currency seems likely to weaken, four baseline strategies should be understood: (1) selling currency futures (or forward contracts), (2) buying puts on the nondollar currency (or puts on currency futures), (3) selling calls, and (4) constructing hybrid hedges, such as collars or corridors, which combine long and short option positions.[1] The choice depends on one's expecta-

---

1. Consult the glossary for a more complete description of these alternative hedge strategies.

tions about the extent of anticipated exchange rate changes as well as one's appetite for risk. In all cases, however, the quantity of nondollar currency units exposed to risk is a moving target, rising or falling as the nondollar value of the portfolio increases or decreases, respectively. The appropriate hedge ratio should thus be recalculated on an ongoing basis, and adjustments should be made as needed.

Consider a portfolio of securities denominated in euros, originally valued at euro 5 million. If the manager decides to hedge the currency exposure with futures, the appropriate hedge would be found simply by taking the value of the portfolio in euros and dividing this amount by the size of the euro currency futures contract (euro 125,000). The initial hedge would thus require selling 40 euro currency futures.

Table 10–1 shows the outcome of the hedge portfolio over three periods, that is, from T0 through T3. During each period, the euro-denominated value of the portfolio increases by 2.5 percent. At the same time, the dollar value of the euro drops by $0.05 in each period.[2] If no currency hedge were employed, the net result of the market change would be a decline in the dollar value of the portfolio of 5.77 percent over the entire period. On the other hand, with a hedge that is adjusted upward each period as the euro-denominated value of the portfolio, moves higher, the dollar value of the portfolio combined with the hedge results, ends up being in excess of $6.4 million, a gain of about 7 percent. Note that this gain reflects the lion's share of the noncurrency-based market appreciation (7.04 percent versus 7.69 percent). The shortfall results because the hedge ratio is always adjusted somewhat belatedly. Put another way, before each adjustment, the investor is slightly underhedged in the example shown. Under such conditions, the compensation generated by the hedge should be expected to be somewhat smaller than the damage done by the weakening euro.

Table 10–2 shows the potential outcome if the euro becomes stronger—contrary to the hedger's expectations. In this case, the

---

2. For simplicity, the example equates spot and futures prices and thus ignores basis risk.

T A B L E 10–1

Hedging the Currency Exposure of a Nondollar Portfolio
When Foreign Exchange Is Weakening

	T0	T1	T2	T3
Portfolio value (euros)	5,000,000	5,125,000	5,253,125	5,384,453
Portfolio growth rate (euros)				
Per period		2.50%	2.50%	2.50%
Cumulative		2.50%	5.06%	7.69%
Spot exchange rate ($/euro)	1.2000	1.1500	1.1000	1.0500
Portfolio value ($)	6,000,000	5,893,750	5,778,436	5,653,676
Portfolio growth rate ($)				
Per period		–1.77%	–1.96%	–2.16%
Cumulative		–1.77%	–3.69%	–5.77%
Euro currency futures	1.2000	1.15000	1.1000	1.0500
Euro contract size	125,000	125,000	125,000	125,000
Theoretical hedge ratio	40.00	41.00	42.03	43.08
Actual hedge ratio	40	41	42	43
Result (individual periods)				
Euro currency futures ($)		250,000	256,250	262,500
Portfolio change ($)		(106,250)	(115,313)	(124,762)
Combined ($)		143,750	140,937	137,738
Hedged portfolio growth rate		2.40%	2.39%	2.38%
Results (cumulative)				
Euro currency futures ($)		250,000	506,250	768,750
Portfolio change ($)		(106,250)	(221,563)	(346,324)
Combined ($)		143,750	284,688	422,426
Hedged portfolio ($)		6,143,750	6,284,688	6,422,426
Hedged portfolio growth rate		2.40%	4.74%	7.04%

hedge immunizes the investor from the beneficial effect of the rising value of the euro. The final result shows a cumulative growth rate of 8.34 percent for the hedged portfolio, which is slightly better than the 7.69 percent growth of the euro-denominated portfolio independent of currency considerations (i.e., in the home currency). Again, the difference arises because of the imperfect hedge adjustment process. This time, however, the

T A B L E 10–2

Hedging the Currency Exposure of a Nondollar Portfolio
When Foreign Exchange Is Strengthening

	T0	T1	T2	T3
Portfolio value (euros)	5,000,000	5,125,000	5,253,125	5,384,453
Portfolio growth rate (euros)				
Per period		2.50%	2.50%	2.50%
Cumulative		2.50%	5.06%	7.69%
Spot exchange rate ($/euro)	1.2000	1.2500	1.3000	1.3500
Portfolio value ($)	6,000,000	6,406,250	6,829,063	7,269,012
Portfolio growth rate ($)				
Per period		6.77%	6.60%	6.44%
Cumulative		6,77%	13.82%	21.15%
Euro currency futures	1.2000	1.25000	1.3000	1.3500
Euro contract size	125,000	125,000	125,000	125,000
Theoretical hedge ratio	40.00	41.00	42.03	43.08
Actual hedge ratio	40	41	42	43
Result (individual periods)				
Euro currency futures ($)		(250,000)	(256,250)	(262,500)
Portfolio change ($)		406,250	422,813	439,949
Combined ($)		156,250	166,563	177,449
Hedged portfolio growth rate		2.60%	2.60%	2.60%
Results (cumulative)				
Euro currency futures ($)		(250,000)	(506,250)	(768,750)
Portfolio change ($)		406,250	829,063	1,269,012
Combined ($)		156,250	322,813	500,262
Hedged portfolio ($)		6,156,250	6,322,813	6,500,262
Hedged portfolio growth rate		2.60%	5.38%	8.34%

underhedging is beneficial, since the futures contracts are generating losses smaller than the currency-based gains accruing to the portfolio.[3]

---

3. If the example reflected a scenario where the securities were falling in value in their home currency, the belated hedge adjustments would result in being chronically overhedged. In such circumstances, the results from the futures hedge would exceed the changes in the portfolio effects due to exchange rate moves.

Choppy markets create a problem for the dynamic hedge adjustment process. Consider, for example, a nondollar portfolio for which the value rises and falls multiple times because of volatility in the home market. The dollar-based investor would likely increase and decrease the size of the hedge accordingly. The profits or losses on such adjustments would depend on the level of the exchange rate at the time of each trade and the degree to which one is overhedged or underhedged. Of course, one couldn't know in advance how serious (or beneficial) this aspect of the hedge would be. In all cases, however, the effect of commissions and bid/ask spreads would be detrimental. Thus, if sufficient volatility develops, whipsaw losses on the hedge could be a problem.

The discussion above pertains to a dynamic hedge using futures, but parallel cases can be shown for long put hedges, short call hedges, or hybrid hedges. In these cases, too, the proper size of the hedge rises and falls as the nondollar currency exposure increases and decreases. Ideally, a dynamic long put hedge will protect the portfolio from the potential adverse effects of a weakening nondollar currency (strengthening dollar) and will allow the benefits of a strengthening currency (weakening dollar). A short call hedge will generate immediate revenue from the sale of the option, providing a finite dollar value of protection. At the same time, it will commit the hedger to forgoing the benefit of a strengthening nondollar currency. Hybrid hedges typically offset currency effects over some predefined range of currency exchange rates, leaving exposures intact outside of these ranges. As is the case with the dynamic futures hedges, these alternative hedging strategies have a certain amount of inherent uncertainty because of the imperfect adjustment procedure and the potential for whipsaw losses.

CONCLUSION

While available exchange-traded currency hedging instruments may not achieve perfect currency exchange rate protection, they do offer the manager of nondollar investment some valuable flexibility. The manager who rules out such hedging devices is left with the choice of either liquidating investments or sweating out periods of declines in nondollar currencies. Dynamic foreign exchange hedging expands investment alternatives and thus offers opportunities for enhanced performance.

Conceptually—or ideally—selling futures locks in the currency exchange rate, thereby eliminating both risk and opportunity. Buying puts on currency futures protects against adverse currency exchange rate moves but leaves open the possibility of a beneficial change in exchange rates—for a price. Selling calls generates income and hence offers a finite amount of protection from an adverse move, but selling calls also obligates the hedger to forgo improved performance associated with a beneficial foreign exchange move. Finally, hybrid hedges, such as collars and corridors, offer a partial measure of protection within some range (or ranges) of currency exchange rates, with exposure if exchange rates move outside of those ranges.

In all cases, the hedger can expect to approach the ideal, but practical considerations still necessarily create some uncertainty. Deviations from the ideal could prove to be either beneficial or adverse. In general, the potential discrepancy will appear to be a relatively minor consideration when compared with either the cost of liquidating a portfolio or the risk of holding it unhedged.

GLOSSARY

Collar Hedge: A collar is constructed by pairing the purchase of a put on the nondollar currency (the same as a call on dollars) with the sale of a call on the nondollar currency (a put on dollars). A collar hedge protects from the effects of a weakening nondollar currency. At the same time, collars limit the benefit that would otherwise accrue from that currency strengthening. The cost of this protection is the net premiums of the two component options, often arranged to be zero cost. Ultimately, a hedge fixes a best-case/worst-case pair of possibilities.

Corridor Hedge: A corridor is constructed by pairing the purchase and sale of two puts on nondollar currency units (the equivalent of two calls on dollars). The long option generates a payoff if the nondollar currency weakens beyond some threshold dictated by that option's strike price. The short option effectively returns this protection if the weakening extends beyond a second threshold level dictated by the short option's strike price. Ultimately, a corridor locks in the currency effects provided the exchange rate stays within the range of the two strike prices. On the other hand, if the exchange rate moves outside of this range, the investor is exposed—to both risk and opportunity.

Dollar/Nondollar Exchange Rate Risk: The potential loss in dollars due to a change of the value of nondollar currency units, or vice-versa.

Dynamic Hedge Adjustment Process: A technique whereby the number of contracts required to hedge a foreign currency exposure is reevaluated periodically and the hedge ratio is adjusted accordingly.

Hedge Ratio: The number of futures contracts (or option contracts) used to manage currency exchange rate risk.

Long Put Hedge: A long put on currency futures "pays off" when the currency weakens relative to the dollar, thereby protecting an investment manager from this exposure. If the nondollar currency unit appreciates, the U.S. investor will enjoy the benefit of a stronger currency, net cost of the put.

Short Call Hedge: By selling calls, the U.S. investor generates income equal to the call premium. The protection derived from this strategy is thus limited to the size of the premium. Any weakening of the nondollar currency beyond this point goes unprotected. With a strengthening currency, the short call hedger gives up the potential of enjoying the benefits of the appreciating currency whenever the exchange rates move beyond the strike price of the call.

CHAPTER 11

Equity Derivatives Strategies and Risk Management

Joanne M. Hill
Co-Head, Global Equity Derivatives Research
Goldman, Sachs & Co.
New York, New York

Maria E. Tsu
Vice President, Equity Derivatives Research
Goldman, Sachs & Co.
New York, New York

Editorial Assistance provided by Barbara Dunn

Equity derivatives have come of age. Stock options have been trading for 25 years and stock index futures and options for some 15 years. In the last decade, over-the-counter trading of stock and index options has grown markedly, as have index swaps, as customers are requiring more customized solutions for investment management problems. According to annual surveys in *Pension and Investment Age*, approximately half of the largest 200 pension funds use equity derivatives, but only 10 to 15 percent of users are investment managers. As we shall see below, applications of equity derivatives are most prominent in index-based or top-down investment strategies. Among stock portfolio managers, however, index futures are increasingly being used to improve benchmark tracking, and stock options are being used to fine-tune stock views. In the last few years, stock option volume has been growing at a rate of over 20 percent. Also, the attention being paid to risk management has encouraged institutional investors to hire equity derivatives experts, who assist in strategy development as well as in establishing the infrastructure for monitoring the risks and measuring the returns of strategies involving these instruments.

EVOLUTION OF EQUITY DERIVATIVES

Strategies involving equity derivatives developed hand-in-hand with new equity products and implementation vehicles. In the early 1970s, the investing world focused on individual stock selection implemented through block trading of specific shares; selection of assets on the basis of portfolio concerns, and efficient frontiers of return versus risk. Index funds were appreciated and studied more in the academic world than by practitioners.

After the first index funds started in the mid-1970s, portfolio structuring based on quantitative principles became more important and stock options began trading. Also, because of flat equity market returns, the 1970s was a great decade for the start-up and growth of covered-call writing.

Strong equity market performance in the 1980s changed the focus of derivatives. Strategies began to center on achieving exposure to U.S. equities, with applications involving tactical asset allocation and synthetic index funds. Portfolio insurance used futures to replicate put options, with the goal of protecting portfolio gains. Derivative strategies primarily involved stock index options and stock index futures.

The failure of portfolio insurance to fully eliminate downside risk and its perceived connection to the stock market crash of 1987, plus the newness of the markets, led participants to reevaluate the use of derivatives. Dynamic hedging fell by the wayside, but synthetic investing with futures and basket, or portfolio, trading have both survived.

Proponents of derivatives adopted a bunker mentality for a few years; they spent most of their time trying to explain to regulators why derivatives were safe. In the 1990s, however, many new applications were developed. Competition from international exchanges and the growth in futures applications in the foreign markets spurred many U.S. institutions to take another look at derivatives.

The biggest growth in derivatives use in the 1990s has been in implementing global asset allocation and stock option strategies. Another factor in the growth of equity derivatives has been the development of long/short strategies, which use long index futures combined with a market-neutral position that is long a group of "in favor" stocks and short stocks that are expected to underperform. OTC options and structured notes in equities fill in the gaps of listed derivatives trading and meet more customized needs. In contrast to fixed income, where the amount of OTC swaps and structured notes outstanding is greater than the amount of exchange-traded derivatives, the notional amount outstanding of OTC equity derivative products is a small fraction of the notional amount of listed equity derivatives.

PRODUCTS MEET STRATEGIES

Derivative products are used to make existing strategies more efficient or to make new strategies possible. Equity derivatives fit into two categories. The first group, stock or portfolio substitutes that have symmetrical returns, includes basket products, listed futures, and swaps. In this group, the derivatives provide the full risk and return of an underlying security or portfolio, but the underlying security's volatility does not affect the pricing. The second group, optionlike securities, encompasses listed options, OTC options, and market indexed notes, which are fixed-income securities whose coupons and/or final payments depend on the return of a stock, portfolio of stocks, or market index. The volatility of the underlying security is a critical parameter in pricing these derivatives.

Equity derivative strategies can be categorized into four different areas:

- Efficient and enhanced fund management
- Asset allocation
- View-driven (active) strategies
- Risk management

Figure 11–1 shows particular applications that fit into each of these categories.

Efficient and Enhanced Fund Management

Using futures for efficient portfolio management is usually the starting point for most portfolio managers' use of equity derivatives. Because futures trading costs are significantly less than those of stocks, futures are critical for managing cash flows to equitize cash and for keeping tracking error to benchmarks low. In most equity markets, the commission and market impact of trading index futures is 10 to 25 percent (or less) of the cost of trading stocks. This means that for positions held for short periods, either as a synthetic investment or for tactical positions based on an index view, futures are much more cost effective than trading stocks. Long/short stock strategies also commonly use futures to provide equitization. Cash holdings can also be converted into international investments by buying a portfolio of international index futures structured to replicate the portfolio manager's international benchmark.

Asset Allocation

Stock index and fixed-income futures and options are also handy for shifting asset class exposure on an overlay basis. Investors use stock index, government bond, and Eurodeposit futures to manage the mix of equities, fixed income, and cash in their portfolios. By shifting country and debt/equity exposures in this way, they can leave the stock and bond holdings undisturbed, allowing them to save on trading costs as well as capitalize on any outperformance of their holding relative to the instrument underlying the future. Options and structured notes are also used for adjusting asset allocation, with options favored over futures when the investor either wants to receive a premium for committing to an asset allocation shift by the sale of an index put or call or wants to limit exposure to downside moves in exchange for less than full participation on the upside via a structured note.

F I G U R E   11–1

Efficient/Enhanced Fund Management	Equitizing cash Futures-related portfolio trading Tighten benchmark tracking with overlay Enhance returns from cheap futures Cash management or market-neutral strategies Synthetic international indexing
Asset Allocation (Domestic, Int'l. Global)	Overlay stock, bond, currency management Country allocation Selling options to improve trading range returns Structured notes with variable index exposure
View-Driven Strategies	Shift benchmark index exposure Short-term stock/sector call sales (bearish/neutral) Call options/warrants as stock substitutes Volatility trading Notes with embedded exposure to single stocks
Risk Management	Overlay future hedges to reduce exposure Option-based hedges: puts, put spreads, collars Selling index calls to trade upside for "range" enhancement Reshaping payoffs with options

View-Driven Strategies

Active managers, including mutual funds, investment advisors, hedge funds, and high-net-worth individuals, use equity derivatives to implement their views on the entire market, sectors, industries, and specific stocks. Top-down market views are typically traded using index futures or options to hedge equity exposure or increase the leverage/exposure to the broad market. The index futures now available on a wide range of global stock indexes, along with U.S. large-cap, mid-cap, and small-cap indexes, are tools that provide a wide range of choices for market-timing and tactical trades.

Since active stock selection is a more "bottom-up" approach, active managers are more inclined to use single stock options or options on specific industries and sectors. Although listed stock options are used extensively, OTC options are also commonly employed for view-driven strategies. Baskets based on a customized group of stocks that the portfolio manager selects can be the basis for an OTC call option or hedge through a put option. Also, because listed options have limited liquidity and expirations, OTC options help when the manager has a longer time horizon, desires an end-of-month or end-of-quarter expiration, or wants the dealer to facilitate a large trade by taking the position in their own book. The most commonly used strategies include writing covered calls against stock holdings, using long-term options as a strategic investment, and using options to hedge downside risk.

Options also provide an opportunity to take a view on stock or index volatility which is embedded in options prices. Some trading accounts and investment managers look for opportunities to speculate on volatility that can be connected to or independent of a view on the underlying security or index. Such strategies include options spread trades, strangles, or volatility swaps, which can be designed to have a high exposure to volatility.

Figures 11–2 and 11–3 provide a perspective on relative volume of equity index derivatives to stock trading as well as the growth of listed futures and options trading over time. In most global markets futures trade a national amount equivalent to the dollar value of stock trading.

FIGURE 11–2

The Ratio of Futures, Options to Stock Volume
(as of December 31, 1998)

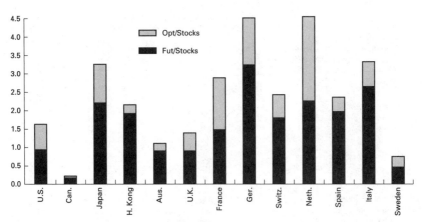

Risk Management

Equity derivative hedging strategies are helpful in reducing the risk of equity portfolios. A sale of futures against a portfolio can be structured to neutralize the risk with respect to the portfolio's sensitivity to the underlying index, creating, in effect, a synthetic cash-equivalent position. The most common option-based hedges include puts, put spreads (long near-the-money put/short out-of-the money put), and collars (long put/short call combinations). Investors have a wide range of choices in terms of horizon, the downside floor, and the method of financing the hedge, including selling a call to limit upside participation, selling a put to restore exposure after an extreme down move, or paying for the hedge outright. Another choice that shifts the risk and return profile of the portfolio is to consider selling index calls to enhance returns for a range in exchange for limiting upside by committing to sell the index at the strike price.

INDEX REPLICATION

One of the basic concepts that underlies many derivatives applications is that they efficiently replicate exposure to an underlying

FIGURE 11–3

Dollar Volume of Listed Index Derivatives

		FUTURES		OPTIONS	
		1998 Avg. Daily Volume (in mil$)	5-yr. Growth* (in contracts)	1998 Avg. Daily Volume (in mil$)	5-yr. Growth* (in contracts)
Country	Index				
North America	Total U.S.	35,982		24,530	
U.S.	S&P 500 Index	32,364	2.9	11,013	10.1
	S&P 500 Fut Opt			5,357	–3.0
	E-Mini S&P 500	962			
	SVX	11	17.2		
	SGX	6	15.9		
	DJIA**	1,206		218	
	S&P 100			6,959	–12.2
	S&P MidCap	210	7.3	37	–18.1
	Russell 2000	226	66.8	143	12.3
	NDX 100	547	42.6	803	1.1
	NYSE	450	–13.3		
Canada	TSE 35	212	31.8	37	12.2
Europe	Eurotop 100	15			
	STOXX 50	24			
	Euro STOXX 50	95			
U.K.	FT-SE 100	2,833	1.4	1,668	–17.8
France	CAC-40	3,304	6.6	3,255	–25.1
Germany	DAX	7,836	14.1	3,351	6.5
Switzerland	SMI	1,708	15.0	623	–9.5
Netherlands	AEX	1,475	36.2	1,557	14.3
Spain	IBEX 35	1,973	52.0	424	36.5
Italy	MIB 30	4,272	71.9	1,182	83.4
Sweden	OMX	325	8.9	234	–15.1
Pacific	Total Japan	5,546		2,662	
Japan	TOPIX	734	–1.5		
	Nikkei 225 (O)	3,333	–3.6	2,467	6.7
	Nikkei 225 (S)	1,282	1.9	195	19.2
	Nikkei 225 (C)	130	6.2		
	Nikkei 300	67	–30.0		
Hong Kong	Hang Seng	1,630	23.1	195	17.8
Australia	All Ords	507	28.3	140	–6.1
Korea	KOSPI	1,087	309.2		
Taiwan	MSCI Taiwan	202	174.7		

NOTE: Derivatives are expressed in terms of the national dollar amount of the underlying index. Historical contract volumes are adjusted to reflect the new contract sizes effective 1/1/99.
*Annualized five-year growth was compounded using the last five years of data unless the contract started trading after 1993: Number of years used for futures: four years (OMX and Nikkei 300; three years (MIB 30); two years (SVX, SGX, NDX 100 and KOSPI); and one year (MSCI Taiwan). Number of years used for options; four years (NDX 100 and Nikkei 225 (O)); and two years (FT-SE 100, CAC-40, DAX, SMI, AEX, MIB 30 and Nikkei 225 (S)).
**Dow Jones option volume is a combination of index option and futures option volume adjusted to the multiplier for the index options. Futures option volume is multiplied by 10. Futures options are 38.05 percent of the total.
Source: Reuters, DataStream, FAME Information Services, and local exchanges and brokers.

index, such as the S&P 500, the Nikkei 225, or the Financial Times-Stock Exchange 100 Share Index (FT-SE 100). Basic derivative products, such as stock index futures and total-return swaps, easily and efficiently replicate the exposure to virtually any index or benchmark.

An investor has three ways of owning an index fund: buy the index, buy the future, or buy the swap (Figure 11–4). Buying

F I G U R E 11–4

Equity Exposure Through Stock Index Futures and Equity
Index Swaps

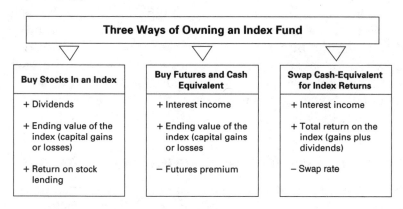

Three Ways of Owning an Index Fund		
Buy Stocks In an Index	**Buy Futures and Cash Equivalent**	**Swap Cash-Equivalent for Index Returns**
+ Dividends	+ Interest income	+ Interest income
+ Ending value of the index (capital gains or losses)	+ Ending value of the index (capital gains or losses	+ Total return on the index (gains plus dividends)
+ Return on stock lending	− Futures premium	− Swap rate

"Fair" futures premium (futures price - index) = index x (interest rate - dividend yield - stock lending return)

"Fair" swap rate = interest rate on cash equivalent.

˙ Note: No cash outlay is required when buying futures. Money can be invested in money market securities. Before transaction costs.

the stocks in an index gives the investor the dividends, the ending value of the index (capital gains or losses), and any return on lending the stock. The alternative to buying the stocks is to buy a futures contract and invest in cash-equivalent portfolios, U.S. T-bills or money market securities. Buying a futures contract on the index gives the investor gains or losses on the future plus the interest income on investing the cash (net of initial margin) that would otherwise be used to buy stocks. The interest income on that portfolio serves in place of the dividend and offsets the loss as futures converge to the index level at expiration.

A swap operates in a similar way, but instead of the gains or losses occurring daily as the investor marks a listed futures position to market, the swap buyer pays interest in exchange for the total return of the index at the reset date, which is usually quarterly. The seller of the swap passes the return—or the move in the underlying portfolio—to the buyer and receives the interest payment. This return can be with or without dividends; the decision is up to the buyer and is reflected in the interest rate. Swap pricing is usually quoted as LIBOR plus or minus a spread in basis points, reflecting current market pricing and supply/demand conditions. As with futures, the buyer typically invests the cash in a money market portfolio. This portfolio generates the interest with which the buyer will pay the dealer for the return of the index via the swap. When the interest income from the money market portfolio method equals the fixed- or floating-rate payment on the swap, it will not matter whether an investor buys the underlying stocks or enters into a swap.

EFFICIENT AND ENHANCED FUND MANAGEMENT

Efficient or enhanced fund management strategies include using futures to equitize cash, tightening benchmark tracking with overlays, futures-related portfolio trading to keep costs down, enhancing returns from cheap futures, cash management or market-neutral strategies, and synthetic international indexing.

Equitizing Cash

Futures provide an efficient way to maintain strategic asset-class weights or a fully invested position. Equitizing cash appeals to investors who require ways to keep cash invested to minimize the unintended risk of the cash flows in positions. This application, using futures to equitize cash or carry an ongoing position of cash in a mutual fund to provide room for withdrawals, is probably the most basic and widely used application of equity derivatives. Investment managers can experience problems with intermittent cash flows caused by money inflows or, worse, large withdrawals in a short period of time, which force the manager to sell stocks. The cost in basis points of carrying cash increases as a portfolio's cash allocation increases and as equity market returns increase. With a cash allocation of 8 percent, for example, the cost of carrying cash is considerably higher when equity market returns are 25 percent than when returns are 6 percent (2 percent per year versus 0.4 percent).

To create the synthetic index (benchmark) exposure, the investor simply buys a quantity of contracts based on the amount of cash to be invested divided by the notional value of each contact (index × multiplier).[1] For benchmarks with no futures contracts, such as the Wilshire 5000, a combination of other index futures (e.g., the S&P 500, S&P MidCap, and Russell 2000 futures) can be determined that will track the benchmark as closely as possible. Precise determination of the number of contracts involves adjusting for the interest rate sensitivity of daily realized gains and losses, which is sometimes called "tailing the hedge."

Tightening Benchmark Tracking

Benchmark tracking is a big concern because performance measurement is increasingly tied to benchmarks. Managers also worry about tracking benchmarks because their compensation is often performance-based. The solution is a simple exercise. For however much cash is taken in, the manager buys a basket of futures to mimic the benchmark for the existing portfolio holding. For every $1 million worth of that basket of futures, the manager might construct a portfolio of DJIA futures, Nasdaq 100 futures, S&P 500 futures—whatever index or mix of indexes has the most similarity to the actual holding. This approach quickly and efficiently achieves exposure to the required benchmark.

Futures-Related Trading

Certain types of portfolio trades tap into the liquidity or ease of dealer hedging from the availability of futures. Portfolio managers can lower stock-trading costs through futures-related trades. The two most commonly used futures-related trades are exchange-for-physical (EFP) trades and basis trades. In a typical EFP trade, a fund manager exchanges portfolios for futures (or vice versa) at a spread negotiated as a markup or markdown to the fair value of the future. Stocks are exchanged at opening or

---

1. Some investors reduce the number of contracts to account for the fact that the price of a future increased slightly more than that of the index. For more details, see *Global Index Futures Betas: Do Futures Amplify Index Moves?* by Joanne M. Hill and Jean-Baptiste Champon, Equity Derivatives Research, Goldman, Sachs & Co., January 1999.

closing prices adjusted for the spread. The cost is generally about one cent per share—a little less for selling stock and buying futures; a little more for the other side. This one cent cost applies to a portfolio that is exactly like the S&P 500. For something that has, say, a 3 percent tracking error with the S&P 500, the price would include a risk premium, so the cost of tracking would be higher. Basically, the dealer at the end of that transaction is long futures/short stocks, or the other way around. This approach is well suited to transition management and takes advantage of a natural hedge to the dealer. It is also a much cheaper way of trading than when a market maker is needed to make a market in individual stocks.

In a basis trade, a portfolio is exchanged for cash, again at a spread negotiated with the dealer. Clients who want to buy stocks ask the dealer to quote a price for giving them the particular stock portfolio as a basis trade. The dealer who wins buys futures over the course of the day, with the timing often directed by the client. Then, based on the average futures price the dealer paid and the negotiated spread, the dealer sells that portfolio to the client. The client never directly takes on a futures position but can take advantage of the fact that the dealer is putting on the hedge in the course of the trading day for the commitment to give the fund manager the portfolio at the end of the day.

Enhanced Equity Returns with Derivatives

Most investors earn their return enhancement from managing the cash available when they establish a long position via futures. One approach is for investors to buy a cash-equivalent (money market) portfolio, invest the dollar amount in a U.S. or international index futures contract, and within the cash-equivalent portfolio, pursue some active strategies that add alpha (excess return). Instead of getting their alpha from stockpicking, they get it from cash management or structured fixed-income products. Another approach is to use market-neutral strategies, such as long/short stock strategies or volatility trading.

STOCK AND INDEX OPTION STRATEGIES

Call selling is the most popular strategy used in conjunction with equity portfolio management. Calls may be sold on a covered or an uncovered basis. When covered calls are sold, the seller owns the underlying stock, which must be delivered if the call is exercised. When calls are sold on an uncovered basis, the seller is speculating that the call will *not* be exercised, so the premium may be kept. If the call is exercised, the call seller would need to deliver stock at the exercise price. Since there is no limit to how high the underlying stock price can go, there is no limit to the potential loss. Hence, selling naked calls is substantially riskier than selling calls against existing stock holdings.

COVERED CALL WRITING

The focus here is on the strategy of selling calls on a covered basis. (Note that when stock is purchased at the same time the calls are sold, the strategy is referred to as a *buy-write*.) There are three main motivations for writing covered calls:

- *To enhance returns:* Calls may be sold against stocks expected to remain in a trading range near-term to enhance returns. In this strategy, the call seller hopes to capture the premium but continue to hold the stock longer term. Therefore, the call seller hopes the calls will *not* be exercised.

- *To reduce downside risk:* Calls may be sold to reduce downside exposure against stocks expected to be modestly weak. Here, the call seller hopes the premium received for selling the calls will provide a cushion against a modest decline in the stock. As in the previous case, the investor typically wishes to maintain the stock position and hopes the calls will *not* be exercised.

- *To exit stock positions:* For this strategy, near-the-money calls are sold against current stock positions as a way to exit or reduce such positions. Here, the call seller may believe the stock is fully valued or overvalued and would be a seller of the stock at current prices. Premium is received in exchange for agreeing to sell stock, which increases the stock's effective sale price.

USING LONG-TERM OPTIONS

Most listed options are short-dated, with terms ranging from one to nine months. As such, short-dated options may be used to implement tactical strategies based on a short-term outlook for a stock. Long-dated options—terms of one year or more—may be more useful for implementing a longer-term strategic investment view or as an alternative to buying the stock. Long-dated listed options called LEAPS® (Long-Term Equity Anticipation Securities®) exist for a number of stocks. If no LEAPS are available or liquidity is limited, long-term options can be traded on an over-the-counter basis.

The main advantages of using long-term options for strategic investment strategies include:

- The time horizon better matches the investor's fundamental view.
- Longer-term means more time for views to be reflected in prices.
- There is more leverage versus buying stocks on margin.
- Time decay is initially slower.
- They may be taxed as long-term capital gains.

Compared to short-term out-of-the-money (OTM) options, long-term in-the-money (ITM) options are less risky. This is because for the same amount of capital at risk, long-term ITM options provide less leverage than short-term OTM options. In addition, long-term ITM options typically have a delta closer to 1.0, which means (1) they are more sensitive to moves in the underlying stock's price, and (2) they are more likely to be in-the-money at expiration.

Because of these characteristics, there has been increasing interest from portfolio managers in using long-term ITM options. Typically, these managers wish to leverage their views on stocks they like. By selectively replacing existing stock holdings with long-term ITM calls, the degree of leverage is increased and capital is freed up for other uses. This strategy can also be implemented on an unleveraged basis by keeping the cash balance in an interest-bearing account. Note that a long-call-plus-cash position is equivalent to a long-stock-plus-put position. Thus, when implemented on an unleveraged basis, the long-term call provides downside protection by virtue of the embedded put.

HEDGING AN ACTIVE PORTFOLIO

Options may be used for hedging downside risk in a portfolio. The main steps in the hedging process are as follows:

1. Identify the risk to be hedged.
2. Choose a hedging vehicle.
3. Choose a strategy.
4. Compare the tradeoff between cost and degree of fit.
5. Use scenario analysis to compare alternative strategies.

Identify the Risk to Be Hedged

The types of risks which may be hedged include market or country risk, sector or industry risk, and company-specific risk. In general, the more specific the risk to be hedged, the more important it is to use a hedging vehicle that matches the risk and, typically, the more costly the hedge. For example, a broad-market hedging strategy using S&P 500 options typically is less costly than a technology-sector hedging strategy, which is less costly than hedging individual technology stock positions within a portfolio.

Choose a Hedging Vehicle

Once the risk to be hedged has been identified, the next step is to select a hedging vehicle or the underlying index for the option strategy. This step typically requires some analysis to determine which index or combination of indexes provides the best fit to the portfolio.

The risk characteristics of the portfolio, including its volatility and correlation or tracking error to an index, may be analyzed using a risk model like BARRA or using historical return analysis. Historical analysis may be preferred when there is high turnover in the portfolio, since (1) current constituents may be less relevant when turnover is high and (2) historical returns may be more indicative of the manager's investment style.

Unless the underlying index for the option is identical to the portfolio being hedged, there will be tracking error between the two. Tracking error is a one-standard-deviation measure of the potential difference in returns between the portfolio and the index. For example, an annual tracking error of 5 percent means that the portfolio returns may match the index returns, plus or minus 5 percent, roughly two out of every three years, or 68 percent of the time.

Choose a Strategy

The most common hedging strategies include the following (see also Figure 11–5):

- *Long put:* Provides protection for declines below the put strike but allows full upside participation.
- *Short call:* Premium received provides cushion against modest declines but upside participation is capped.
- *Collar (long put, short call):* Put cost is reduced by selling an out-of-the-money call. Strategy provides downside protection but caps upside participation above the call strike.
- *Put-spread (long near OTM put, short far OTM put):* Reduces downside exposure for declines between the put strikes.
- *Put-spread collar (long put spread, short call):* Reduces cost of put-spread but caps upside participation above the call strike.

Compare Hedging Costs and Degree of Fit

There are three types of costs for each hedging strategy: (1) upfront net cost of options based on the underlying index, strategy,

F I G U R E 11–5

S&P 500 Index at 1280

	Put	Put-Spread	Collar
Long put strike	1225	1225	1225
(% below index)	–4.27	–4.27	–4.27
Short put strike		1050	
(% below index)		–17.95	
Short call strike			1350
(% below index)			5.50
Cost %	4.58	2.85	0.36
Max loss/floor %	–8.8		–4.6
Max gain %			5.1
Break-Even	1338	1316	1284

Prices are indicative for Jun 99 options, as of 01/29/99.

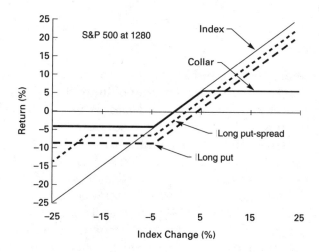

Prices are indicative for Jun 99 options, as of 01/29/99.

and liquidity of the options; (2) opportunity costs of short call (which caps upside participation) or put strike that is too low; and (3) potential costs due to imperfect tracking between the portfolio and the underlying index. Typically, there is a tradeoff among the three. For example, buying a far OTM put is less expensive but increases the "deductible" before put protection begins; or likewise, buying an S&P 500 put option might be less costly than a put on a technology index but would provide a poor fit for a portfolio laden with technology stocks.

Scenario Analysis

At a minimum, the potential returns of each strategy (at expiration) should be calculated for changes in the underlying index. Scenario analysis may also be used to examine the sensitivity of the strategy to potential changes in other assumptions. For example, analysis of an option strategy at various times prior to expiration may require assumptions about the path of volatility. Given the sensitivity of option values to volatility, this type of analysis is perhaps the most difficult but also the most important to perform. At expiration, analysis of the potential returns for different amounts of tracking error may be more relevant.

CONCLUSION

Effective risk management and strategy development with equity derivatives is based on an understanding of liquidity, pricing, performance measurement, and strategy design issues. In this chapter, we have explained some of the most common strategies employed by institutional investors that utilize equity options, index futures, and index swaps. Portfolio managers should try to use resources at their firms, at broker dealers, or derivative exchanges to help them understand the markets and the trading and risk issues for these derivative products. This will help them use these products in a manner that best accomplishes their strategy goals within their risk-tolerance levels. Whether derivatives are being used for efficient portfolio management, asset allocation, view-driven strategies, or risk management, they greatly expand the toolkit for managers of equity portfolios.

CHAPTER 12

Value at Risk for Asset Managers

Christopher Culp
Managing Director
CP Risk Management, LLC
and
Adjunct Associate Professor of Finance
The University of Chicago Graduate School of Business
Chicago, Illinois

Ron Mensink
Director of Quantitative Research and Risk Analytics
State of Wisconsin Investment Board
Madison, Wisconsin

Andrea M.P. Neves
Vice President
CP Risk Management, LLC
Chicago, Illinois

INTRODUCTION

Value at risk (VaR) is a probability-based metric for quantifying the market risk of assets and portfolios.[1] VaR is often used as an approximation of the "maximum reasonable loss" over a chosen time horizon. Its primary appeal—widespread amongst commercial bankers, derivatives dealers, and corporate treasury risk

---

We are grateful to Brian Heimsoth and Geoff Ihle for work with us on this subject. Nevertheless, the usual disclaimer applies and we alone are responsible for any errors and omissions. In particular, the views herein do not necessarily represent those of the State of Wisconsin Investment Board, CP Risk Management, or any CPRM client.

1. *Market risk* is the risk that the value of an asset or portfolio will decline because of adverse movements in market prices, such as interest rates, exchange rates, and security prices. Market risk is distinct from other types of financial risk, such as default risk or liquidity risk. In this chapter, our attention is limited to market risk, primarily because that risk is the main financial risk that VaR was developed to measure.

managers—is its ease of interpretation as a *summary* measure of risk as well as its *consistent* treatment of risk across different financial instruments and asset classes.

Value at risk is not nearly as well accepted in the institutional investment community as it is elsewhere.[2] The main reason is that asset managers are typically in the business of *taking* risks, either to fund uncertain liability streams or to generate positive excess risk-adjusted returns. Not surprisingly, asset managers—mutual funds, private banks, hedge funds, pension plans, endowments, and foundations—often view risk management in general and value at risk in particular as inherently at odds with their primary business mandate. Nevertheless, VaR can be a useful tool by which asset managers can better ascertain whether the risks they are taking are those risks they want or need to be taking and think they are taking. Investors as well are becoming increasingly aware of the benefits of VaR as a monitoring tool, causing them to further prod their fiduciary asset managers toward the regular calculation and disclosure of this measure of market risk.[3]

In this chapter, some of the applications of VaR to asset management are explored, with particular attention to the importance of VaR for multicurrency asset managers.[4] We first explain what VaR is and why it is so appealing conceptually. In the subsequent section, the mechanics of calculating VaR are explained, including the importance of some of the assumptions underlying the most common VaR measurement methodology. Bearing in mind the measurement difficulties with VaR, we then summarize four concrete applications of VaR to asset management. These applications involve the use of VaR to (1) monitor managers, portfolios, and

---

2. See Christopher L. Culp, Merton H. Miller, and Andrea M.P. Neves, "Value at Risk: Uses and Abuses," *Journal of Applied Corporate Finance*, Vol. 10, Winter 1998.

3. Throughout this article, we shall define *managers* as those who invest funds on behalf of outsiders. The outsiders placing capital with the asset manager are called *investors*. In a pension plan, for example, the managers are those internal and external portfolio managers (and their senior supervisors) who invest capital on behalf of retirees. The retiree beneficiaries, in turn, are the investors. At a hedge fund, mutual fund, or private bank, the managers again represent the portfolio manager(s) or general partner, whereas the investors are the outside depositors, purchasers, and limited partners.

4. For a more specific discussion of the use of VaR by pension plans, see Christopher L. Culp, Kamaryn T. Tanner, and Ron Mensink, "Risks, Returns and Retirement," *Risk*, Vol. 10, October 1987.

hedging programs; (2) eliminate *ex ante* transactional approval requirements; (3) define a formal system of risk targets and thresholds; and (4) implement a "risk budget."

WHAT IS VaR?

Value at risk is a statistic that summarizes the exposure of an asset or portfolio to market risk.[5] VaR allows managers to quantify and express risk as in the statement: "We do not expect losses to exceed 10 percent of the fund's net asset value in more than one out of the next twenty quarters."[6]

To arrive at a VaR measure for a given portfolio, a manager must generate a probability distribution of possible returns or changes in the value of that portfolio (or its component assets) over a specific time horizon. The distribution of possible portfolio returns or future values is called the *VaR distribution*.[7] The VaR statistic for the portfolio is the return or absolute dollar loss corresponding to some predefined probability level—usually 5 percent or less—as defined by the left-hand tail of the VaR distribution. Alternatively, VaR is the adverse return or dollar loss that is expected to occur no more than 5 percent of the time over the specified time horizon.

VaR is often considered a useful summary measure of market risk for several reasons. One feature of VaR is its *consistency* as a measure of financial risk. By expressing risk using a possible dollar-loss, or adverse-return, metric, VaR facilitates direct comparisons of risk across different portfolios (e.g., equity vs. fixed-income) and distinct financial products (e.g., interest rate swaps vs. common stock).

In addition to consistency, VaR enables managers or investors to examine potential losses over the particular time horizons with which they are concerned. Any measure of VaR requires the specification of such a *risk horizon*. A judicious choice

---

5. Portions of this section draw heavily from Culp, Miller, and Neves, op. cit..
6. For a general description of VaR, see Philippe Jorion, *Value at Risk*, Irwin Professional Publishing, Chicago, 1997.
7. The VaR distribution may be expressed in returns or in dollars. Return distributions often are empirically more tractable, and these can always be converted to a corresponding potential dollar loss given the current portfolio value.

of that risk horizon can aid asset managers in numerous risk management and disclosure matters. An asset manager's choice of an appropriate risk horizon may depend upon the timing of events, including the following: outside manager evaluations; board or trustee meetings; performance disclosures to investors, limited partners, or third-party tracking services (e.g., MAR or AIMR); regulatory examinations; tax assessments; key client meetings; and the like.[8]

Another advantage of VaR derives from its roots in probability theory. With whatever degree of confidence a portfolio manager wants to specify, VaR allows a specific potential loss over the risk horizon to be associated with that level of confidence. For example, a 95 percent confidence level with a one-month risk horizon, tells the portfolio manager, strictly speaking, that returns can be expected to dip below, say, x percent in the next month with 95 percent confidence. Some often go on to assume that the 5 percent confidence level means they stand to experience returns below x percent in no more than five months out of every hundred, an inference that is true only if strong assumptions are made about the stability of the underlying probability distributions.[9] Either way, VaR measures are *forward-looking* approximations of market risk, unlike traditionally backward-looking measures of actual historical performance, such as the Sharpe ratio that is calculated for performance evaluation purposes using *realized* manager returns.[10] VaR thus complements such conventional methods, rather than displacing them.

A related advantage of VaR that often appeals to asset managers is that it is largely tactical neutral. In other words, VaR is calculated by examining the market risk of the individual instruments in a portfolio, *not* using actual historical performance.[11]

---

8. See James V. Jordan and Robert J. Mackay, "Assessing Value at Risk for Equity Portfolios: Implementing Alternative Techniques," in *Derivatives Handbook*, R.J. Schwartz and C.W. Smith, Jr., eds., Wiley, New York, 1997.
9. This interpretation assumes that asset price changes are independently and identically distributed, i.e., that price changes are drawn from essentially the same distribution every period.
10. See William F. Sharpe, "The Sharpe Ratio," *Journal of Portfolio Management*, Fall 1994.
11. This is a source of some confusion in the institutional investment community. When the actual returns of a manager or portfolio serve as the basis for calculating a sum-

Whereas typical performance measurements reflect manager performance, VaR reveals the market risk borne by an investor based
solely on the asset mix and current security holdings.
Nevertheless, VaR is not totally neutral to *all* active strategies. If a
manager loads up on a higher volatility sector, technology, for
example, that strategy-induced volatility is picked up by VaR.
Managers' tactical shifts and market-timing decisions, by contrast, are not reflected in VaR measures, nor, as we shall see later,
should they be.[12]

THE MECHANICS OF VaR ESTIMATION

Creating a VaR distribution for a particular portfolio and a given
risk horizon can be viewed as a two-step process.[13] In the first
step, the price or return distribution for each individual security
in the portfolio is generated. These distributions represent possible value changes in all the component assets over the risk horizon. Next, the individual distributions somehow must be
aggregated into a single portfolio distribution using appropriate
measures of covariation, such as correlation. The resulting portfolio distribution then serves as the basis for the VaR summary
measure.

Methods for generating both individual asset and portfolio
VaR distributions range from the simplistic to the incredibly complex. The more realistic approaches to VaR measurement generate
the VaR distribution by revaluing all the assets in a portfolio for
the most realistic market risk scenarios possible. These *full-
revaluation* methods, however, can be very costly from a computational stand point. Accordingly, simpler approaches often make
a number of statistical assumptions intended to reduce
data requirements and computing costs. One is to assume that
small changes in portfolio values around its current value are
representative of larger potential value changes. This is known as

---

mary statistic, the resulting metric can be used for performance evaluation but *not*
for VaR.
12. See Culp and Mensink, op. cit.
13. In practice, VaR is not often implemented in a clean two-step manner, but covering it
in this way simplifies our discussion, without any loss of generality.

the *partial revaluation* approach to VaR measurement and is analogous to using a bond's duration as an approximation of risk, while ignoring its convexity.[14] Other simplifications made with the intention of relieving computing costs include a variety of distributional assumptions, most of which will be covered below.

To date, most asset managers who have implemented VaR used the more simplified computational approaches. Accordingly, we explore in this section the mechanics of simplified VaR calculations using an international equity portfolio as an example. We begin with a simple historical calculation of VaR that relies exclusively on historical time series data. We then discuss the most common method of VaR estimation—called *variance-based* VaR measurement—which was popularized by J.P. Morgan with its 1994 introduction of RiskMetrics™. The section concludes with a short discussion of the shortcomings of the variance-based approach and a survey of other alternatives.

HISTORICAL VaR

One way to calculate VaR is simply to assume that the future will behave precisely like the past. VaR can then be calculated using a sample time series of past security returns. An example will help illustrate.

Figure 12–1 shows a frequency distribution (histogram) of monthly returns on the FTSE 100 stock index from January 1988 to January 1995, as well as the summary statistics for that time series. The horizontal axis shows returns, and the vertical axis shows the percentage of the total sample of historical returns associated with each return interval on the horizontal axis. By assuming the future behaves like the past, we can say this frequency of past represents returns the "probability" that these same return levels will be realized in the future. The rightmost bar, for example, indicates that approximately 1 percent of

---

14. The full revaluation and partial revaluation methods are compared in J.P. Morgan, *RiskMetrics Technical Document*, 4th ed., December 1996.

FIGURE 12–1

FTSE-100 Monthly Returns (1/88–1/95)

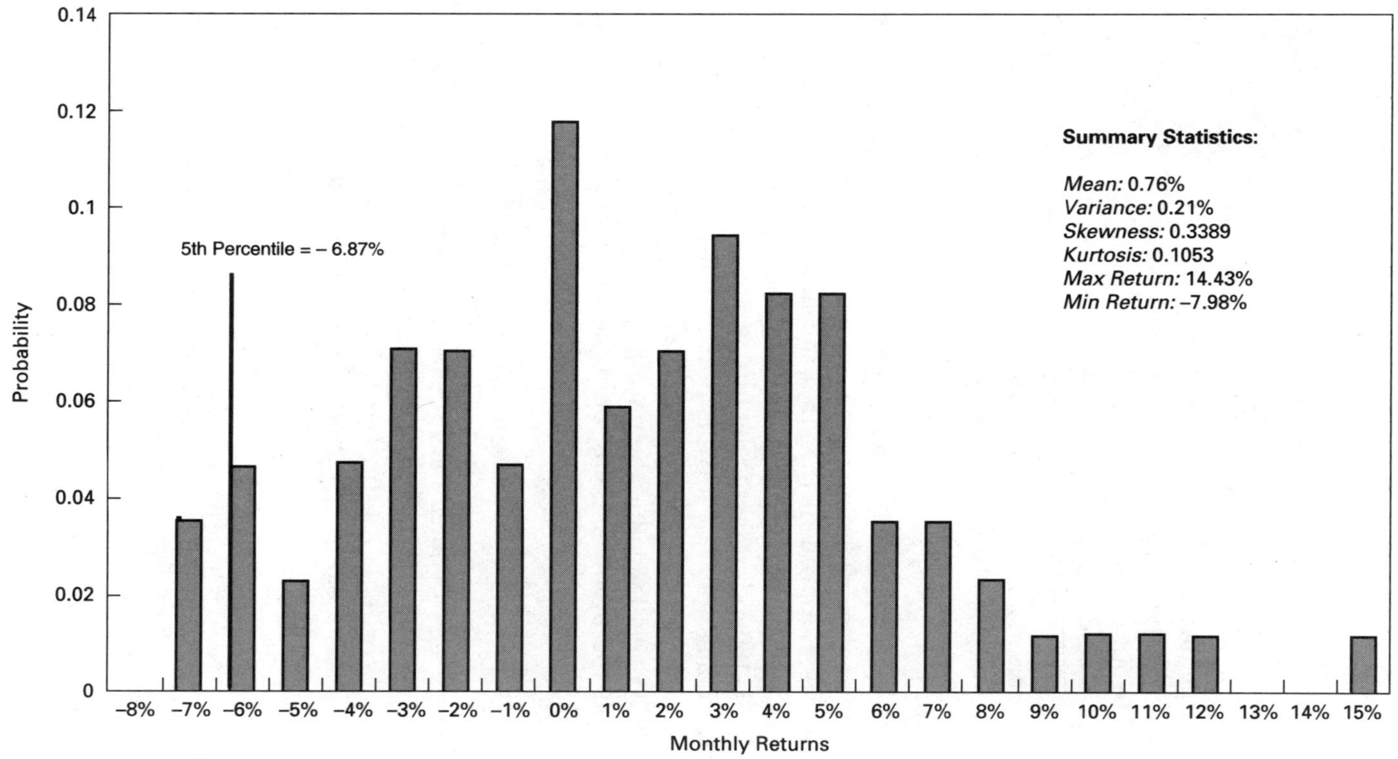

0.14
0.12
0.1
0.08
0.06
0.04
0.02
0
Probability
5th Percentile = – 6.87%
Summary Statistics:
Mean: 0.76%
Variance: 0.21%
Skewness: 0.3389
Kurtosis: 0.1053
Max Return: 14.43%
Min Return: –7.98%
–8% –7% –6% –5% –4% –3% –2% –1% 0% 1% 2% 3% 4% 5% 6% 7% 8% 9% 10% 11% 12% 13% 14% 15%
Monthly Returns

historical monthly returns were greater than 14 percent.[15] Assuming the next month in the future behaves like prior months, we can interpret this to mean that there is a 1 percent probability of a return in excess of 14 percent next month.

As the summary statistics and Figure 12–1 show, this return distribution is positively skewed—more probability lies in the right-hand tail than the left-hand tail. In other words, the probability of a return x percent above the mean is *higher* than the probability of a return x percent below the mean. We also can see that the excess kurtosis is positive, indicating that the distribution shown in Figure 12–1 has fatter tails than the normal distribution.[16]

Suppose a British asset manager has an equity portfolio with a current market value of £1 million invested entirely in FTSE-100 stocks. Suppose further that the manager holds the equities in exactly the same proportion as their portfolio weights in the FTSE-100 index, that is the fund is an index fund.[17] If the manager calculates the VaR for this portfolio at the 95 percent confidence level over a one-month risk horizon, the resulting VaR measure will reveal the value the portfolio is expected to match five of the next 100 months. Using only the historical data in Figure 12–1, this VaR can be calculated as follows:

$$VaR = £1,000,000 * R^{.05}$$

where $R^{.05}$ denotes the fifth percentile historical monthly return for the FTSE-100. This fifth percentile return, indicated with a bold vertical line on Figure 12–1, was –6.87 percent in the 1988–1995 sample period. So, the sterling-denominated one-

---

15. The x-axis labels on the figure correspond to the upper tick. For example, the 15 percent label lies between two tick marks, and the bar above that number that implies approximately 1 percent of the historical data was less than or equal to 15 percent and greater than 14 percent.

16. Excess kurtosis is the amount by which the kurtosis of a distribution exceeds the kurtosis of the normal distribution, which is 3. A positive excess kurtosis statistic indicates that the distribution has a more peaked center and fatter tails than the normal distribution.

17. For the purpose of this example, we thus treat the FTSE-100 "portfolio" as a single asset.

month VaR for this portfolio is £68,700.[18] We thus expect the net asset value (NAV) of this portfolio to decline by more than £68,700 in only five of the next 100 months.[19]

For large portfolios with numerous assets and exposures, the historical approach quickly becomes intractable. The data requirements alone can render this simplistic approach virtually worthless for large portfolios. Suppose, for example, we want to calculate the VaR of a portfolio comprised of FTSE-100 stocks, but in which the portfolio weights for each stock are now different from the weights used to calculate the FTSE-100 index. In that case, each stock would need to be examined directly. In other words, you would obtain historical time series for each of the 100 stocks and calculate the VaR using the new portfolio weights and the historical correlation matrix.

VARIANCE-BASED VaR

J.P. Morgan and Reuters greatly simplified the data problems of the pure historical approach by proposing a more simplified method of VaR measurement. This RiskMetrics™ VaR calculation methodology circumvents the data problems associated with using actual historical data in two ways. First, the RiskMetrics approach relies on *primitive securities* rather than actual security-level portfolio holdings. Primitive securities are securities intended to *represent* actual security holdings for the purpose of VaR calculations. The cash flows on a given portfolio of actual securities are "mapped" into corresponding cash flows on primitive securities in order to perform the VaR calculation. Second, RiskMetrics makes available the relevant data on those primitive securities so that virtually no historical data collection is required. As an example, RiskMetrics *does not* furnish data on coupon-bearing U.S. Treasury securities, but it does on zero-coupon Treasuries. So a portfolio of coupon-bearing Treasuries (i.e., actual holdings) can be mapped into a portfolio of corresponding

---

18. By convention, we drop the negative sign when reporting VaR.
19. VaR, however, does not give any indication of how far beyond this amount the portfolio could decline; it could be £68,701 or £1,000,000.

zero-coupon Treasury securities (i.e., primitive securities) for which data is available. The primitive securities available through RiskMetrics include government bonds, swap rates (which double as corporate bond rates), exchange rates, equity index levels, commodity prices, and money market rates, all of which are available for various countries and currency denominations.

Aside from addressing the data problems associated with historical VaR, the RiskMetrics approach makes a number of statistical assumptions that also simplify the *computational* side of the VaR calculation. Most important, the approach assumes that all primitive security returns are distributed normally. An attractive property of the normal distribution is that it is symmetric. Mean and variance thus are "sufficient statistics" to fully characterize a normal distribution. The variance of an asset whose return is normally distributed is all that is needed to summarize the risk of that asset.

So simplistic is Morgan's calculation method that many managers now use it with primitive securities of their own—without using the RiskMetrics data set. The approach thus has come to be known more generally as simply, the *variance-based approach*. Because this is by far the most predominant—and affordable—method of calculating VaR, the following subsections explore the mechanics of this methodology in more detail.

SINGLE-ASSET, SINGLE-PERIOD VaR

To calculate VaR using the variance-based approach, we rely on the fact that the probability in the left-hand tail of a normal distribution is a known function of the standard deviation of the distribution. Five percent of the normal distribution, for example, lies 1.65 standard deviations below the mean. Again, the mechanics of this approach are best illustrated by example.

Consider again the FTSE-100 index portfolio from the standpoint of the sterling-based asset manager. From the summary statistics provided in Figure 12–1, we know that the average monthly return is 0.76 percent and the monthly variance is 0.21 percent. With a current portfolio NAV of £1,000,000, the one-month VaR at the 95 percent confidence level is calculated as follows:

$$\text{VaR}_e = £1,000,000 \cdot (0.0076 - 1.65 \cdot 0.045)$$
$$= £1,000,000 \cdot (-0.068) = £68,012$$

On Figure 12–2, the historical distribution of returns from Figure 1 is superimposed with a normal distribution whose mean and variance are equal to the historical sample mean and variance. Figure 12–2 then depicts this variance-based VaR estimate (expressed as a percentage return) with a vertical line. Note that the variance-based VaR expressed as a return is the same (to the second decimal) as the fifth percentile return of the actual frequency distribution. Not surprisingly, the variance-based £68,012 VaR is only trivially different from the £68,700 one-month VaR calculated earlier using only the sample frequency distribution.

For a measure of the standard deviation used in the variance-based VaR calculation, we used the *unconditional* variance of the historical time series, i.e., the standard deviation of all 85 monthly returns shown in Figures 12–1 and 12–2. Alternatively, we could have used a different method to estimate the volatility input to the variance-based VaR estimate.[20] If we chose to recalculate this number on a regular basis, for example, we might have used a moving average of return variance as our estimate for volatility.[21] Because moving-average volatility is calculated using equal weights for all observations in the historical time series, the calculations are very simple. The result, however, is a smoothing effect that causes sharp changes in volatility to appear as plateaus over longer periods of time, failing to capture some dramatic volatility changes.

In order to remedy this problem, the RiskMetrics data sets provided by J.P. Morgan and Reuters include volatilities for all the supported primitive securities, computed at both the daily and monthly frequencies using an exponentially weighted moving average.[22] Unlike the unconditional variance or the simple

---

20. For a review of these methods, see Culp, Miller, and Neves, op. cit., and Jorion, op. cit.
21. To get a moving average estimate of variance, the average is taken over a rolling window of historical volatility data. Given a 20-month rolling window, for example, the variance used for one-month VaR calculations would be the average monthly variance over the most recent 20 months.
22. The data sets also include correlations.

Monthly VaR Distribution for FTSE 100 (1/88–1/95)

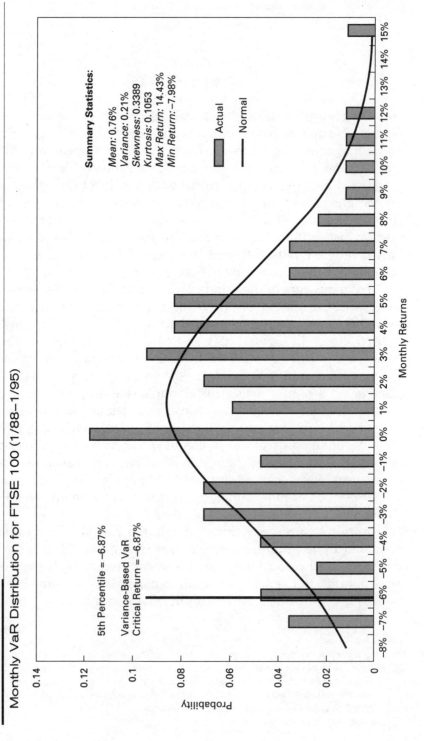

moving-average volatility estimate, an exponentially weighted moving average allows the most recent observations to be more influential in the calculation than observations further in the past. This has the advantage of capturing shocks in the market better than the simple moving average and thus is often regarded as producing a better volatility for variance-based VaR.

MULTIASSET, SINGLE-PERIOD VaR

The real savings in data and computing costs delivered by the variance-based VaR approach comes into play when the VaR is desired for a large portfolio of multiple assets and currency denominations. We can illustrate the simplicity of this approach, even in the two-asset case, by assuming in our earlier example that the FTSE-100 portfolio is now run by a *dollar-based* asset manager. The total portfolio thus consists now of two positions, a sterling-denominated equity exposure and a spot foreign exchange position to convert sterling into dollars.

Suppose the sterling price of U.S. dollars is £1.629/US$. The equity portfolio then is worth US$613,874 at the prevailing exchange rate. The combined portfolio of the dollar-denominated investor thus includes a US$613,874 position in the FTSE-100 (the equity primitive security) and an equivalent spot exchange rate position (the FX primitive). The one-month VaR of the equity is now[23]

$$VaR_e = US\$613,874 \cdot (0.0076 - 1.65 \cdot 0.045) = US\$40,915$$

Because this considers the VaR of the equity portfolio in isolation, this risk measure is called the *undiversified VaR* of the equity position.

We now can calculate the undiversified VaR of the spot exchange rate position:

$$VaR_{fx} = US\$613,874 \cdot (\mu_{fx} - 1.65\sigma_{fx})$$

---

23. We could have come to the same result (save for rounding error) by taking our original equity VaR calculation and simply converting that VaR into U.S. dollars at the prevailing spot rate.

where μ_{fx} and σ_{fx} are the mean and standard deviation of the monthly percentage change in the sterling/dollar rate. Again using the unconditional standard deviation (from January 1988 to January 1995) as our volatility estimate, we calculate σ_{fx} as 0.0368 and μ_{fx} as −0.001. Substituting into the above equation, we ascertain that the undiversified VaR of the currency exposure is

$$VaR_{fx} = US\$613,874 \cdot (-0.001 - 1.65 \cdot 0.0368) = US\$37,888$$

We now can calculate the total portfolio VaR using a powerful property of the bivariate normal probability distribution.[24] Specifically,

$$VaR_p{}^2 = VaR_e{}^2 + VaR_{fx}{}^2 + 2\rho VaR_e VaR_{fx}$$

where ρ is the correlation between FTSE-100 returns and monthly percentage changes in the sterling/dollar rate. We estimate ρ to be −0.2136 from our 1988–1995 sample, i.e., the FTSE-100 varies *inversely* with changes in the sterling/dollar spot rate. Substituting that correlation coefficient and the other values into the above equation, we thus calculate the one-month portfolio VaR as follows:

$$VaR_p = [(\$40,915)^2 + (\$37,888)^2 + 2(-0.2136)(\$40,915)(\$37,888)]^{1/2}$$
$$= \$49,470$$

This number represents the *diversified* VaR, or the one-month VaR (at the 95 percent confidence level) that reflects both the equity and currency exposures as well as the correlation between the two. The fund manager thus should expect the portfolio to lose 8 percent or more of its current NAV in five of the next 100 months from its combined FTSE and sterling exposure. As one would expect, diversified VaR benefits from the lack of perfect correla-

---

24. The property on which we implicitly rely is that the variance of a portfolio of two assets whose returns are distributed bivariate normal is a linear function of the variance of each asset return plus twice the correlation of the two returns times the two standard deviations. This result can be extended to portfolios comprised of more than two assets if returns are distributed multivariate normal.

tion—and, indeed, the negative correlation in this case—and is considerably less than the sum of the two undiversified VaRs.

MULTI-PERIOD VaR

The examples above have used monthly data to generate VaR measures for a one-month risk horizon. Because RiskMetrics data is indeed available at the monthly frequency,[25] no further adjustments need to be made if we care about a monthly risk horizon. To compute the VaR for longer risk horizons, however, the one-period VaR must be adjusted. This calculation is performed with the aid of *another* simplifying assumption in the variance-based approach: return distributions are assumed to be independent and stable over time (collectively, "distributional stationarity"). This means that the VaR distribution we use to calculate one-month VaR is presumed to be identical to the distribution from which successive monthly returns are drawn. The multiperiod VaR is then just the one-period VaR multiplied by the square root of the number of periods in the risk horizon.

Suppose we now wish to compute the diversified FTSE portfolio VaR at the 95 percent confidence level for a *one-quarter* risk horizon. To accomplish this, we need only multiply the one-month diversified VaR by the square root of three ($49,470 × 1.7321 = $85,685). So, we expect losses in our international equity portfolio not to exceed $85,685 in 95 of the next 100 quarters.

ALTERNATIVES TO THE VARIANCE-BASED VaR APPROACH

As we saw in Figures 12–1 and 12–2, the undiversified variance-based VaR is almost exactly the same as the undiversified VaR computed using actual historical data. At first glance, this may seem surprising. Figure 12–2 and the sample statistics for the actual historical show quite clearly, after all, that the frequency distribution does *not* resemble the normal distribution.[26]

---

25. Volatility and correlation data also is available for the daily frequency.
26. Note in Figure 12–2 the fat tails of the actual distribution relative to the normal. This is consistent with the positive excess kurtosis statistic examined earlier.

Nevertheless, even when the underlying data is not normally distributed, managers can sometimes get lucky, i.e., the normal approximation is sometimes realistic enough for VaR calculations, but not always and perhaps not even often.

Figure 12–3 shows the frequency distribution of monthly returns on the Nikkei 225 Japanese stock index from January 1988 through January 1995. As in Figure 12–2, a normal distribution is superimposed on the frequency distribution, whose mean and variance come from the underlying historical return data. Figure 12–3 and the sample statistics show this distribution is negatively skewed and has even fatter tails relative to the normal distribution than the FTSE-100. Not surprisingly, the variance-based undiversified critical VaR return, –11.68 percent when expressed as a return(is higher than the historical fifth percentile return of –12.62 percent. An undiversified VaR calculated using the assumption of normality thus *understates* the true risk of the Nikkei 225 portfolio.

As a general rule, variance-based VaR understates the risk of an asset or portfolio whenever the underlying distribution is negatively skewed and has tails fatter than the normal distribution (i.e., "leptokurtic"). Quite a few asset classes fall into this category, including real estate, commodities, private placements, and some bonds. Many asset managers, not surprisingly, are unsatisfied with the assumption that variance is a complete measure of risk for all asset classes. In addition, long-term asset managers with risk horizons of a quarter or more often are equally displeased with the assumption of distributional stationarity in the variance-based VaR approach. Some investors thus opt to calculate VaR using a measurement methodology that does *not* rely on variance and distributional stationarity.[27] Two such methods include Monte Carlo simulation and historical simulation.[28]

Non-variance-based VaR can be quite expensive computationally, Advanced VaR calculation systems that do not force the user to rely on the assumption of normally distributed asset

27. Some investors also avoid VaR for this reason, as well, choosing instead to focus on "downside risk" measures such as below-target risk or downside semivariance. See Culp, Tanner, and Mensink, op. cit.
28. For examples of these approaches, see Jordan and Mackay, op. cit.

FIGURE 12-3

Monthly VaR Distribution for Nikkei 225 (1/88–1/95)

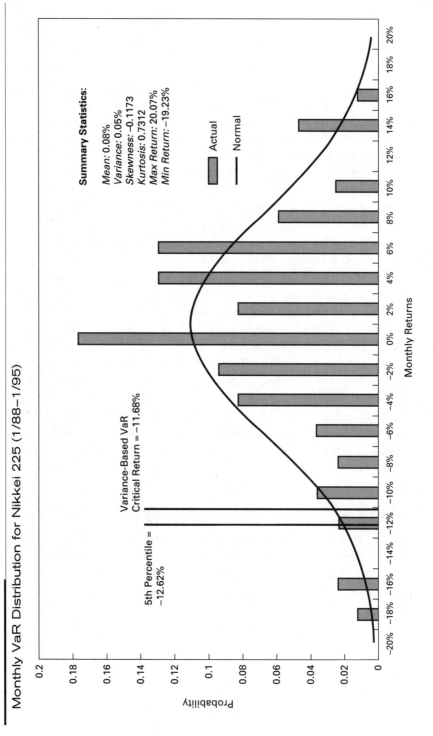

Summary Statistics:

Mean: 0.08%
Variance: 0.05%
Skewness: -0.1173
Kurtosis: 0.7312
Max Return: 20.07%
Min Return: -19.23%

Actual
Normal

Variance-Based VaR
Critical Return = -11.68%

5th Percentile =
-12.62%

Probability

Monthly Returns

returns often cost over $1 million, sometimes $1 million *per annum* in leasing fees. Beyond that purchase/leasing price, more advanced calculation methods also typically necessitate significantly more *data* e.g., historical security returns. In some cases, the cost of obtaining and maintaining this data can be as much if not more than the cost of the system itself.

Aside from the systems and data costs of advanced VaR measurement, the more complex the system, the more costly it is to implement and maintain from a *labor cost* standpoint. A very advanced system often necessitates the creation of a full-time job to manage the inputs and outputs of the system. And the more complex the system, the more savvy its user must be.

Asset managers thus often face a relatively unpleasant trade-off between cost and precision (realism) in their VaR estimates. Not surprisingly, many managers just eschew VaR altogether, especially when the applications of VaR are far from obvious for many asset managers. If the job of an asset manager is to take risk in order to fund an uncertain liability stream and earn a competitive return on invested capital, why should that manager spend over a million dollars on a VaR measurement system? In the next section, we attempt to answer that question by proposing some applications of VaR that neither require a huge expenditure on a VaR system nor needlessly attenuate the investment autonomy of portfolio managers.

APPLICATIONS OF VaR TO ASSET MANAGEMENT

In order for VaR to make sense to most asset managers, the investment policy must first be accepted as sacrosanct. VaR should complement rather than compete with the primary investment management goals of the asset manager. It is a tool for helping managers determine whether the risks to which they are exposed are those risks to which they think they are and want to be exposed. Value at risk will never tell an asset manager how much risk to take. It will only tell a manager how much risk is being taken.

Taking the investment policy as a given, asset managers can apply VaR in at least four ways to the operation of their funds.

MONITORING

One of the primary benefits of VaR for asset managers is that it facilitates the consistent and regular monitoring of market risk. Institutional investors can calculate and monitor VaR on a variety of different levels. When calculated and monitored at the *portfolio* level, the risks taken by individual asset managers—whether internal traders and portfolio managers or external account managers—can be evaluated on an ongoing basis. Market risk also can be tracked and monitored at the aggregate fund level, as well as by asset class, by issuer/counterparty, and the like. Three specific monitoring applications of VaR are discussed in the subsections below.

INTERNAL MANAGER/PORTFOLIO MONITORING

Suppose that Pension Plan Dearborn is a defined-benefit plan with a current NAV of US$1 billion invested through internal and external fund managers in all traditional asset classes. Pension Plan Dearborn calculates the quarterly VaR once a week for all of its portfolio managers. Suppose that external account manager Rush manages a $100 million international bond portfolio for Dearborn. If the VaR for account manager Rush is monitored each week, major departures of Rush's VaR from various established comparison risk measures should trigger an inquiry into Rush's recent investment activities, transactions that Pension Plan Dearborn's senior managers might otherwise have no reason to scrutinize.

Consider the specific case in which external account manager Rush has a quarterly diversified VaR that has averaged $10 million (at the 95 percent confidence level) over the last two years. That means that Pension Plan Dearborn expects to lose no more than 10 percent of its total investment with manager Rush in 95 of the next 100 quarters. If the diversified VaR for manager Rush is recalculated every week and suddenly jumps to $50 million from the historical average of $10 million, the senior managers of Plan Dearborn might be inclined to wonder—and to ask—why. Because VaR is strategy-neutral, only two answers are possible. First, the volatility in manager Rush's international bond holdings has gone up (e.g., following the Asian currency crisis), in which case the risk of the position simply reflects the risks of the asset allocation decision. Alternatively, manager Rush has acquired new securities that expose Dearborn to significant additional market risks that were not contemplated by the asset allocation decision.

Aside from monitoring a manager's risk relative to its own historical risk profile, VaR also facilitates comparisons of the risks of one portfolio or manager with other portfolios or managers. To continue the above example, the increase in manager Rush's VaR might not appear problematic if the VaRs of other international bond managers engaged by Plan Dearborn rise at the same time. The same is true if the VaR of the benchmark used to evaluate the performance of manager Rush rises proportionately. In these cases, Plan Dearborn might conclude that its market risk has increased because of its exposure to international fixed income as an asset class rather than because of its particular exposure to the investment strategies of manager Rush.

For VaR to provide a useful monitoring benefit, precision in the measurement of VaR is not absolutely essential. In fact, the primary benefit of VaR monitoring comes from examining relative VaR, or the VaR of a manager or portfolio compared to the VaR of a benchmark portfolio, peer group portfolios, other internal or external managers, or the same manager over time. Even if the actual levels of VaR—$10 million and $50 million above—are imprecisely measured, the same measurement bias may affect other portfolios in the same way.[29] The theory is that these measurement errors "cancel out" when relative VaR is the focus instead of the absolute level of the VaR measure in question. Consequently, asset managers can derive a surprising amount of marginal benefit from monitoring even a variance-based VaR.

External Monitoring

The monitoring benefit of VaR is not restricted to internal and external portfolio management. Especially for asset managers

---

29. This also may not be the case. Each situation should be evaluated on its own to identify sources of measurement error in the VaR statistic, in particular, whether measurement error is consistent across assets and portfolios.

whose portfolio holdings are not transparently available to investors at all times, e.g., most hedge funds, a VaR reported to investors can help assuage any investors' concerns about market risk without necessitating disclosure of portfolio holdings. Similarly, regular reports of VaR to boards of directors or trustees can go a long way toward reassuring these bodies that market risk is within the specified risk tolerance of the investment pool.

Hedge-Effectiveness Monitoring

Asset managers may use diversified VaR to monitor the extent to which their hedging strategies are accomplishing the desired objectives. To take a simple example, consider a $500 million mutual fund invested in domestic and international equities that hedges its exchange rate risk using currency forwards and futures. Suppose the one-quarter diversified VaR for the fund is 15 percent of NAV *without* including the currency hedges in the VaR calculation. The mutual fund manager can evaluate the effectiveness of the hedge (and analyze the extent to which returns and risks are affected by currency risk) by recalculating diversified VaR *with* the hedges. If the diversified VaR of the hedged portfolio is 14.5 percent of NAV, the fund manager might question whether the hedging is worthwhile or whether the hedges have been properly implemented.

The use of VaR to evaluate the effectiveness of a hedging program depends strongly on the type of hedging program in place *and* on how the investment policy defines the hedging objective. To see why, consider two different examples, both of which concern a pension plan invested in international bonds and equities with a mandate to control its currency risk.[30] In the first case, suppose the pension plan specifies in its investment policy that no more than 1 percent of the current value of any particular portfolio can be exposed to exchange rate risk and that portfolio managers are left to hedge those risks on their own. The effectiveness of each manager's hedge can be evaluated by examining the

---

30. This situation is explored in more detail in Geoffrey Ihle, "Forward Hedges that Increase Value at Risk," *Derivatives Quarterly*, vol. 4, no. 4, Summer 1998.

diversified VaRs of each portfolio separately, with and without the inclusion of the hedging contracts.

Now suppose the same pension plan specifies in its investment policy that no more than 1 percent of the current NAV *of the whole plan* can be exposed to exchange rate risk. Suppose further those managers do not do their own hedging, but that the plan engages an FX overlay manager to hedge its consolidated currency risk. The effectiveness of the overlay plan can be evaluated by comparing the plan's aggregate diversified VaR with and without the overlay program included.

Some interesting problems can arise when hedge effectiveness is monitored at a level different from the one specified in the investment policy as the hedging objective. Specifically, suppose the plan's international equity is invested entirely in Canadian dollar-denominated equities and that its international bonds are denominated entirely in Austrian shillings.[31] These two currencies happen to be negatively correlated. Consequently, if the pension plan specifies a hedging policy by portfolio, the independent hedging decisions of the bond and equity managers may achieve the plan's desired VaR reduction on an individual portfolio basis but may also increase the plan's aggregate diversified VaR. By partially hedging two portfolios whose currency risks are negatively correlated, the "natural hedge" is removed and the plan's consolidated diversified VaR rises.[32]

An overlay manager could, of course, construct a partial hedge that incorporates the negative correlation between the ATS and CAD holdings. For a plan interested in hedging its aggregate exchange rate risk, the overlay manager thus can achieve the desired VaR reduction. At the same time, if an overlay manager is used and the diversified VaRs of the individual portfolios are then evaluated, at least one of the portfolios will look riskier when the hedges are taken into account.

The usefulness of VaR in evaluating hedging programs thus depends strongly on the particular hedging objectives specified by the asset manager in the investment policy. Some asset managers may be more concerned about currency risk at the manager level

31. This example follows from Ihle, op. cit.
32. This is illustrated numerically in Ihle, op. cit.

than at the aggregate fund level. The fund may, for example, want to control the independent currency bets made by outside managers and thus may opt to require portfolio-specific hedging for management purposes. In that case, the fund would specify portfolio-level hedging requirements but then must monitor hedge effectiveness at the portfolio level. In the end, the plan will likely end up overhedged (i.e., speculating on currencies) in aggregate when some of the currencies held are negatively correlated. Such plans, therefore, should also carefully monitor their aggregate diversified VaR to ensure this residual FX exposure does not become an unexpected (and possibly significant) risk factor.

By contrast, an asset manager whose appetite for currency risk is defined at the aggregate level should both hedge at the aggregate level and monitor the management of that risk using aggregate fund-level diversified VaR.

WHAT-IF MODELING OF CANDIDATE TRADES

VaR also can be beneficial to asset managers who wish to eliminate transactional scrutiny by senior managers or directors and trustees. In this way, VaR can actually help give portfolio managers more autonomy than they might otherwise have without a formalized, VaR-based risk management process.

After the "great derivatives disasters" of the early 1990s, many directors and trustees of institutional investors became concerned with the risks posed by derivatives transactions. As a result, such transactions were prohibited in numerous investment policies and were subject to board-level approval in many others. Transactional monitoring using VaR can be an effective way of addressing this issue.

Suppose, for example, that the limited partners of a hedge fund are concerned about the possibility that the fund managers will engage in leveraged derivatives to augment their returns.[33] Because most hedge funds do not report their portfolio holdings

---

33. Not all derivatives are leveraged. Our use of the term here refers to formula leverage rather than margin. A swap in which the hedge fund receives a fixed rate of 8 percent and pays LIBOR against a notional amount of $1 million would not be formula leveraged. A swap in which the fund receives 8 percent fixed and pays LIBOR *squared* would be.

on a regular basis, the limited partners might be inclined to ask the general partner to prohibit such investments. As a better alternative, the general partner might simply agree not to engage in any transactions that would increase the fund's VaR by more than x percent of the fund's capital.

In order to minimize unnecessary scrutiny of particular trades, an asset manager need not require that VaR be calculated and reported *ex ante*, especially if the cost of a VaR system is an issue. Few affordable VaR systems allow for this type of real-time computation. Nevertheless, the requirement could be instituted and enforced *ex post*, with the corresponding requirement that any trades in violation of the "maximum marginal VaR" requirement would be liquidated or hedged within, say, a week of the deal.

As a cautionary note, asset managers must be attentive to the means by which the VaR of a particular transaction is calculated in order for this application of VaR to make sense. One VaR-like statistic, proposed by Mark Garman, is called DelVaR and examines the impact of a particular trade on the VaR of a portfolio.[34] Although quite useful in its own right, DelVaR would not be appropriate for the application of VaR discussed here. The particular measurement method proposed by Garman is useful for evaluating the impact of a particular security on the VaR of a portfolio only for small presumed changes in underlying prices. DelVaR badly underestimates, however, the marginal risk of certain trades for wide price swings. In order to apply VaR in the manner discussed here, the portfolio VaR would have to be fully re-estimated with and without the candidate trade rather than simply approximated using a measure like DelVaR.

RISK TARGETS AND THRESHOLDS

A third application of VaR to asset management involves measuring and monitoring market risk using a formal system of predefined risk targets or thresholds. In essence, risk thresholds take ad hoc risk monitoring one step further and systematize the

---

34. Mark Garman, "Improving on VAR," *Risk*, vol.9, no. 5, 1996.

process by which VaR levels are evaluated and discussed for portfolios or managers—or in some cases, for the whole investment fund.

A system of risk thresholds is tantamount to setting up a tripwire around an investment "field," where the field is characterized by a fund's investment policy and risk tolerance. This tripwire is defined in terms of the maximum tolerable VaR allocated to a manager or portfolio and then is monitored by regularly, e.g., weekly, comparing actual VaRs to these predefined targets. Investment managers are permitted to leave the field when they wish, but the tripwire signals senior managers that they have done so. When a tripwire is hit, i.e., a VaR threshold is breached, an "exception report" is generated and discussions and explanations are required.

Risk targets can be specified in terms of absolute or relative VaR. A private bank might conclude, for example, that a particular client's capital should never be placed at risk above a certain amount, regardless of the risks taken by other clients or managers. In that case, the traders on that client's account could be subject to an absolute VaR threshold. A mutual fund, by contrast, might prefer to specify its risk targets relative to the VaR of its benchmark portfolio or peer group.

The hallmark of a well-functioning risk target system is not that targets are never breached or that all exceptions are rectified through liquidating or hedging current holdings. Rather, the primary benefit of a risk target system is the formalization of a process by which exceptions are discussed, addressed, and analyzed. Risk thresholds thus are a useful means by which asset managers can systematically monitor and control their market risks without attenuating the autonomy of their portfolio managers. Because the primary purpose of risk limits is to systematize discussions about actual market risk exposures relative to defined risk tolerances, huge investments in VaR calculation systems, moreover, typically are not required. Even an imprecise measure of VaR will usually accomplish the desired result of formalizing the risk-monitoring process.

RISK LIMITS AND RISK BUDGETS

A more extreme version of risk targets and risk thresholds is a system of rigid risk limits. This application of VaR is also known as a *risk budget*. In a risk budget, the fund's total VaR is calculated and then allocated to asset classes and specific portfolios in terms of absolute and benchmark-relative VaR, as well as shortfall at risk (SaR).[35] Managers are then required to remain within their allocated risk budget along these risk dimensions. So whereas a risk target resembles a tripwire around a field that a manager must account, *ex post*, for crossing, a true risk budget instead acts as an electric fence around the field that managers simply cannot cross, *ex ante*.

A total risk budget defined across all portfolios can create numerous problems for an asset manager. First, risk budgeting relies at some level on the absolute VaR of a fund and its portfolios. To the extent that the measurement methodology is flawed, the risk budget will be wrong. If the VaR measurement methodology is more biased for some asset classes or security types than others, moreover, some managers could be penalized or rewarded simply because of flaws in the measurement methodology. In the extreme, relatively riskier funds could be given a risk budget that is too high, whereas relatively safer funds could be allocated too little VaR.

Second, risk budgeting defined across both asset classes and portfolios can contradict and call into question the fund's asset allocation decision. This can be especially problematic when a fund manager's board must approve changes in the asset allocation unless hitting a risk limit in the risk budget triggers the change. Suppose a pension plan allocates capital into asset classes annually using traditional mean-variance asset allocation and portfolio optimization techniques. Then suppose the plan defines a VaR budget for asset classes and portfolios in which VaR is measured using a variance-based approach. If the risk budget is enforced more frequently than annually, the risk budget will call

---

35. SaR is directly analogous to VaR, with the net asset/liability position subjected to the risk calculation and summary measure. See Culp, Tanner, and Mensink, op. cit.

into question the asset allocation simply because volatility changes in the markets on a regular basis. Variance-induced changes in VaR thus prompt a shift in the asset allocation through the risk budget. Even though the practical consequence is a change in the asset allocation itself, the actual trigger is the risk budget; the board may never be consulted.[36]

To avoid this problem, risk budgeting should be limited to rebalancing funds between portfolios within the same asset class. Even then, asset managers contemplating a risk budget will need to allocate a considerable sum of money for the VaR calculation system to ensure that the calculation method is not biased against particular managers or financial instruments.

CONCLUSION

Many asset managers have avoided or criticized VaR based on the notion that systematic measurements and disclosures of risk serve only to attenuate the autonomous nature of the investment management process. On the contrary, measuring VaR and using it as the basis for internal monitoring and risk targets, external risk disclosures, and transactional risk evaluations can actually give the asset manager more autonomy than if investors or senior managers are unsure of what the fund's market risk exposures actually are. A sound VaR-based risk management system should take the investment policy as given and should seek only to help managers and investors ensure that the risks to which the fund is exposed are those risks to which it thinks it is and wants or needs to be exposed.

Most cost-effective systems for measuring VaR rely on simplistic and often unrealistic assumptions. Nevertheless, the benefit of most VaR applications for asset managers comes from how the VaR estimate is used rather than the calculation methodology. Especially for asset managers with exposures in multiple curren-

---

36. Ironically, a risk budget may be supported by a board, which thinks the budget reduces the need for board-level micromanagement. Yet to the extent that the risk budget simply grants fund managers license to circumvent the board-approved asset allocation, the opposite intention will have been achieved.

cies, even simplified VaR can be an invaluable tool for distilling market risk into one summary statistic. It is no panacea, but an asset manager that measures its VaR may be better able to manage its primary investment business than one that is largely unaware of its consolidated market risk exposures.

This article originally appeared in *Derivatives Quarterly*, Vol. 5, No. 2 (Winter 1998).

CHAPTER 13

Trading Risks in International Investments—Why Market-Neutral Strategies Sometimes Fail

Ezra Zask
Manager
Gibson Capital Management, Ltd.
Lakeville, Connecticut

Relative value and market-neutral programs, also commonly known as *long-short programs,* are among the most intellectually appealing and widely misunderstood investment strategies. They seek to attain low-volatility profits in rising or declining markets. Essentially, the strategy entails the construction of a portfolio of long and short positions. The portfolio profits if the manager's relative valuation leads to a rise in the value of the long position(s) and/or a decline in the value of the short position(s). Relative value strategies differ from "directional" investment, in which the gain or loss comes from the rise or fall in price of a single asset rather than the relative movement of two or more assets.

Closely related to relative value programs are market-neutral programs. Market-neutral portfolios are constructed so that the portfolio's assets are relatively insensitive to the up-and-down movements of major markets, whether stocks, bonds, currencies, or commodities. In contrast to relative value, where two or more offsetting assets are meant to neutralize or reduce risk, market-neutral strategies reduce risk to a wider market movement.

In theory, market-neutral investments should be less risky than relative value investments, since they afford protection against large-scale market movements. In practice, however, market-neutral strategies tend to be more highly leveraged, reducing the difference between the strategies.

Given the recent upheaval at Long Term Capital Management, it might appear inappropriate to place relative value and market-neutral strategies in a section on risk management methods. In their genesis and in practice, however, these strategies are meant to reduce the risk of investments. Relative value models are used to statistically measure the historical correlation between the prices of related assets, be they bonds, stocks, or currencies. Often, the analysis shows a divergence from historical price patterns, presenting an opportunity to profit from the reversion of prices to historical norms. At other times, the calculation is based on the assumption that prices and relationships will remain stable, allowing a profit from the differential in yield between assets. In recent years, examples of the former include buying Italian government bonds and selling German government bonds, looking to profit from the convergence of interest rates as the European markets converged (Figure 13–1). An example of the latter would include the purchase of mortgage securities hedged by U.S. government bonds, the goal being to lock in the interest rate differential.

The attractiveness of market-neutral and relative value strategies is their "built-in" hedge. If properly structured under the right market conditions, these spreads are able to produce relatively low-volatility returns in a wide range of market conditions. There are many types of market-neutral and relative value strategies, as shown in Table 13–1.

PROBLEMS WITH MARKET-NEUTRAL STRATEGIES

It is obvious that market-neutral and relative value strategies also have some severe problems, both in theory and in practice. Many of these problems have to do with the trading and execution of relative value positions, especially during times of market distress.

F I G U R E 13–1

Italian-German 10-Year Bond Yields

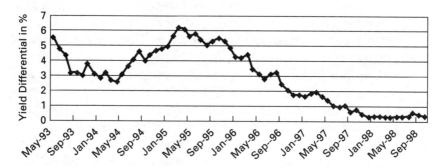

T A B L E 13–1

Examples of Market-Neutral and Relative-Value Strategies

Markets	Market-Neutral/Relative-Value Strategy
Equity	Long one group of stocks; short one group of stocks
	Long-short stock index and/or futures
	Long stock of company being acquired; short stock of acquiring company
	Long stock market index of one country; short index of another country
Fixed-income	Long mortgage-backed securities;short U.S. Treasuries
	Long one country's bonds; short another country's bonds
	Long short-duration bond; short long-duration bond
	Long convertible bond; short underlying stock
Currencies	Long one currency against another
	Long portfolio of high-yield securities; short low-yield currencies
	Long one block of currencies against another

Pricing and Mispricing of Risks

One of the most baffling aspects of the Asian crisis of 1997–1998 was the speedy turnaround in the investors' perception of risk and, consequently, of risk premium. This change led to a dramatic increase in the spread between higher- and lower-risk assets and to divergences between assets that had previously moved in the same direction. Many of the losses suffered by investors during this time period came from this increase in risk premium. For example, emerging market spreads over U.S. Treasury bonds in 1998 exceeded those of the third-world debt crisis of the early 1980s. Spreads on U.S. high-yield corporate debt (junk bonds) rose to 600 basis points over U.S. Treasuries. The same was true of a wide range of bond and equity investments.

The proper specification of risk and risk premium is a key element of relative value programs. The rapid fluctuations in risk premium can disrupt the most carefully planned program. One of the problems here is differentiating between the psychological aspects of risk perception (often referred to as "financial panic attack") and the fundamental factors that lead to actual changes in risk. Often, the changes in risk premium come down to the question of whether the world has really become riskier or are there changes only in the perception of risk. However, the financial world has only begun to deal with this important issue. Most treatments are journalistic or anecdotal and not very useful for investment risk management. Complicating the answer is the fact that a panic attack could well bring on additional risk, as described below.

Liquidity Problems

The behavior of market participants during a crisis has been compared to a herd of elephants trying to rush out a small door at the same time. Risk management systems take as their starting point an often unspoken assumption that there are markets. Moreover, the assumption is that these markets are orderly, nearly infinite in size, and able to buy and sell securities in relatively tight spreads. Most models, whether relative value, market-neutral, or value-at-risk, implicitly assume that investors can always get out of their positions. This is the basis on which positions can be priced and hedges calculated. Once liquidity, and therefore pricing, becomes a problem, relative value and market-neutral positions fall apart.

In a financial crisis, there is little liquidity and disappearing markets, and that turns market risk into event risk and credit risk. There are common features during market declines, as bubbles burst and cycles reverse. Once investors reevaluate their perceptions of the risks and rewards of investing in high-flying markets, a chain of events occurs whose impact is largely felt in the trading environment and whose eventual outcome is a sharp decline in asset prices. Along the way, investors are treated to high volatility, debt rescheduling and defaults, liquidity and credit pressures, and overshooting markets.

With the onset of a crisis, banks become less willing to buy assets, especially if they already have similar assets in their portfolios. At the same time, they are likely to increase margin requirements, forcing investors to sell positions at reduced market prices. Volatility tends to increase as prices collapse, setting off another cycle of margin calls, volatility, forced liquidation, and price declines.

With high levels of leverage on the part of investors, the snowballing effect can happen quickly. When Russia declared a moratorium on its debt in 1998, the immediate effect was a lack of liquidity in the Russian bond market. Investors were forced to liquidate other assets—Latin American, U.S. high-yield, mortgage bonds—to raise needed capital. Obviously, this forced up the yields in these markets in a process that has now been dubbed "contagion."

It is interesting to note the similarity between the effects that a lack of liquidity had on the quantitative models of the 1990s and portfolio insurance hedge strategies in 1987. Portfolio insurance could only work properly with a liquid market. However, the stock market's collapse in 1987 happened too quickly to allow the rehedging needed for portfolio insurance, leading to large losses.

In 1998, the markets also came face-to-face with the ultimate lack of liquidity: default. After Russia's default, prices became impossible to find, and hedges were impossible to execute. The Russian default also throws into doubt the implicit assumption behind much of the growth in international investment in the past decade: that no country will default on its debt.

Correlation Breakdowns and Market Contagion

Like a collapsing chain of dominoes, once started, the crisis spread with seeming inevitability from one market to another.

However, most market-neutral and relative value strategies have stable correlation as their core assumption. In fact, the reduced risk of these strategies comes specifically from the assumption that historical correlation between markets and assets will hold into the future.

The breakdown in correlation has a number of adverse effects on these strategies. First, the notion of diversification as a risk management strategy disappears as all assets and markets move in the same direction. Second, risks that are supposed to cancel each other out instead reinforce each other. In addition, the order of magnitude of these movements tends to exceed historical levels.

Political Risk

At its core, the Asian crisis was a political problem. In any exercise of market forecasting and relative value strategies, predicting political outcomes remains the most complicated task. It is possible to measure the ability of governments to act in certain ways given their economic positions. It is extremely difficult to measure their willingness to act in certain ways. This is best exemplified in the assumption that the Russian government would not default on its debt. Banks and hedge funds made billions of dollars of market-neutral and relative value spreads based on this assumption. That these investments were made after the Asian crisis was well along its destructive path is even more indicative of the difficulty of integrating political risk with market-neutral investing.

THE GAMBLER'S DILEMMA RISK

Leverage combined with high volatility and correlated market movements brings some investors to the edge of the gambler's dilemma and beyond. Actors in the financial market calculate their capital or cash positions based on historical levels of risk and volatility. This calculation is also used to determine the size of investment positions that will allow an entity to carry on under all market movements. However, the combination of leverage and large-scale market movements forces many investors beyond the pain threshold or, equally significant, drives their creditor banks beyond their lending tolerance. As a result, hedge funds and banks are forced to liquidate assets at fire sale prices in order to meet margin or capital requirements or prevent ruin. This gambler's dilemma flows directly from the dramatic difference in pricing of assets during normal times versus during times of crisis.

VaR and Model Risk

Value-at-risk models have become the accepted norm for risk measurement and risk management in the banking and investment community. However, VaR models also have well-known limitations. For example, prior to the Asian crisis, Lehman reported that it was 95 percent certain that it would not lose more than $14.8 million in a day's trading. Credit Suisse Group asserted that it was 99 percent certain that it would lose no more than Sf257.7 million over the course of one day's trading. And Bankers Trust reported a maximum $156.8 million 10-day VaR to a 99 percent confidence level. These figures were derived using accepted assumptions, including a normal distribution of market movements and extreme movements rarely occurring. Obviously, the Asian crisis created losses that vastly exceeded those predicted by the banks.

One method for compensating for the normal distribution assumptions is stress testing and scenario analysis, which assumes extreme market movements. However, there is no consensus on how these analyses are to be conducted. By assuming extreme market movements, it is possible to conclude that no investment should be made. On the other hand, assuming smaller movements may allow investments that prove to be highly volatile.

The potential problem with the simple application of value at risk is illustrated by an analysis of emerging market Brady bonds performed just before the collapse of that market in 1997. A VaR analysis of Brady bonds from Algeria, Argentina, Colombia, Bolivia, Bulgaria, Mexico, Peru, Russia, Turkey, Ukraine, and Venezuela showed a 95 percent probability that losses would be less than 3 percent of the portfolio over a month. The low volatility and low correlation that preceded the Asian crisis gave a misleading measure of risk and was a far cry from the 30 to 50 percent collapse in the price of many of these instruments (see Figure 13–2).

F I G U R E 13–2

Brady Bond Spread Over U.S. Treasuries

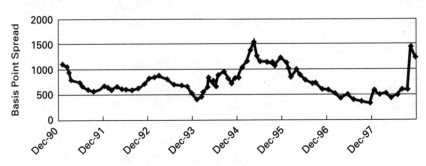

Trading Savvy Risk

This leads logically to the final risk that belongs in this list: the risk of missing trading experience. Many of the risks discussed in this article cannot be precisely quantified, yet they cannot be ignored. The missing ingredient is often the trading experience necessary to gauge the appropriate scenario analysis or the effects of market illiquidity on a portfolio. Trading experience is especially important in predicting correlation, political risk, the effects of a crisis on market movements, and the likes. None of these can be captured by a purely statistical approach to portfolio management.

CONCLUSION

Market-neutral and relative value strategies will continue to be used in the future. The self-hedging nature of these spreads, when applied to the right markets and with the proper risk management guidelines, gives them an important place in global investment risk management. In addition, the experiences of the past several years should highlight the importance of trading capabilities and crisis and risk management as well as sophisticated statistical models.

CHAPTER 14

Managing Global Emerging Markets Risk

Richard Johnston
Managing Director
OFFITBANK
New York, New York

Jason Cook
Senior Research Analyst
Emerging Markets Investment Group
OFFITBANK
New York, New York

The topic of managing the risks of emerging markets investments is especially poignant as of this writing. Events in recent years have demonstrated the new realities of global investing and are forcing us to construct a new framework for defining and addressing the risks of investing in emerging markets.

A global financial crisis was touched off by the devaluation of the Thai baht and spread to southeast Asian countries once held to be models for development, such as Indonesia and Malaysia. The crisis then consumed a global economic powerhouse, Korea, whose economic importance dwarfed that of its southerly neighbors. Russia was next to fall, forced into devaluation and domestic default. Then it was Brazil and the rest of Latin America, who remain under assault from what became a global crisis of investor confidence.

This chain of events connecteds countries and regions with vastly different economic characteristics, political institutions, and cultures. The importance of each of these countries to the global economy varies in terms of GDP and share of trade. Their interconnection ranges from meaningful levels of trade and financial flows to the insignificant. Russia's significance stems more from its geopolitical significance as a potential military power than its US$ 400 billion economy (on a par with Argentina and Mexico; half that of Brazil).

The global impact of events in these small and isolated (at least from each other) regions and countries, previously considered economically insignificant, introduced a new term to the financial lexicon: *contagion.*

DEFINING RISK–CONTAGION

Contagion has been cited both in the popular press and by investment professionals to explain how events a world away can afflict an economy with minimal trade or financial ties with the source, but the mechanisms which transmit these events are poorly defined. In order to address risk management for emerging markets investments in the new reality of integrated global financial markets, it is necessary to understand what contagion means, or more precisely, to give it meaning. To begin, a clear understanding of the different aspects of risk an investor faces in emerging markets is necessary.

WHAT ARE EMERGING MARKETS AND THEIR UNIQUE RISKS?

The most basic tenet of investing is that risk and return are balanced in a tradeoff of one for the other. You cannot have higher returns without taking on additional risk. This is as true for emerging markets investing as for any other asset class. In addressing the subject of managing emerging markets risk, we must first accept that in order to enjoy the higher returns promised by these investments, we must also embrace the higher level of risk.

The first order of business is to identify an investable emerging market and explain the nature of emerging markets risk and why it deserves special attention.

Defining an Investable Emerging Market

Defining an investable emerging market is the first step in making an allocation to that asset class. There is no consensus on this subject, though the predominant view is best illustrated in the International Finance Corporation's approach to its indexes of emerging markets equities. For their purposes, the IFC defines an emerging stock market as any stock market in a country classified as either low- or middle-income by the World Bank Group (GDP per capita below approximately US$ 10,000 per annum).

The IFC recognizes the limitations of such a definition and has refined its approach to present its Investable Indices, which screen for liquidity and ownership restrictions that could affect the ability of foreign investors to own the equity. There are 31 such country indices.

The most commonly quoted emerging markets index for fixed-income instruments is the J.P. Morgan Emerging Markets Bond Index, which tracks a portfolio of external currency denominated debt of emerging markets. This index contains 13 countries. J.P. Morgan also tracks local-market fixed-income investment opportunities through its Emerging Markets Local Markets Index, which contains nine countries. Both of these indices strive to take into account trading liquidity and any legal or tax barriers to foreign investing.

Citing indices to distinguish investable emerging markets is an unsatisfactory approach, of course, but these indices do illustrate that the investability of an emerging market is a function not only of the country's status as a "developing nation" but also of the liquidity and accessibility of the market.

To extend this analysis even further, when delineating the universe of investable emerging markets, the investor should also take into account regulatory oversight of the market, taxes, standard of disclosures, attitudes to foreign ownership, and legal recourse. A last consideration is how diverse a market is in terms of investing options. In some equity markets, there may be only a handful of stocks with significant trading liquidity, and they may or may not be representative of the overall economy of the country. Local debt markets, as mentioned before, often are limited to short maturities.

Barriers for the foreign investor include absolute bars on owning certain companies or participating in certain industries, onerous taxes on entering or exiting the market, or regulatory requirements for setting up special accounts for custody of cash or securities. In some cases, the investability of the market may be, as much as anything else, a function of the investor's willingness to hold investments for a certain time period (to avoid taxes) or to comply with complex documentation requirements.

Though touched on above, the importance of trading liquidity to this definition of investable emerging markets is worth underlining. For the institutional investor, liquidity means the ability to put millions of dollars to work in a market in a reasonably short time period, or sometimes more important, to sell millions of dollars in investments rather rapidly.

What Are Unique Emerging Markets Risks?

The surprising truth about emerging markets risk is that emerging markets investing does not confront the investor with any new or unique fundamental risks. The basic risks present in emerging markets are the same as those affecting any global investor: interest rate risk, currency risk, economic risk, default risk, and political risk, to name a few. The difference lies not in the nature but in the magnitude of these risks. The volatility and unpredictability of movements in these factors is simply much greater than in developed markets.

The investor cannot expect to hedge away or otherwise avoid all the risks associated with emerging markets and at the same time garner all the potential rewards. In fact, many of these risks cannot be hedged practicably due to high costs or the lack of available hedges. Therefore, the emphasis of the analysis will be on managing these risks through thorough analysis of the fundamentals and vigilance regarding technical market forces in order to make informed and appropriate asset allocations.

The Greater Importance of Political Risk

Political risk deserves special attention. The investor who has never ventured to invest outside the United States or Europe may not be accustomed to thinking about political risk, except perhaps in its more subtle forms: fiscal policy, monetary policy, and regulatory environment. Political risk in emerging markets is not a different species; it is just a larger, faster, and more powerful breed that assumes greater relative importance in the analysis of investment alternatives.

One reason for the greater importance of political risk analysis in emerging markets investing is simply the larger role governments play in these economies. Government ownership of assets and development initiatives has significant impact on these countries' economies. Furthermore, the relative fragility of emerging markets economies demands greater involvement from government through fiscal and monetary policy. The larger presence of the government in the economy often gives rise to "crony capitalism," or corruption, which raises the cost of doing business and can distort economic incentives. Such corruption may also make the direction of policy unclear to the outsider, as private motives may overwhelm more visible macroeconomic concerns.

Often, the political system itself is underdeveloped and government institutions lack strength, making continuity of policy uncertain. The lack of institutional integrity may also give rise to irresponsible policy, as vocal minorities may exert undue influence on policy decisions or make policy changes frequent and unpredictable. Judicial independence and integrity may also be compromised, making legal recourse for the investor difficult, lengthy, and costly at best.

This institutional weakness is also reflected in the lack of independent regulatory bodies. One result is inadequate regulatory oversight due either to the lack of well formulated regulations or simply to lax enforcement of existing regulations. Another effect of such institutional weakness is the lack of transparency in company reporting, since companies may not be required or accustomed to divulging essential financial and operating information to any authority, much less an outside investor.

Over the last decade, political risk in emerging markets has indeed been tamed to some degree. The threats of nationalization, confiscation, currency controls, and revocation of fundamental property rights have become remote considerations. While events in Russia, Malaysia, and Indonesia in 1998 raised the specter of these concerns again, they remain isolated cases. Once such concerns become real risks, however, most likely the best risk management strategy is to exit the country.

Liquidity, Sophistication, and Culture as Elements of Risk

Emerging markets are by definition markets that have yet to reach maturity. Therefore, one aspect of risk that is different from most developed markets is the relative illiquidity of the markets. Trading liquidity may be low, the diversity of investment opportunities may be limited, and the available maturities of investments may be limited to the short and medium term in the case of fixed-income investing. In fact, this phenomenon of well-developed short-term markets and essentially nonexistent long-term markets is a hallmark of emerging markets.

Governments, financial institutions, and companies may also lack financial sophistication. They therefore may not always take appropriate actions in response to events. This is not unique to emerging markets. It is simply more prevalent, requiring the investor to be more vigilant.

The immaturity of these financial markets is often reflected in a high concentration of market power among a few financial institutions in the country. In addition to impinging on liquidity, such concentration of financial markets access also creates essentially captive markets. Since they cannot choose freely among many institutions, nonfinancial companies and private investors (or depositors) are faced with inefficient pricing of financial services. Coupled with inadequate oversight, such concentration in financial markets can also lead to market manipulation.

The culture of each country is reflected in everything from manners, tastes, and customs to standards of disclosure, willingness to choose profitability over market share, and attitudes toward outside investors. While differing cultures are not in and of themselves a risk, they do require understanding from the investor. This doesn't mean that in order to invest in emerging markets one must learn a dozen new languages or adopt local dress when traveling. It does mean that ignorance of the culture and the resulting behavioral tendencies is an unacceptable and avoidable risk.

While emerging markets investing does not present the investor with a unique set of risks, the risks do vary in importance and degree from those present in other markets. However, in order to grapple with the consequences of globally integrated financial markets and the effects of contagion, it is necessary to take a step back and differentiate between even more fundamental concepts of risk: interim price volatility and default risk.

Default Risk

Default risk is the ultimate risk of losing all invested capital. For the fixed-income investor, it is easy to define as the failure of the borrower to repay principal and interest. For the equity investor, it is when a firm goes bankrupt and the franchise value of the firm essentially becomes zero, i.e., the business is no longer a going concern, and the liquidation of assets is impossible or results in minimal salvage value.[1]

Default risk is generally the domain of traditional fundamental analysis, which would take into account the factors of country risk analysis (monetary policy, balance of payments, fiscal deficits, and political risk, among others) as well as industry analysis and financial analysis at the company level. Default risk is best addressed through the rigorous application of these disciplines in a thorough analysis of improving long-term trends (an essential assumption to emerging markets investing) and of short-term vulnerabilities.

Default Risk and Global Liquidity

One fundamental risk factor not adequately acknowledged prior to the 1998 crisis was the importance of global liquidity conditions as measured by the direction of monetary policy globally. Emerging markets economies are generally net demanders of financing, either to fund long-term investments or current consumption. Past borrowings also place a demand on financing through debt-servicing and refinancing needs. These demands

---

1. In emerging markets, events of effective default or bankruptcy can be triggered by sovereign actions, such as confiscation, nationalization, or nullification of contractual rights. This level of risk is best addressed through fundamental sovereign risk analysis and asset allocation. However, in today's environment, these risks are generally low.

will be evidenced either in current account or fiscal deficits, which serve as the measurement for the size of this financing need.

While it is generally agreed that it is undesirable for emerging economies to borrow in order to fund current consumption (and this is a fundamental factor for analysis), productive investments in infrastructure or plant are necessary to fulfill the primary thesis of emerging markets investing: superior long-term rates of growth.

This financing need is the most important short-term vulnerability for emerging markets countries. Therefore the backdrop of global availability and pricing of financing is an essential starting point for analyzing risk. In an environment of global tightening, emerging markets are vulnerable, and the stage is set for contagion.

If one creditor fails, or was expected to fail, and the market's previously held perception of default probability was unrealistically low, the pricing of emerging markets risk is increased globally and all borrowers face higher financing costs. In such an instance, historical benchmarks for pricing risk can become obsolete, and totally new parameters come into effect. There is no regression to the established mean; the mean is itself unstable and apt to shift. This increase in financing costs triggered by one borrower's problems can create real problems for an otherwise sound borrower, who must now pay higher prices for scarcer resources (if they remain available at all).

Price Volatility Risk

Almost by definition, price volatility in emerging markets is high relative to other asset classes. The financial crisis of 1997–1998 has made it clear that this price volatility is itself subject to periods of higher and lower intensity. Prices of assets can be moved by either fundamental or technical factors. Fundamental price movements reflect the financial health of the asset; technical factors reflect the health of the market.

One caveat to this distinction is when expectations become self-fulfilling and technical market weakness creates fundamental vulnerabilities. Perception changes reality. An example of this reflexivity is the closing of capital markets' access to issuers as the result of high price volatility.[2] Investors demand higher premiums in order to absorb the volatility, and issuers are weakened by the higher rates they must pay.

Unforeseen increases in price volatility can have dramatic effects when markets have accepted a large amount of leveraged investing. *Leverage,* increasing invested exposure through borrowing, results in increased volatility of investment returns as the magnitude of profits or losses become a multiple of the actual price movement of the investable asset. When large amounts of leverage are put to work in a given asset class, that entire market becomes subject to exaggerated swings in prices that do not reflect fundamental reality.

When prices decline dramatically, it can trigger margin calls that force users of leverage to liquidate positions, creating a short-term surplus of assets for sale and subsequently driving down market clearing prices. More perversely, such an investor may often sell not the individual asset whose price has fallen but another investment which has not suffered a dramatic price decline. While the aggressive selling of one asset due to price declines in another unrelated investment seems rational when spread across a marketplace that is highly leveraged, it is one of the most powerful mechanisms contributing to contagion.

A similar phenomenon is the "portfolio effect," investors having to sell one class of assets (for example, industrial classification, nationality, or currency) in order to reduce an overweight in the portfolio that has arisen due to the dramatic underperformance of another class of assets. A similar effect arises when mutual investors aggressively exit an asset class, causing fund managers to sell the most liquid investments to fund redemptions, regardless of absolute or relative value considerations.

Likewise, hedging activities can create contagion when highly correlated assets are used in crosshedging strategies. One asset is sold in order to protect the position of another, potentially unrelated asset.

---

2. *Reflexivity* as a concept has been championed by global investor George Soros in numerous publications.

APPROACHES TO MANAGING PRICE VOLATILITY AND DEFAULT RISK

What we have set out above are the most powerful drivers of contagion. What we are charged with is to answer how the investor can manage this risk. There are two basic answers: hedging and asset allocation. Hedging is more appropriate for managing price volatility. Dynamic asset allocation based on well-done fundamental analysis presents the best method for managing default risk.

Managing Price Volatility—Hedging

Hedging emerging markets investments is a difficult and expensive prospect. The most problematic aspect of this approach is the lack of natural buyers for emerging markets risk.

Hedging by using options or other derivatives suffers from similar problems. Only a few counterparties make an over-the-counter (OTC) market (and few exchange-traded options) to cover these risks, and the high volatility of the assets creates high prices and wide bid-offer spreads for the hedge. In addition to the low liquidity of this OTC market, there is the inability to hedge beyond the very short term; market makers are mostly unwilling to extend beyond 12 months. Many market participants do take advantage of these short-term hedges with the intention of rolling them over at expiration, but the ability to roll over such positions is yet another risk to consider.

As witnessed in the Russian domestic debt default, hedges also present significant counterparty risk, in which hedges are invalidated by the default of many direct and indirect counterparties.

Hedging may also fail in the event sovereign policy actions are responsible for significant market moves. Most OTC hedging agreements contain *force-majeure* clauses that render the contract null and void in the event a sovereign government's policy change prevents the execution of the contract. Furthermore, many foreign exchange hedge contracts specify a particular reference rate that may or may not be allowed to reflect true market prices in a dual exchange system.

The uneven trading liquidity of emerging markets assets has led to the widespread use of cross-hedging techniques to take advantage of historical price movement relationships between more-liquid assets (and therefore less expensive to hedge) and less-liquid assets. Such strategies introduce basis risk, since the hedge and long asset do not move in tandem, one-for-one.

This basis risk, in turn, requires the investor to practice dynamic hedging, that is, adjusting the hedge or long position constantly in order to maintain the hedge, a process that is itself costly. If historic correlation relationships break down, the cross-hedge fails and the unintended consequences for the overall portfolio can be quite damaging. What has become apparent in this period of heightened volatility is the instability of such relationships, with the end effect that positions thought to be hedged weren't.

Low and uneven levels of emerging markets trading liquidity also hinders the use of short positions as hedges, though it does not eliminate it for the most-liquid instruments. Covering a short position can be problematic when prices move against you swiftly and by a large amount. The asset the investor is short may prove hard to find at fair prices.

Managing Default Risk—Asset Allocation

While there are facilities for exporters and direct investors to purchase sovereign risk insurance, no such cost-effective insurance exists for portfolio investors. A nascent market for emerging market default swaps is evolving, but it is yet to represent a viable option. Therefore, asset allocation remains the most important tool for managing default risk in emerging markets.

Asset allocation begins with an assessment of the risk tolerance and time horizon of the investor. In turn, these two factors determine the appropriate asset mix for the investor (cash, equity, fixed-income, and real estate weights; currency allocations; developed versus emerging markets; etc.). The final step entails regional, industry, and issuer allocations.

Once the decision to invest in emerging markets is made, allocating within the asset class requires a deep understanding of the fundamental differences between individual issuers and the operating environments they face. It also requires an understanding that emerging markets is not a region, but an asset class, with a diversity of issuers and countries who demonstrate a vast range of credit quality, earnings prospects, trading liquidity, and risk dimensions. It must also be emphasized that this is a dynamic process requiring constant vigilance and testing of assumptions.

Asset Allocation—the Top-Down Bottom-Up Approach

Given the limitations of hedging strategies, asset allocation is the primary option the investor has to manage risk in emerging markets. Asset allocation is often not thought of as a risk management approach, but it is through the rigorous application of all the tools of asset allocation—sovereign risk analysis, industry analysis, and issuer analysis—that the investor can address the multitude of risks present in emerging markets.

Among institutional investors, the dominant approach to investing in emerging markets is best described as *top-down bottom-up*. *Top-down bottom-up* investing begins with sovereign analysis to determine the overarching political and macroeconomic risks and opportunities, then moves on to industry analysis to select those industries best positioned to prosper in the current environment. It concludes with detailed financial analysis of individual issuers to determine company-specific strengths and vulnerabilities.

This approach assumes that country allocation is the primary determinant of investment performance and therefore is the first area to be analyzed. In any economy, there is no shelter from macroeconomic meltdowns, the likes of which were experienced in Russia in 1998 and Mexico in 1994. The list of factors to consider is extensive and includes political risk analysis, macroeconomic trends, balance of payments analysis, investment (foreign and domestic), the health of the banking system, and monetary and fiscal policy.

A careful country analysis begins by differentiating long-term trends from short-term vulnerabilities. Current account concerns, financing needs, and transitory fiscal deficits are examples of short-term weaknesses that may introduce volatility and uncertainty into a near-term outlook. However, it is the longer-term trends that must be most fully understood. In most emerging markets, the commitment to long-term economic and governmental reform is perhaps the most important long-term factor to gauge. In order for emerging markets to deliver on their potential for sustained high levels of economic growth, long-term reform prospects hold the key.

Industry analysis in emerging markets poses challenges distinct from those in the developed world. Regulatory regimes may be nonexistent or in a state of rapid transformation, foreign competition may be increasing, or consolidation may be occurring. Development initiatives may favor one industry over another. In addition, heavy industries in emerging markets tend to be highly concentrated, with a few large players having substantial pricing power.

Issuer analysis in emerging markets has the added challenges of different accounting systems, lower levels of disclosure, and often, complex corporate structures. Valuation exercises also require a thorough understanding of the oftentimes unique situations of companies in order to avoid overlooking potential value or poorly disclosed liabilities. Ownership and management take on a heightened level of importance in emerging markets, since weak regulatory oversight and economic volatility place the competence and character of ownership and management at a premium.

CONTAGION AND THE NEED FOR A NEW APPROACH

As long as investors fail to recognize the fundamental differences in the quality of emerging markets investments, the threat of contagion remains significant. However, the default risk triggered by the effects of contagion can be mitigated by recognizing those investments most vulnerable to financing availability or to their operating business franchise.

Price volatility in emerging markets can be effectively managed only through the selection of the appropriate time horizon for investment. Emerging markets investment requires a horizon sufficiently long to endure interim pricing volatility as well as rigorous fundamental research to substantiate the intrinsic worth of the investment.

CHAPTER 15

Financial Meltdowns and Exchange Rate Regimes

Steve H. Hanke
Professor of Applied Economics
The Johns Hopkins University
Baltimore, Maryland

Recent dramatic economic events in Asia and Russia have generated a torrent of commentary about exchange rates, hot money, and exchange controls. As someone whose views about exchange rates in Asia have been vindicated[1] and who predicted that the ruble would collapse by midyear 1998,[2] I offer my thoughts as to why most of the commentary has been either half-baked or dead wrong. Indeed, the international chattering classes have misdiagnosed the patient, and in consequence, have prescribed the wrong medicine.

EXCHANGE RATE REGIMES

There are three types of exchange-rate regimes: floating, fixed, and pegged rates. Each type has different characteristics and generates different results. Although floating and fixed rates appear to be dissimilar, they are members of the same family. Both are free-market mechanisms for international payments. With a floating rate, a monetary authority sets a monetary policy but has no exchange rate policy. The exchange rate is on autopilot. In

---

1. "Monetary Mischief," *Far Eastern Economic Review,* July 2, 1998.
2. S.H. Hanke, "Is the Ruble Next?" *Forbes,* March 9, 1998.

consequence, the monetary base is determined domestically by a monetary authority. With a fixed rate, a monetary authority sets the exchange rate but has no monetary policy. Monetary policy is on autopilot. In consequence, under a fixed-rate regime, the monetary base is determined by the balance of payments. In other words, when a country's official net foreign reserves increase, its monetary base increases and vice versa. With both of these free-market exchange rate mechanisms, there cannot be conflicts between exchange rate and monetary policies, and consequently, balance of payment crises cannot occur. Indeed, under floating and fixed-rate regimes, market forces act to automatically rebalance financial flows and avert balance of payments crises.

While both floating and fixed-rate regimes are equally desirable in principle, it must be stressed that floating rates, unlike fixed rates, do not perform well in developing countries because these countries usually have weak monetary authorities and histories of monetary instability. For recent dramatic examples, we need look no further than Thailand, Korea, Indonesia, and Russia.

Fixed and pegged rates appear to be the same. However, they are fundamentally different. Pegged rates are not free-market mechanisms for international payments. Pegged rates, such as those that were employed throughout most of Asia and in Russia before the recent currency crises, require a monetary authority to manage both the exchange rate and monetary policy. With a pegged rate, the monetary base contains both domestic and foreign components. Unlike floating and fixed rates, pegged rates invariably result in conflicts between exchange rate and monetary policies. For example, when capital inflows become "excessive" under a pegged system, a monetary authority often attempts to sterilize the ensuing increase in the foreign component of the monetary base by reducing the domestic component of the monetary base. And when outflows become "excessive," an authority attempts to offset the decrease in the foreign component of the base with an increase in the domestic component of the monetary base. Balance of payments crises erupt as a monetary authority begins to offset more and more of the reduction in the foreign component of the monetary base with domestically created base money. When this occurs, it's only a matter of time before currency speculators spot the contradictions between exchange rate and monetary policies and force a devaluation. This is what happened in Europe's Exchange Rate Mechanism in 1992 and 1993 and in Mexico and Turkey in 1994. The same story repeated itself in the summer of 1997 in Thailand and in the other Asian countries with pegged exchange rates and in Russia in the fall of 1998. See Table 15–1 for a summary of the main characteristics and results anticipated with floating, fixed, and pegged exchange rates.

HOT MONEY AND EXCHANGE CONTROLS

Hot money flows are principally associated with pegged exchange rates. Most analysts have misdiagnosed the hot money problem because they have failed to appreciate this all-important linkage. Consequently, they have prescribed exchange controls as a cure-all to cool off the hot money. That prescription treats the symptoms. It fails to treat the disease, which is pegged exchange rates. Until pegged rates are abandoned, there will be volatile hot

T A B L E 15–1

Exchange Rate Regimes

Type of Regime	Exchange Rate Policy	Monetary Policy	Source of Monetary Base	Conflicts Between Exchange Rate and Monetary Policy	Balance of Payments Crisis
Floating Rate[1]	No	Yes	Domestic	No	No
Fixed Rate[2]	Yes	No	Foreign	No	No
Pegged Rate[3]	Yes	Yes	Domestic and foreign	Yes	Yes

1 Floating rates are employed in most developed countries.
2 Fixed rates are employed in several developing countries or regions: Hong Kong (1983), Argentina (1991), Estonia (1992), Lithuania (1994), Bulgaria (1997), and Bosnia (1998).
3 Pegged rates are employed in most developing countries and also among the countries that are members of Europe's Exchange Rate Mechanism.

Source: Steve H. Hanke, "How to Establish Monetary Stability in Asia," *The Cato Journal,* vol. 17, no. 3, Winter 1998.

money flows and calls to cool the hot money with exchange controls.

Professor Paul Krugman of MIT is the most notable promoter of exchange controls.[3] Malaysia's mercurial prime minister, Dr. Mahathir Mohamad, has taken Krugman's bait and imposed the following draconian controls:

- The Malaysian ringgit was pegged to the U.S. dollar at RM3.8 to US $1.
- All export and import settlements must be done in foreign currencies.
- Malaysians will need approval to invest more than RM10,000 abroad.
- Malaysians and foreigners who have ringgit accounts in Singapore and elsewhere have one month to repatriate them to Malaysia. Incidentally, there is an estimated RM100 million cash held overseas and RM25 billion in off-shore accounts.
- From October 1, 1998 travelers into and out of Malaysia may not carry more than RM1000. Visitors will not be allowed to take out more foreign currency than they brought in.
- In an effort to reduce smuggling, RM500 and RM1000 notes will be taken out of circulation.

Like all pyromaniacs, Professor Krugman has now washed his hands of this dastardly deed. Perhaps this is the most devastating critique of controls. But there is more.

Currency convertibility is a simple concept. Essentially, it means residents and nonresidents are able to exchange domestic currency for foreign currency. However, there are many degrees of convertibility, with each denoting the extent to which governments impose controls on the exchange and use of currency.

The pedigree of exchange controls can be traced back to Plato, the father of statism. Inspired by Sparta of Lycurgus, Plato

---

3. "Saving Asia, It's Time To Get Radical," *Fortune*, September 7, 1998.

embraced the idea of an inconvertible currency as a means to preserve the autonomy of the state from outside interference. It's no wonder, therefore, that the so-called Red-Brown (communist-fascist) coalition in the Russian Duma has recently rallied around the idea of exchange controls and an inconvertible ruble. This also explains why the leadership in Beijing finds the idea so user-friendly.

The temptation to turn to exchange controls in the face of disruption caused by "hot money" flows is hardly new. Tsar Nicholas II first pioneered limitations on convertibility in modern times, ordering the State Bank of Russia to introduce, in 1905–1906, a limited form of exchange control to discourage speculative purchases of foreign exchange. The bank did so by refusing to sell foreign exchange, except where it could be shown that it was required to buy imported goods; otherwise, foreign exchange was limited to 50,000 German marks per person. The Tsar's rationale for exchange controls was limiting hot money flows so that foreign reserves and the exchange rate could be maintained. The more things change, the more they remain the same.

But before more politicians come under the spell of exchange controls, they should ponder the following footnote in Nobelist Friederich von Hayek's 1944 classic, *The Road to Serfdom:*

> The extent of the control over all life that economic control confers is nowhere better illustrated that in the field of foreign exchanges. Nothing would at first seem to affect private life less than a state control of the dealings in foreign exchange, and most people will regard its introduction with complete indifference. Yet the experience of most continental countries has taught thoughtful people to regard this step as the decisive advance on the path to totalitarianism and the suppression of individual liberty. It is in fact the complete delivery of the individual to the tyranny of the state, the final suppression of all means of escape—not merely for the rich, but for everybody.

Hayek's message about convertibility has regrettably been overlooked by many contemporary economists. Exchange controls are nothing more than a ring fence within which governments can expropriate their subjects' property. Open exchange and capital markets in fact protect the individual from exactions because governments must reckon with the possibility of capital flight.

From this, it follows that the imposition of exchange controls leads to an instantaneous reduction in the wealth of the country, because all assets decline in value. To see why, let's review how assets are priced.

The value of any asset is the sum of the expected future installments of income it generates discounted to present value. For example, the price of a stock represents the value to the investor now of his share of the company's future profits, whether issued as dividends or reinvested. The present value of future income is calculated using an appropriate interest rate that is adjusted for the various risks that the income may not materialize.

When convertibility is restricted, risk increases, and so the risk-adjusted interest rate employed to value assets is higher than it would be with full convertibility. That's because property is held hostage and subject to a potential ransom through expropriation. As a result, investors are willing to pay less for each dollar of prospective income, and the value of property is less than it would be with full convertibility.

This, incidentally, is the case even when convertibility is allowed for profit remittances. With less than full convertibility, there is still a danger the government will confiscate property without compensation. This explains why foreign investors are less willing to invest new money in a country with such controls, even with guarantees on profit remittances.

So investors become justifiably nervous when it seems a government is considering imposition of exchange controls. At this point, settled money becomes "hot" and capital flight occurs. Asset owners liquidate their property and get out while the getting is good. Contrary to popular wisdom, restrictions on convertibility do not retard capital flight, they promote it.

This type of capital flight (and dollarization) has been occurring on a grand scale in capital-starved Russia. Indeed, Russians swapped $13 billion worth of rubles for greenbacks in 1997, a year in which the dollar-ruble rate was stable and inflation was falling rapidly. This dollarization amounted to a capital export that exceeded all capital imports to Russia that year. The actions of the Russian people in 1997 indicate that, among other things, they anticipated the possibility of the imposition of exchange controls.

Restrictions on convertibility also promote other noxious activities. For example, if capital account convertibility is restricted or limited and convertibility on the current account is allowed, a two-tier currency market will be either formally or informally established. In that case, the "investment currency" will trade at a premium over the price of the relevant foreign currency on the official market for current account transactions. With two prices for the same currency, there are profits to be derived from having capital account transactions "reclassified" as current account transactions. That ad hoc reclassification can usually be bought by crony capitalists, for a price.

Full convertibility is the only guarantee that protects people's right to what belongs to them. Even if governments are not compelled by arguments on the grounds of freedom, the prospect of seeing every asset in the country suddenly lose value as a result of exchange controls should give them pause.

EXCHANGE RATES FOR THE NEW MILLENNIUM

As we enter the 21st century, globalization (the liberalization of financial and trade flows) is threatened. Volatile hot money flows are identified as the problem and exchange controls the remedy. This prescription, which is based on a wrongheaded diagnosis, will lead to monetary nationalism and the type of chaos the world encountered during the interwar years. The only way to avoid such a disaster is for developing countries to unify their currencies with stronger ones via fixed exchange rates supported by currency board monetary constitutions.

This conclusion troubles some analysts, who fret about the inflexibility of fixed exchange rates and currency boards. *The Economist* summarized these sentiments in a piece, "The Great Escape," which appeared in the May 3, 1997 issue. That article asserted that currency board systems cannot cope with external shocks; that they are vulnerable to surges in inflation triggered by capital inflows; and that with limited lender of last resort capacities, they cannot deal effectively with financial emergencies.

The evidence does not support these oft-repeated assertions, however. Let's look at the data from 98 developing countries during the period from 1950 to 1993 and separate it into two categories: countries that have pegged exchange rates and those that have fixed rates. The latter category includes countries with currency boards, monetary institutes, and those that rely solely on foreign currency. On average, the growth rates, measured in terms of GDP per capita, in countries with fixed exchange rates were 54 percent greater than those with pegged exchange rates. Furthermore, the variability of those growth rates (as measured by their standard deviations) was virtually identical, indicating that the lack of discretionary monetary policy with fixed exchange rates did not result in any greater incidence or vulnerability to external economic shocks. As for inflation, fixed rates have proved far superior to pegged rates, with average inflation rates being 4.9 times higher in countries with pegged rates, and 4.2 times more variable. In terms of budget deficits as a percent of GDP, those countries utilizing pegged rates had deficits which on average were 65 percent larger and 1.4 times more variable. Finally, countries with fixed rates experienced fewer financial emergencies.

Until recently, most economists have refused to consider currency boards or to look at the facts. Many have just declared that fixed rates are "inappropriate" or claimed that the facts are "erroneous." There's nothing new here. Indeed, Michael Polanyi concluded in his 1958 book, *Personal Knowledge*, that it is "the normal practice of scientists to ignore evidence which appears incompatible with the accepted system of scientific knowledge." With the failure of pegged and floating rates in Asia and Russia, the tide has begun to shift.[4] This shift is welcome and has left me feeling a bit like Winston Churchill on his return from the Boer War, when he remarked: "Nothing in life is so exhilarating as to be shot at without success."

---

4. See, for example, Stanley Fischer, "Reforming World Finance: Lessons from a Crisis," *The Economist*, October 3, 1998.

CHAPTER 16

Asia Questions Risk?

Michael J. Howell
Managing Director
CrossBorder Capital
London, England

What is risk? According to the conventional definition, future risk can be measured from the standard deviation of past returns. Indeed, it has become a common practice among investment professionals to diversify away from this volatility risk. However, not only is volatility one of several possible risk measures, it is also a hopelessly inadequate gauge, in large part because the future rarely mirrors the past. The summer 1997 Asian crisis provides a clear recent example (see Figure 16–1). Volatility ahead of the crisis was low. But the resulting volatility jump will almost unquestionably force portfolio managers to reduce their future exposure to Asian markets. Perhaps wrongly.

In mature financial markets, it has been well-documented that investors are rewarded for taking extra systematic risk. Indeed, this is the basis for the CAPM (Capital Asset Pricing Model) which uses beta to measure systematic risk. However, Harvey (1994) has shown that there is no relationship between beta and expected returns in several emerging markets.

What's more, Baekaert and Harvey (1995) confirm that emerging market returns depart from statistical normality. The higher order moments of these return distributions show both greater positive skewness than developed stock markets and far greater kurtosis. Summarizing the empirical evidence, emerging markets have:

FIGURE 16-1

Ups and Downs—Emerging Stock Market Price Volatility,
1988–1997 (rolling 3-year standard deviation)

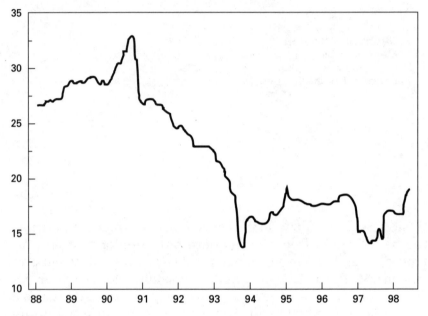

Source: CrossBorder Capital.

1. A high *average rate of return* relative to the mature stock
   markets.
2. A wide *variance* of returns.
3. A *fat-tailed (or leptokurtonic) return distribution,* indicating
   the higher frequency of "large" share price rises and
   "large" share price falls.
4. Low cross-correlations between emerging and developed
   stock markets, and increasingly low cross-correlations
   between emerging market regions, e.g., Europe, Asia, and
   Latin America.

Taken together, these four features suggest that emerging
financial market investment will be very different from the
process of investing in mature financial markets. High relative

volatility, low cross-correlations, and P/E multiples that range from single figures for Russia to high double-digits in China together highlight the lack of integration of emerging markets with world capital markets. Emerging markets are quite simply different.

We shall focus on two particular risk characteristics:

- Why emerging markets experience "large" share price movements.
- Why broad emerging market regions are becoming less well-correlated, but intraregional association is rising.

Both characteristics can be explained by liquidity factors. Large share price swings result from similar swings in the *absolute* volume of financial liquidity. And the falling interregional correlation of emerging markets arises from the appearance of three de facto currency zones, i.e., because of relative *liquidity* movements.

"LARGE" SHARE PRICE MOVEMENTS

Emerging market returns do not follow normal statistical distributions. They are subject to high event risk and have a tendency to "overshoot" both upwards and downwards. For this reason, the standard deviation is an inadequate measure of investment risk, and the traditional mean-variance approach to optimal asset allocation cannot be safely used. In *Euromoney* (1994) Howell also notes that despite their low cross-correlations with developed stock markets, the high relative volatility of emerging market returns severely limits their ability to reduce overall portfolio risk.[1]

Essentially, risk represents the unforeseen or absolute cost of holding an investment. It can be thought of as a measure of our ignorance of the future, but it does not necessarily equate to volatility. Ironically, handled correctly, volatile investments can often prove to be highly profitable.

---

1. Consequently, we believe that return enhancement rather than risk reduction is the major spur pushing funds internationally.

Like the 1987 global stock market crash before it, the 1997 Asian crisis highlights that the real risk faced by investment managers is transactions risk. Can they transact in the required size and at the desired time in order to realize the value of their investments? In short, can they emerge from an emerging market investment in an emergency? After all, for every seller, there must be a buyer. This is another way of asking whether sufficient liquidity exists in financial markets to complete the trade. Therefore, the essence of risk is financial liquidity and not price volatility. Price volatility is a consequence of risk, not a cause.

Strangely, liquidity factors are nearly always ignored by investment analysts. Yet they are implicit in the investment process. Changes in financial liquidity affect the P/E multiple rather the E. In other words, portfolio managers must ask who will be the marginal buyer. This approach is alien to traditional value analysis, which unrealistically and wrongly assumes that investors face a constant P/E multiple, or, in other words, a constant transactions environment inhabited by a fictitious "Mr. Market" who is guaranteed to bid you for stock in unlimited volumes at the current price.[2]

The crucial role of liquidity can be seen by looking inside the P/E multiple. Investment returns depend upon two factors:

- A stream of dividends or earnings (E)
- A valuation multiplier (P/E)

Investment analysts labor over the future path of earnings (E). For the most part, the future path of earnings should be broadly predictable from a knowledge of costs, revenues, and past business cycle savings. However, changes in the prospective multiplier (P/E) are rarely analyzed. These changes are largely

---

2. The constant P/E assumption applies between different markets at one time, and in the same market at different points in time. There may be a clear value arbitrage between two securities trading in two different markets at the same point in time. If liquidity conditions do not change and remain roughly equal between both markets, then the cheap security will always outperform the expensive one. But if relative liquidity conditions change, then the cheap security may underperform the expensive one.

determined by liquidity factors. At the market or economy level, we can write:

$$\frac{P}{E} = \frac{P}{M} \times \frac{M}{GDP} \times \frac{GDP}{E}$$

| Valuation | Relative Ownership | Financial Liquidity | Profit Margins (inverted) |

Or,

$$\frac{P}{E} = \frac{P/M \times M/GDP}{m}$$

where P = market capitalization
   E = aggregate earning
   M = some definition of money
  GDP = national income
   m = profit margins

The two ratios—P/M and M/GDP—are key, and both relate to financial markets rather than to the real economy. The P/M term represents the quotient between the value of equity holdings (P) and liquid assets (M). It measures portfolio structure because the greater the preference for equities over cash, the higher the ratio. Similarly, vice versa. The M/GDP measures the volume of financial or surplus liquidity. In other words, it denotes the overall level of cash (M) scaled by the amount required to finance transactions in the real economy. The greater the availability of cash and the less the needs of the real economy, the larger the volume of financial liquidity.

Assuming that changes in profit margins are a long-term or secular factor, then shifts in the P/E multiple arise because of changes in the volume of financial liquidity (M/GDP) and/or because of changes in portfolio preferences between cash (M) and stocks (P). So, what determines the levels of relative ownership (P/M) and financial liquidity (M/GDP)?

WHAT DRIVES EQUITY OWNERSHIP?

Relative equity ownership is a function of four factors:

- Inflation
- Investor sentiment
- Tax structure
- Demographics

Of these, the last two are typically long-term factors that tend to change over periods of 10–20 years. They may still be important. For example, aging populations and tax incentives are two powerful arguments currently favoring a higher equity exposure of investment portfolios. However, investor sentiment and inflation tend to be the main drivers of relative asset ownership over the short and medium terms, respectively.

Low inflation has been a major factor behind greater equity exposure. One reason may be the ease with which cross-border valuation comparisons can be made in a generally low-inflation environment. Another may simply be the low returns available from competing tangible assets, e.g., real estate and physical commodities. Figure 16–2 shows the strong statistical relationship that exists between low inflation and high equity exposure. Equity exposure is measured on the left-hand scale by the P/M ratio. World inflation of around 10 percent per annum has historically been associated with a P/M ratio of 0.6. In other words, global investors hold 60 cents in equities for every US$1 they hold in cash. However, when world inflation drops to around 2 percent per annum, the P/M ratio jumps to 1.6 times, i.e., global investors are now prepared to hold US$1.60 equity for every US$1 they own in cash, nearly a threefold leap.

The displacement of data around the fitted regression line in Figure 16–2 demonstrates the influence of sentiment. Sentiment factors tend to be important over a one-to-two year period. They often stretch markets to extremes, both upwards and downwards. Our sentiment indicators measure the deviation of the actual P/M ratio from a target P/M that is based on the prevailing inflation trend (see Figure 16–3). Periods when the sentiment indicator lies more than two standard deviations above this "norm" are risky periods for markets because they show extremely high equity

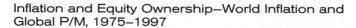

FIGURE 16–2

Inflation and Equity Ownership—World Inflation and
Global P/M, 1975–1997

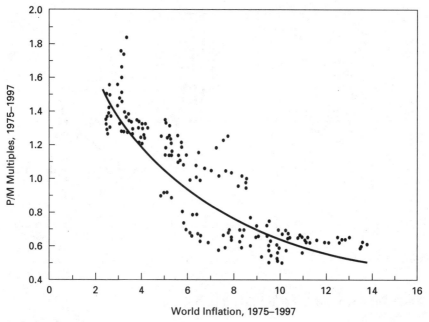

Source: CrossBorder Capital.

ownership relative to inflation, in other words, when the last
investor has bought who is left to buy. Equally, when the sentiment indicator lies more than two standard deviations below this
"norm," then equities are low risk because substantial cash lies on
the sidelines.

According to Figure 16–3, investor sentiment toward Asian
equity markets is (not surprisingly) at a low ebb. However,
despite the waves of bad news hitting us from the region,
investor sentiment is not at rock-bottom levels. In other words,
Asian stock markets are not yet "bargain basement." Any decision to invest must also depend upon our second factor, financial
liquidity. What's more, experience shows that sentiment often follows the same direction set by financial liquidity. In other words,
money talks. We tend to be more bullish with cash in our wallets
and more bearish without it.

FIGURE 16–3

Investor Sentiment Toward Asian Emerging Stock Markets, 1990–1998. (index range 0–100%; 50% = "normal").

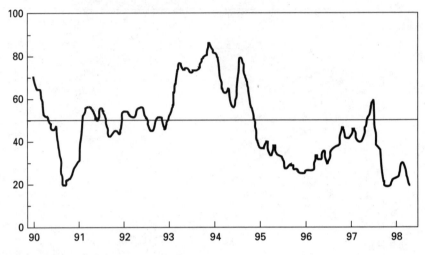

Source: CrossBorder Capital.

THE FINANCIAL LIQUIDITY CYCLE

The 1997 Asian crisis was caused by a regional loss of liquidity. Figures 16–4 shows the outflow of private capital from the region on a monthly basis through 1997. This loss of foreign liquidity led, in turn, to a leveraged collapse in overall Asian liquidity. This decline triggered a collapse in Asian asset prices and currencies, and is set to inflict recession across the region.

In fact, overall financial liquidity is determined by four factors:

- Central bank activity
- Net buying by foreign investors
- Real economy's appetite for credit
- Domestic savings behavior

Periods of weak economic growth, easy monetary policy, active foreign buyers, and strong domestic savings flows support rising financial liquidity and hence buoyant financial markets. Similarly, vice versa. Figure 16–5 shows our calculations of overall

F I G U R E 16–4

Monthly Private Capital Outflows from Asia, 1996–1998
(US $ millions)

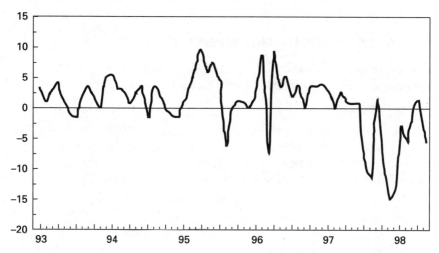

Source: CrossBorder Capital.

F I G U R E 16–5

The Asian Liquidity Cycle, 1990–1998 (index range 0–100%;
50% = "normal").

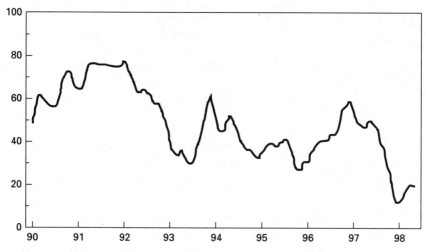

Source: CrossBorder Capital.

Asian financial liquidity. Financial liquidity clearly plummeted some months before the collapse in Asian financial markets. Moreover, it shows few signs of revival, yet.

FINANCIAL VERSUS ECONOMIC RISKS

Therefore, the "fat-tailed" return distribution for emerging markets results from the interaction of these two dominant factors:

- *Financial liquidity*   For example, the sudden large and lumpy outflows of Western capital, mainly associated with major shifts in monetary policy and the relaxation of controls on outward foreign investment, e.g., the ending of UK exchange controls in May 1979 by Mrs. Thatcher's incoming conservative government.
- *Investors' sentiment*   Such as sweeping local political change in the emerging countries themselves, e.g., the fall of the Berlin Wall in November 1989 or China's Tiananmen Square incident in June 1989.

Our preferred valuation measure for emerging markets in P/E-to-growth rather than simply the P/E (see Appendix: The "Big Bang" Growth Model). Therefore, rewriting the above expression:

$$\frac{P/E}{g} = \frac{P/M \times M/GDP}{g \times m}$$

Or,

$$\text{Valuation} = \frac{\text{sentiment} \times \text{liquidity}}{\text{growth} \times \text{margins}}$$

In other words, valuation measures consist of two elements: (1) a financially determined numerator, i.e., sentiment × liquidity, and (2) an economically determined denominator, i.e., growth × margins. Risk can then be gauged in terms of possible changes in these financial and economic risk components. Sentiment and liquidity tend to change over the short-to-medium term, e.g., one-to-five years. In contrast, economic growth and profit margins tend to record secular or long-term shifts, e.g., five to twenty years. Consequently, financial risks are likely to dominate over the typical investment horizon.

FINANCIAL STRUCTURE OF EMERGING ECONOMIES

Although these financial risks are common to all emerging markets, their timing and frequency are not. While Mexico suffered a steep financial correction in 1994–1995, Asian markets still managed to show contemporaneous gains. Similarly, the 1997 Asian crisis occurred against a background of rising Latin American share prices. In short, relative liquidity conditions often vary greatly across the emerging markets.

The key to relative liquidity is an understanding of cross-border capital flows and currency zones. The last 20 years have seen two major changes in the structure of the world economy:

1. *Direction of capital:* International capital now flows procyclicaly toward strong core economies, as opposed to anticyclically toward weak core economies. This is because the pool of global capital is dominated by institutional investors and multinationals rather than by banks. This capital, therefore, tends to seek out high returns, compared to previously, when banking capital was pulled in by high money market interest rates.

2. *Leverage of capital:* Emerging markets lack both capital and an efficient financial market structure. Consequently, emerging market banking systems tend to be significantly leveraged to foreign capital inflows. Thus, when capital is flowing into a core economic zone, some of this liquidity spills over into the neighboring emerging markets, thereby causing dramatic jumps in emerging markets' credit growth.

Figure 16–6 highlights this leverage. It shows the ratio between broad liquidity and the monetary base—i.e., the money multiplier—for a number of selected economies charted against the ratio between foreign exchange reserves and the monetary base. Thus, not only do emerging markets have large money

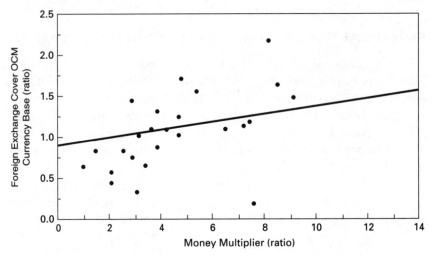

F I G U R E 16–6

The Vulnerability of Emerging Markets–Money Multipliers
Versus Forex Cover of Monetary Base, 1990–1997 Average

Source: CrossBorder Capital.

multipliers, but holdings of foreign exchange reserves largely
determine the size of their monetary bases. Thus, a capital outflow will cause both foreign exchange reserves and the monetary
base to drop virtually one-for-one, whereas a large money
multiplier will translate this into a large fall in domestic money
supply.

Figure 16–7 illustrates how these features explain the 1997
Asian crisis. Three de facto currency zones exist: euro, U.S. dollar,
and Japanese yen. At the center of each zone is a major economy:
core Europe, i.e., Germany, France, and Benelux; U.S., and Japan.
And surrounding each core economy is an emerging market
periphery: emerging Europe, Latin America, and the Pacific Rim.
Liquidity in each emerging market is highly leveraged to conditions in its respective core.

The 1997 Asian crisis started in the core of the Asian zones,
i.e., Japan, and not in the rim, e.g., Thailand or Korea. Japanese
economic weakness in the wake of the spring 1997 tax hikes and
the crippling rise in the yen caused global capital to flee toward
the safety of the sound U.S. economy. Consequently, liquidity

FIGURE 16-7

Core Currency Zones

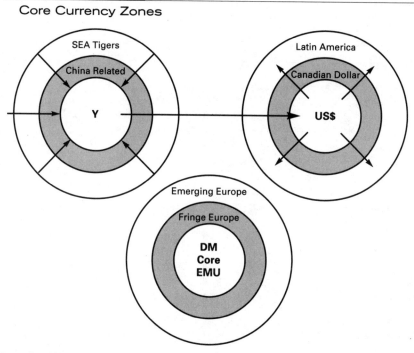

Source: CrossBorder Capital.

conditions in Japan tightened, which caused an even greater collapse of liquidity across the leveraged Asian emerging markets.

Figure 16–8 shows the scale of this private capital exodus. Total outflows in 1997 were roughly equal to the two previous years' net inflows. What's more, there appear to be few signs of stability. Annualized data for the first four months of 1998 show a continued hemorrhage of money. This is probably not surprising, because the cause of emerging Asia's plight was economic weakness in the core, and Japan's economic prospects around mid-1998 still looked bleak.

FUNDAMENTAL WARNING SIGNS

What are the warning signs that emerging market investors must look out for in order to avoid these negative liquidity shocks?

FIGURE 16-8

Private Sector Capital Flows to Asia, 1994-1997
(US $ billions)

	1994	1995	1996	1997	1998E	1997 as % GDP
China	-8.3	-13.5	-17.8	-25.3	-38.0	-3.4
Hong Kong	15.3	25.2	11.0	32.2	12.9	20.9
Taiwan	3.5	-6.5	-12.0	-9.5	-0.2	-13.3
Korea	11.6	17.5	27.2	-13.0	-28.5	-2.8
Singapore	-6.1	-8.5	-7.2	-15.5	-11.2	-16.4
Malaysia	-1.7	1.3	2,8	-14.0	-6.4	-14.2
Thailand	12.0	19.3	15.1	-10.8	-8.9	-5.9
Philippines	2.7	-0.1	7.8	0.3	1.0	0.4
Indonesia	2.1	4.8	4.9	-6.7	-8.7	-3.0
Japan			-10.9	-53.4	-57.0	-1.2
Asia ex. China	39.4	52.9	48.8	-36.9	-34.2	-2.7
ASEAN 5	9.0	16.8	22.6	-46.7	-34.2	-6.8
Asia Total*	31.2	39.4	31.0	-62.2	-87.9	-2.9
China Hong Kong	7.0	11.7	-6.8	6.9	-25.1	0.8

* Asia Total excludes Japan.
Source: CrossBorder Capital.

Two factors are important. In general terms, the rate of change
(not the level) of foreign exchange reserves is critical. Traditionally, economists have favored the level of foreign exchange
reserves as an indicator, expressed in terms of the number of
months of import cover they represent. This probably worked
well during an era when economies were linked more through
trade than capital flows, but it does not stand up today, when
capital dominates. In short, 21 months of import cover could
easily prove to be a mere 21 minutes of portfolio capital cover.
Therefore, falling foreign exchange reserves will give some
warning.

However, an earlier and more specific warning signal is the
fundamental balance. A deteriorating fundamental balance offered
investors several months warning of economic problems in both
Mexico and Asia ahead of their respective crises.

The fundamental balance is simply a measure of the current
account position of an economy, but adjusted for large-scale

imports of capital equipment by multinational corporations. It is important to exclude these imports because they tell us nothing about the imbalances in the domestic economy. For example, during the early 1990s, Malaysia suffered a current account deficit of over 5 percent of GDP. Most economists argued that this was a dangerous rate until it was pointed out that foreign multinationals were directly investing over 6 percent of GDP annually into Malaysia, much of which as imported. Consequently, adding back the 6 percent foreign direct investment (FDI) to the 5 percent current account deficit gives a fundamental surplus of 1 percent.

Thus, the fundamental balance is the best gauge of a domestic imbalance between aggregate economic demand and supply for an emerging economy attracting significant inflows of FDI. Figure 16–9 shows why a falling fundamental balance correctly spotted the Asian and Mexican crises.

Using the flow of funds identified for national income (aggregate sources = aggregate uses of funds), the fundamental balance equals the amount of "free savings" less domestic investment, where free savings are defined as total private sector savings less government borrowings.

The 1994–1995 Mexico crisis was caused by excess demand, which led to rapid import growth. A symptom of this excess demand was a rising rate of consumer spending and a falling savings ratio. Thus, according to Figure 16–9, Mexico's falling rate of

F I G U R E   16–9

The Asian and Mexican Crises—Different Causes, Same Result

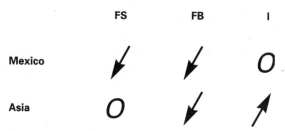

Free saving = fundamental balance + investment

	FS	FB	I
Mexico	↙	↙	O
Asia	O	↙	↗

Source: CrossBorder Capital.

F I G U R E 16–10

Warning Sign—Mexico's Fundamental Balance, 1990–1997
(US $ billions)

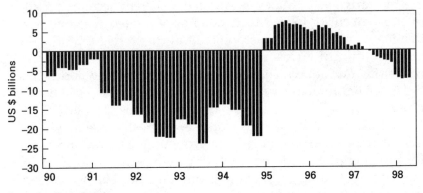

Source: CrossBorder Capital.

free savings (FS) matched its deteriorating fundamental balance
(FB). In contrast, the 1997 Asian crisis was an overproduction
problem, i.e., too much supply. This was reflected in rising
imports and skidding exports. Overproduction resulted from
overinvestment. The counterpart to sharply rising domestic
investment (I) was a falling fundamental balance (FB).

Figure 16–10 highlights the dramatic deterioration of
Mexico's fundamental balance in the early 1990s and its subsequent improvement back to health through 1995 and 1996. Similar
worsening trends were obvious across Asia during 1996 and 1997.
Both Thailand and Korea, for example, recorded whopping fundamental deficits in 1996 and 1997.

But the fundamental balance is especially important because
it leads the movements of international capital. These flows are
driven by rates of return in the business sector, and the fundamental balance summarizes the net competitive position of an
economy. For example, countries with a competitive advantage in
production will likely generate high returns on capital. Similarly,
vice versa. Therefore, fundamental surpluses tend to attract portfolio capital in search of these returns, and fundamental deficits
repel portfolio capital. What's more, there also tends to be a leveraged effect because small changes in the fundamental balance can
often trigger huge swings of portfolio capital, i.e.:

$$\Delta FX \quad = \quad FB \quad + \quad PF \quad + \quad B$$

| Change in foreign exchange reserves | Fundamental balance | Portfolio capital flows | Banking flows |

Or, since

$$PF \quad = \quad k\Delta FB$$

where k>0

$$\Delta FX \quad = \quad FB \quad + \quad k\Delta FB \quad + \quad B$$

Therefore, a falling fundamental balance is likely to result in falling foreign exchange reserves. And because of the leverage of emerging market financial systems, falling foreign exchange reserves likely mean a shrinking monetary base. This, in turn, will translate into a sizeable shrinkage in domestic credit because most emerging markets have high money multipliers between base money and overall money supply. For example, assuming a money multiplier of 20 times; a monetary base largely consisting of foreign exchange, and a k-factor linking portfolio flows to changes in the fundamental balance of two times, then each US$100 million fall in the fundamental balance will mean a US$4 billion drop in money supply, i.e., a forty-fold difference.

CONCLUSION: LIQUIDITY MATTERS MOST

Contrary to conventional wisdom, portfolio managers often ought to buy into volatility rather than diversify away from it. If markets have fallen sharply because of cyclically low levels of liquidity and investor sentiment, then they should rise when sentiment and, particularly, liquidity recover.

Emerging markets such as Asia are especially leveraged to foreign liquidity flows. These foreign inflows drive up rates of domestic credit growth and generate economic imbalances, such as overproduction and overconsumption. The 1997 Asian crisis resulted from regional overproduction, which was exacerbated by a demand slowdown in Japan and China. In contrast, the

F I G U R E 16–11

The Dance of the Rim—Flows to Emerging Markets and
Financial Crises

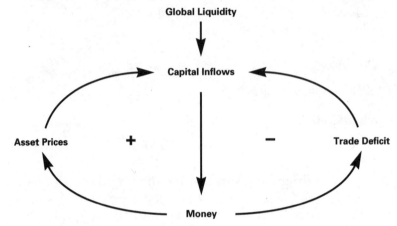

Source: CrossBorder Capital.

1994–1995 Mexico crisis was an excess demand problem. However, both led to financial market collapses, and both featured
falling fundamental balances and plunging real exchange rates
(see Figure 16–11).

According to Figure 16–11, there are two paths that the
money created by capital inflow can take: (1) it can positively
boost asset prices, which excites still greater capital inflows, ad
infinitem, or (2) it can negatively increase the trade deficit, which
ultimately will scare off both new and existing international capital. This exodus of foreign money will trigger the previous virtuous circle of asset price gains to run rapidly and violently in
reserve. The dislocation caused by slumping asset prices destroys
financial wealth, threatens the integrity of banks, and triggers economic recession.

Thus, Asia and Mexico's loss of financial liquidity reduced
investors' wealth and buying power and destroyed investors' sentiment. Financial market volatility jumped as a result. But market
volatility is simply a symptom of risk, not a cause. The true measure of risk is the ability to transact in size and at prevailing
prices. In short, liquidity is key.

REFERENCES

Bekaert, G., C.B. Erb, C.R. Harvey, and T.E. Viskanta, "The Behavior of Emerging Market Returns." Paper presented to The Future of Emerging Market Capital Flows Conference, May 23–24, 1996, New York University Leonard N. Stern School of Business.

Bekaert, G. and C.R. Harvey, "Time-Varying World Market Integration," *Journal of Finance,* vol. 1, no. 2, June 1995, pp. 403–444.

Euromoney/World Bank, *Investing In Emerging Markets,* M.J. Howell, (ed.), Euromoney Publications, 1994.

Harvey, C.R., "The Risk Exposure of Emerging Markets," in Euromoney/World Bank, *Investing In Emerging Markets,* Euromoney Publications, 1994.

Howell, M.J., "The Financial Silk Road," vols. 1 and 2, ING/Baring Securities, 1995.

Mobius, M., "The Investor's Guide to Emerging Markets," Pitman Publishing, 1994.

A P P E N D I X : 16–1

Evaluating Emerging Equity Markets—The "Big Bang" Growth Model

P/E multiples are probably still the most common tool used to analyze emerging equity markets. A low multiple is taken to be the key target of investors. However, a P/E multiple by itself says nothing about the further growth potential. Indeed, most investment errors in emerging markets come back to this simple point: A low P/E stock is not necessarily "cheap" if it is at the same time a low-growth stock. *Therefore, it is essential to adjust the P/E by an estimate of future growth. For many emerging markets, this adjustment is "large."*

Our preferred method is to divide the current year P/E multiple by the five-year compound rate of future real growth (i.e., inflation-adjusted). For example, if the current P/E is 20 times and five-year real growth is estimated to be 5 percent per annum, then the P/E growth ratio is four times (i.e., 20 ÷ 5 percent). We have found that P/E growth ratios below around 4.5 times offer excellent value.

The theoretical basis for this adjustment comes from the earnings (or dividend) discount model:

$$P = \frac{E}{r-g}$$

where P = share prices
       r = discount factor
       g = the growth rate in perpetuity
       E = earnings per share

Earnings per share can be calculated using U.S. Generally Accepted Accounting Practices (GAAP), which have become increasingly commonplace across the emerging world.[4] However, in the cases where these still do not apply, we suggest using cash flows rather than earnings. Experience shows that cash flows can eliminate up to 70 percent of the variations in national earnings definitions.

Rewriting this expression:

$$\frac{P}{E} = \frac{1}{r-g}$$

$$= \frac{1}{r} \times \frac{r}{r-g}$$

Adding one to both sides:

$$= \frac{1}{r} \times [\, 1 - \frac{r}{r-g} + \frac{r}{r-g} \,]$$

---

4. Mobius (1994) describes a case in which it took 11,000 man hours of expert time to restate one Chinese company's three-year accounts into U.S. GAAP.

$$= \frac{1}{r} \times [1 + \frac{g}{r-g}]$$

$$= \frac{1}{r} \times [1 + G]$$

where $G = \frac{g}{r-g}$

The G-factor represents the present value of all future growth opportunities. It can be thought of as "big bang" growth. The stream of future receipts has been reduced to an equivalent single lump sum in today's money. This, of course, is the essence of discounting, but what we have done is to separate out the growth elements, captured by G, from the known value, represented by the existing rate of earnings and capitalized at a rate, r.

Rearranging:

$$P/E = \frac{1}{r} + \frac{G}{r}$$

In words:

Price/earnings (P/E) = Base P/E + Growth P/E

Two important observations follow from this formula:

- $1/r$ represents the "base," or zero-growth P/E. Thus an investment with zero growth potential would not have a zero P/E. Rather, its P/E would equal its base P/E of $1/r$. Each unit of present value growth (G) raises the base P/E by $1/r$. The higher G, the larger the "fair-value" multiple investors should be prepared to pay. And because of the fixed contribution of each investment's base P/E ($1/r$), the relationship between growth and value is linear but not one-for-one.
- It is the size of G, not the time profile of the underlying stream of earnings or dividends, that matters. In other words, several different earnings streams are capable of generating the same G-factor. What's more, G-factors can

be calculated for earnings and dividends, as well as for sales, investment, or aggregate GDP.

The P/E multiple moves up and down according to the extent of growth. It can be "normalized" with respect to growth by forming the "P/E-growth" ratio:

$$\frac{P/E}{(1+G)} = \frac{1}{r} = \text{base, or zero-growth, } P/E$$

Alternatively, this can be written as:

$$\frac{P}{E.(1+G)} = \frac{P}{E^*} = \frac{P}{E + \Delta E}$$

E^* denotes the present value of all future earnings, and ΔE represents the present value increment in earnings, i.e., $E^* - E$ or G.E. And where $1/r$ (the reciprocal of bond yields, which is equivalent to bond prices), the base, or zero-growth, P/E can be thought of as being a constant over the long term.

This model is especially useful for analyzing emerging markets because it highlights the problem of "fast growth" economies. Consider the value of G, the present value of all future additions to earnings. If an economy is "ex growth," then the value of G will be close to zero, i.e., $\Delta E = 0$. Equally, if an economy enjoys rapid growth, then G will be "large." In this latter case, it is likely that the present value of all future growth opportunities will easily exceed current earnings, i.e., $\Delta E \gg E$.

This model allows us more insight into the equity valuation process. It follows that the P/E multiple, the favored tool used by investors in the developed stock markets, will work well if G is close to zero.

This would seem a reasonable assumption in the case of the developed economies, which, by definition, are already a long way up the S-shaped development curve.

For emerging markets, where G is plainly not close to zero, the simple P/E is an inappropriate tool. In fact, in those cases of especially fast growth, where $\Delta E \gg E$, then the $P/\Delta E$ ratio is a more useful valuation measure (see Figure 16–12).

FIGURE 16–12

The S-Curve and Valuation Regimes

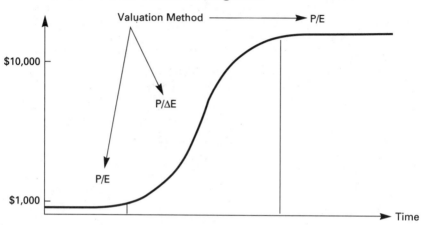

Source: CrossBorder Capital.

Figure 16–12 shows the typical S-shaped development path that is often experienced by products, industries, and national economies. Three broad development phases can be discerned: (1) take-off; (2) growth; and (3) maturity. During the "flat" period of the S-curve, when growth is low, i.e., take-off or maturity, the P/E multiple serves as a sound measure of value. However, during the middle phase of rapid growth, when the S-curve slopes steeply upwards, the P/E multiple should be replaced by the P/ΔE ratio.

Therefore, we have two extreme valuation cases:

- Ex-growth ⇒ P/E
- Fast growth ⇒ P/ΔE

Emerging market investors should use the second model (P/ΔE). However, estimating the present value of all future increments to growth is no easy task. Consequently, we suggest using a "rule of thumb," such as the ratio between the P/E multiple and the five-year compound real (i.e., inflation-adjusted) growth rate (g^*):

$$P/\Delta E \cong \frac{P/E}{g^*}$$

CHAPTER 17

Managing Latin American Investment Risk

Richard Johnston
Managing Director
OFFITBANK
New York, New York

Jason Cook
Senior Research Analyst
Emerging Markets Investment Group
OFFITBANK
New York, New York

Latin America does not necessarily present the investor with unique risk parameters that would be alien to an investor experienced in developed markets. Rather, like all emerging markets, Latin America has a heightened sensitivity to fundamental macroeconomic vulnerabilities and political risks and immature financial markets that are illiquid and volatile relative to the developed world.

The first illusion that must be dispelled is the perception of a monolithic Latin American marketplace, with homogenous culture, business practices, laws, and history. While the region's countries and people do share broad commonalities of heritage, existing differences are real and meaningful. An investor must understand the country-specific drivers of risk and evaluate the overall level of risk attached to each country separately.

We will proceed by discussing the general risk factors as well as risk mitigants that apply to the region as whole and then detail specific factors applicable to the largest and most important markets in the region. The general regional risks are largely structural macroeconomic risks that cannot be hedged in any meaningful way. They are the features of an economy that differentiate emerging economies from developed ones. We will not endeavor to explore every country in the region in detail, since that would entail a massive undertaking beyond the scope of this chapter.

We will then present a few tools for managing these risks, with a focus on various forms of scenario analysis to establish the limits of risk and return in making the allocation decision. Unfortunately, the use of derivatives to hedge risks in the region is limited. The local options and futures markets in Latin America are, with the notable exception of Brazil, underdeveloped. Likewise, listed instruments for hedging Latin American exposure in the U.S. have mixed liquidity, and the over-the-counter (OTC) market in options and futures for Latin America is the domain of a few brokerages whose willingness and ability to make a market for hedges is dependent on market conditions. Because hedging risks in Latin America is an expensive and potentially ineffective approach to portfolio risk management, the best approach is to fully understand and closely monitor fundamental risks and make appropriate asset allocation decisions based on such information.

GENERAL REGIONAL RISKS

Commodity Prices

Latin American economies, broadly speaking, remain largely dependent on commodity products and are therefore vulnerable to global commodity price cycles. This vulnerability is expressed primarily through the current account balance and secondarily in GDP growth. The magnitude of exposure must be viewed not only through the importance of each commodity in the export basket but also through the overall importance of exports to the economy.

It must be emphasized that not every economy is equally exposed to every commodity. Oil is very important to Venezuela and Mexico as a generator of foreign currency, but for Brazil it is an important import. Natural gas is a significant natural resource of Argentina. Copper, gold, and other minerals are significant to Peru and Chile, and Argentina is rapidly expanding its mining industry. Brazil and Argentina are significant producers and exporters of soy and wheat, whereas Mexico often is a net importer of food. This brief sampling is indicative of the complex nature of commodity sensitivity in the region and emphasizes the need for careful, thorough analysis of each country.

Not only are such natural resource commodities important to Latin America, but low value-added manufactured products, whose price behavior is equally commoditylike, are important components of many Latin American economies. Such products include steel coil and slab, pulp and paper, and petrochemicals.

While hedging such exposure via commodity futures and options may be intellectually appealing, the basis risk associated with such a strategy makes it cumbersome. Such a hedge is dynamic in nature and poses significant costs for constant monitoring and rebalancing.

Low Savings

Symptomatic of developing markets is the low savings rate of the region, estimated at 20 percent. Low domestic savings are insufficient to finance the aggressive investment (particularly infrastructure) necessary for these economies to generate high levels of sustainable growth. Therefore, low savings leave these economies in need of external financing, either in the form of direct investment or portfolio flows, including lending. This dependence on external funds makes the economies of Latin America vulnerable to global liquidity conditions and binds them to a global competition for investable funds.

Low savings rates have also led to the creation of large external debt burdens and, in turn indirectly heightened concern for current account deficits. Furthermore, the lack of a domestic pool of investable funds contributes to the underdevelopment of local capital markets as well as structurally weak banking systems.

The lack of a strong base of domestic financial actors can lead to markets dominated by foreign investors. This is best illustrated in contrasting Mexico to Brazil. The Mexican equity market has a high level of foreign participation, as high as 70 percent of capitalization at times, versus 20 percent participation for Brazil at its peak (approximately 13 percent as of this writing). The higher participation of foreign investors can be a positive from the standpoint of increasing price efficiency, but it can be a negative if market movements reflect exogenous factors rather than country fundamentals.

Income Distribution

Latin America's nations present income distributions among the worst in the world. Such disparities inevitably represent the potential for social unrest. Fiscal reform programs, privatizations, and falling trade barriers may face rising opposition if the mass populace perceives the benefits only accruing to the already prosperous elite.

Less acknowledged are the perverse effects of such inequality on economic activity. Extreme disparities in income distribution can lead to trade account pressures as economic growth translates into higher consumption of luxury consumer goods instead of stimulating demand for domestically produced goods. Credit growth may lead to an explosion in demand as low-income consumers access credit for the first time, but a swift contraction is likely, since lenders and borrowers unfamiliar to the use of consumer debt overextend themselves and rising nonperforming loans weaken the banking system.

Recent experience with the cessation of high inflation has left the low-income classes with a realization that economic stability is in their best interest. Dramatic declines in inflation have most positively impacted the living standards of the poor, since they lacked the ability to avoid the inflationary erosion of their incomes. As long as the memory of life under inflation persists and reforms continue to deliver rising employment and incomes, the lower classes will remain supportive of reform.

Education

In the long run, Latin America faces a high hurdle in overcoming low educational levels. In the integrated global marketplace, the ability of these countries to educate the populace with sufficient skills to compete will come increasingly into focus. The key issue will be Latin America's ability to attract investment in high-productivity, technologically advanced industries and avoid being relegated to producing low-value-added goods based on low-cost labor as its sole comparative advantage. Given government financing constraints, solutions to this problem may ultimately rest with the private sector.

Political Risk

Political risk in Latin America has diminished to the extent that nationalization, confiscation, or nullification of property rights is largely removed from normal risk analysis. Latin America emerged from the debt crisis of the 1980s with a commitment to modern norms of conducting policy and has largely rejected development models that call for extensive state intervention. Most important, democratic forms of government that recognize the rule of law now hold sway in the region.

Democratization ultimately reduces political risk. Democracy renders coups and other forced changes in governments illegitimate. Respect for property rights, reduced corruption, and predictable, consistent policy are the ultimate outcomes of this process. However, it can be a traumatic transition. Officials used to acting with independent power often chafe under new restrictions. Furthermore, these evolving democracies are learning the processes of governance and the stridency of debate can at times subject the investor to "headline risk." Finally, democratic governments in pursuit of deep structural reforms may be forced to move slowly in order to assure building the proper consensus for such measures. Such a gradualist approach can run into problems as external conditions change and threaten the entire reform program unless decisive leadership emerges.

Political risk can be hedged indirectly through hedging sovereign debt issues, either through the use of put options or futures or simply short-selling an issue. Such a hedge is somewhat imprecise and therefore introduces basis risk, but it presents the most effective hedge on political risk. The risk of this approach is that other fundamental or technical factors may overwhelm the impact of political risks. When political risk becomes heightened, a better approach is to manage exposure by reducing allocation to the sovereign in question.

Business Culture

Culture is important to the investor in that it influences behavioral tendencies. This is especially true in the specific case of business culture. Much as economic policy was transformed by the experiences of the debt crisis of the 1980s and subsequent difficulties in accessing capital markets, the same factors have led to a no less dramatic change in business practices in the region. Likewise, businesses forced to confront increased competition as their markets opened and foreign investment increased have come to terms with the realities of competition or have perished.

The result has been a reduction in investment risk in the region as companies have adapted to high standards of transparency and disclosure. More fundamentally, businesses recognize that they can no longer hide behind political favoritism and collusion to protect themselves from competition, but must embrace efficiency, productivity, and profitability.

REGIONAL STRENGTHS

Experience with Global Financial Markets

In comparison to the rest of the developing world, Latin America has a long track record of experience with foreign investors and global financial markets. While this experience has not always been positive, it does contribute a higher level of understanding and acknowledgment of economic reality. This greater familiarity with global investors fosters a level of transparency and disclosure that is generally among the best in emerging markets. This realization of the necessity of good market relations has increased the recognition of the rights of bondholders and minority shareholders

Strengthening Banking Systems

The banking systems of Latin America survived the debt crisis of the 1980s and the liquidity shortage associated with the Tequila Crisis of 1994 to emerge as stronger institutions with significant safeguards to protect themselves against similar problems in the future. Increased stringency and activism on the part of regulators has contributed to this evolution and is an evolving strength of these banking systems. Increased regulatory activity is also encouraging a consolidation of these banking systems, which should lead to the elimination of many weak, undercapitalized banks that cannot adapt to heightened competition.

In many markets, especially Brazil and Argentina, foreign banks have taken market leadership through the acquisition of existing banks. This process has led to both a transformation of many weak banks into reinvigorated entities with solid capitalization and consolidation of the system through acquisition. Foreign investors are also improving the technology and management practices of these banks.

Regional Conflicts

While there are small, isolated disputes in the region, such as Ecuador and Peru's recent border hostilities, Latin America is generally free of serious international political, religious, or ethnic conflicts.

The region is fairly homogenous in term of religious belief. Ethnic disputes are relatively limited to conflicts over historical rights of indigenous peoples. Such ethnic conflicts are generally limited to particular problems within a single nation and do not represent the potential to blossom into regional warfare as in sub-Saharan Africa.

Insurgent guerrilla activities currently represent a limited problem in Mexico and Colombia. This could not have been said a decade ago, when insurgents in Peru and Colombia and ongoing conflicts in Central America presented significant risks to the region as a whole.

We do not suggest that Latin America is an utopian world of egalitarianism or tolerance, but rather that ethnic, political, and religious difference are not on the verge of sparking large-scale conflicts.

Trade Agreements

Latin America is at the forefront of creating viable and vibrant trade agreements that are increasing trade and creating a rational framework for resolving economic disputes. The most notable of these arrangements is the Common Market of the Southern Cone (Mercosur), which represents Brazil, Argentina, Paraguay, Uruguay, and Chile. Mercosur is itself in negotiations with the Andean Pact to create a trade agreement. Mexico, in addition to

NAFTA, has embarked on an aggressive program of multilateral and bilateral trade agreements throughout the region.

While such arrangements promote trade and stimulate growth, they do increase intraregional economic dependencies, thereby reducing the benefits of diversification.

ARGENTINA

Argentina's specific risks are most closely associated with the currency board that is the cornerstone of its current economic regime. The plan guarantees that the peso and dollar are freely convertible on a one-to-one basis and requires the monetary base to be fully backed by U.S. dollar assets. As a result, Argentina no longer has the flexibility to institute monetary policy in order to adjust to external pressures; interest rates and money supply must be allowed to adjust freely. Furthermore, the success of the plan requires the continued solvency of banking system and fiscal discipline.

For the investor, convertibility reduces currency volatility as a meaningful risk, but it leaves Argentine economic risk more strongly influenced by U.S. economic factors as expressed through U.S. monetary policy.

Argentina's large and growing trade ties to Brazil represent a potential risk. Such an interrelationship reduces the independence of Argentine risk from Brazilian risk and therefore reduces the diversification benefits of investing in Argentina.

A disappointing feature of investing in Argentina is the lack of diversity in the investable universe and a failure of these investments to fully reflect the economy of the country. The local stock market is small and relatively illiquid overall. The most dynamic aspects of the Argentine economy, agriculture and mining, are all but uninvestable via publicly traded securities.

As mentioned earlier, Argentina has significant exposure to commodity prices, in particular soy, wheat, oil, natural gas, and minerals.

A long-run positive trend for investing in Argentina is the rapid growth of mutual and privatized pension funds. Currently growing at 30 percent per year, they have US$16 billion in assets under management as of this writing. Such funds are driving a rising demand for a longer domestic currency yield curve and new equity opportunities. The risk of such domestic fund growth is an ultimate decline in liquidity if funds buy up the majority of the float of existing companies and new investments are not introduced. Likewise, as experienced in Chile, if improperly incentivized and regulated, fund managers have a tendency to "herd," or to make similar investment decisions in order to avoid underperforming their peers.

Argentina's domestic forwards and options market is small, illiquid, and underdeveloped. Options and futures for the Argentine floating rate bond (FRB) and par bond are listed on the Chicago Mercantile Exchange (CME) but are thinly traded, with a combined average daily trading volume of six contracts in 1997 (each contract represents 100,000 face value of bonds). Currency hedging in Argentina can be accomplished most readily through the offshore over-the-counter nondeliverable forward (NDF) market. Hedging out the foreign exchange risk generally reduces the return to the extent that the investment is no longer appealing.

CHILE

Chile has long been viewed as a textbook example of development in Latin America. While Chile should be given credit for its tremendous accomplishments in creating economic stability and high growth, reform has stagnated in recent years. The economy remains largely indexed to inflation, labor market flexibilization remains undone, and large state-owned enterprises (most notably COLDECO, the state-owned copper company) are not slated for privatization.

The oft-cited privatized pension funds in Chile have done a remarkable job of mobilizing savings, but they face regulatory constraints that now limit further development of the capital markets. The incentives for the funds penalize underperformance of the peer group and encourage herding. Regulation also does not promote diversification of fund objectives: younger investors cannot choose funds that emphasize equities, and older investors cannot move into more conservative funds. Many funds are also pushing up against the limits placed on what percentage of a company's equity they can hold.

The pension funds have sufficient power to be a key determinant of local market movements. This power is largely the byproduct of currency controls in Chile, which have limited foreign participation in the local securities market. The majority of foreign investor participation in Chile, therefore, occurs with American depositary receipts (ADRs) which do not directly affect capital flows. These controls have been put in place to prevent economic disruption caused by unpredictable flows that may be attracted to the high real rates offered in the local Chilean fixed-income market. The persistence of high rates is itself a result of continuing inflation expectations and indexation.

The Chilean economy, despite its strengths of efficiency and a sound financial system, presents the risks of high commodity dependence. Copper, pulp, and agricultural products are large components of both Chile's GDP and its trade.

A strength of many Chilean companies is increasing investment within the region. Utilities in particular are major exporters of capital to the rest of Latin America, with significant investments in Argentina, Peru, Brazil, and Colombia. The higher growth and diversification benefits of these investments are obvious. However, the exposure to less-mature, more-volatile operating environments introduces a new element of risk into these companies and interdependency within the region.

Despite the perceived sophistication of the Chilean capital markets, the local futures and options market is virtually nonexistent. Regulatory views on the use of derivatives as "speculation" have retarded the growth of such instruments. Partial capital controls (in the form of minimum holding periods and reserve requirements) also render hedging the currency difficult, though an offshore, over-the-counter NDF market does exist.

MEXICO

Mexico is often the first stop for investors venturing into Latin American. It's physical nearness to the U.S. and large number of listed ADRs makes Mexico the most accessible market in the region.

Mexico offers the only freely floating currency in the region. The free float of the Mexican peso benefits investors by providing an accurate reflection of relative costs, but it also introduces currency volatility into the investor's risk set. The peso tends to move with high volatility that often is not related to Mexican fundamentals. As the most prominent and liquid floating currency in emerging markets, the Mexican peso attracts investors who may use it as a proxy for betting for or against all emerging markets. Investors may short peso investments in order to hedge all emerging markets exposure.

Mexico's banking system remains fragile as a result of the dramatic liquidity contraction that accompanied the peso devaluation of 1994. The banks have yet to fully recognize and address their undercapitalization. The process of consolidation and rising foreign participation is moving ahead slowly.

Political risk in Mexico is a critical variable. The longstanding power of the Institutional Revolutionary Party (PRI), which has held effective control of the federal government for six decades is eroding. While increased democratization is in the long-term interests of Mexico and the investor, the immediate future will continue to be punctuated by often-fierce debate unusual to Mexican politics. This debate rages not only between opposition parties and the PRI but also within the PRI. Politicians accustomed to the quietly negotiated arrangements that typified politics in Mexico in the past are resisting the increasing democratization of the party and resisting many reform initiatives.

The upcoming presidential election in 2000 will be a flashpoint for this risk, since President Ernesto Zedillo has announced that he will not follow the tradition of choosing his own successor. Initial indications are that the PRI will follow a primary system for choosing their candidate. This will set the stage for unprecedented open debate within the party.

Mexico's history of repeated currency maxidevaluations accompanying presidential elections deserves mention as well. While the economic fundamentals confronting Mexico today do not presage a maxidevaluation, the pressures that may come into play around the elections bear close monitoring.

In order to hedge Mexican risk, including currency, interest rates, and sovereign risk, the investor can take advantage of

CME-listed options and futures on the Mexican peso, 91-day Mexican Treasury bills (CETES), the Mexican par Brady bonds, the 28-day Mexican Interbank Rate (TIE), and the Mexican IPC Stock Index. CETES and Mexican peso CME-listed futures represent fairly liquid vehicles for hedging Mexican exposure. In 1997, futures for the peso traded an average of 6750 contracts per day (500,000 pesos per contract), and CETES futures traded an average of 34 contracts per day (2,000,000 pesos per contract). Peso futures require physical delivery of the currency.

BRAZIL

Brazil is the largest economy in the region, with a GDP of approximately US$800 billion, nearly twice the size of Mexico or Argentina. As of this writing, Brazil is the focal point of a global crisis of confidence. Its managed exchange rate regime is under assault as investors focus on the need for structural reform to rein in its fiscal deficit. The exchange rate regime is the focal point, but it is the fiscal deficit which is the true vulnerability of the Brazilian economy. Also as of this writing, the government is putting in place a package to address the fiscal deficit on a sustainable basis.

Short-term political risk is largely assuaged in Brazil as President Fernando Henrique Cardoso's successful reelection ensures policy continuity. However, the large and fragmented coalition that supports the government in Congress is unwieldy and can lead to slow progress. This coalition will also literally erode over the next four years, as parties and candidates attempt to differentiate themselves in anticipation of the next national elections.

In contrast to most other emerging markets, Brazil boasts a deep, liquid, and broad financial market. The large domestic pension and mutual fund industry generates a substantial source of domestic financing and supports substantial trading liquidity in both equity and fixed income.

The BM&F, Brazil's options and futures market, is the third largest futures exchange in the world in terms of contracts traded, in excess of 120 million annually. The market allows for hedging all manner of economic exposure, including financial assets such as gold, the local stock exchange index (BOVESPA), interest rates, and dollars. Agricultural goods, such as sugar, cotton, cattle, coffee, corn, and soybeans, are also traded; the market is one of the two most important futures markets in the world for such commodities. Traded instruments include swaps, futures, and options denominated in either reals or dollars, although to hedge for periods longer than six months is difficult at best, and such short-term hedges introduce significant rollover risk.

Additionally, the CME lists futures and options on the Brazilian real, and Brazilian sovereign dollar denominated Brady Bonds (the C and EI). Real futures do not require physical delivery of currency due to partial capital controls in Brazil. Real futures traded an average of 194 contracts per day in 1997 (100,000 reals per contract). EI futures are very illiquid, while the futures on the C bond traded an average of nearly 3000 contracts per day in 1997 (each contract represents US$100,000 face value of C bonds).

RISK MANAGEMENT

While we have spent an exceptional amount of effort to identify some of the more salient risks to the region, we have only briefly addressed how to manage such risk. Hedging risks in Latin America through options, futures, or other derivatives is costly and difficult. Therefore, the most appropriate methods of managing the risks of investing in Latin America involve setting an appropriate time horizon in order to be able to absorb interim price volatility and managing risk through a dynamic and constant process of asset allocation based on rigorous fundamental research.

Tools—Fixed Income

There are certain tools applicable to managing the risks of Latin American investing. The following examples are essentially different versions of horizon analysis, one applied to local currency investments (in this case Mexican peso-denominated CETES), the other to a dollar denominated Eurobond.

Local Currency

Take a look at Table 17–1. This analysis looks at the returns on an investment in a 91-day CETES (Mexican T-bill) under different assumptions of price movements of the CETES (represented by future yields on the left vertical axis) and different levels of the peso (top horizontal axis). Note that a hold-to-maturity strategy provides a higher likelihood of positive returns.

Such an analysis should be performed for any local currency fixed-income investment and for a range of maturities. The most important component of this type of analysis is to illustrate the sensitivity of return to the key variables of currency, price, and time.

External Currency Debt

One the toughest problems for the fixed-income investor in Latin America is the lack of well-developed sovereign yield curves. These incomplete yield curves make pricing of risk difficult, since there may not be a useful benchmark for pricing a corporate bond of a given maturity (as a function of a credit spread over the sovereign). The issue by Latin American governments of dollar denominated bonds of longer tenors, up to 30 years, has recently reduced this problem and created sovereign yield curves to enable more efficient pricing of corporate debt of increasing maturities.

Pricing of this risk, as measured by the spread over U.S. Treasuries (the difference between the risky asset and the yield of a Treasury of similar maturity or duration), for an emerging markets issuer is composed of two factors. The first of these factors is the risk associated with the country where the company is domiciled; the second factor involves the company-specific risks associated with its capital structure, industry, strategy, and operating environment. Relative value decisions between companies domiciled within the same country are therefore an exercise in judging the appropriate spread above their country's yield curve, rather than simply above U.S. Treasuries.

A useful exercise in this regard is to perform a horizon analysis to judge the total return of a bond under varying assumptions of spread compression/widening. Such an exercise can either

T A B L E 17–1

Investment Analysis: 91-Day Mexican "CETE" Investment

YTM: 36.55% p.s.
91-day CETE Purchase Price 9.1542375
Entry Peso/US$: 10.194

U.S. Dollar Total Return for a 28-Day Holding Period
Implied Devaluation & Peso/U.S. $ Exchange Rate at End of Period

	Implied Deval.	7.19% 11.00 Ps/$	5.45% 10.75 Ps/$	3.00% 10.50 Ps/$	0.00% 10.19 Ps/$	(1.90%) 10.00 Ps/$
	46.55%	(6.4%)	(4.2%)	(1.9%)		3.0%
	44.05%	(6.0%)	(3.8%)	(1.3%)		3.4%
CETE	41.55%	(5.6%)	(3.4%)	(1.1%)		3.8%
yields at	39.05%	(5.2%)	(3.0%)	(0.7%)		4.2%
end of	36.55%					
period	34.05%	(4.5%)	(2.2%)	0.1%		5.1%
	31.55%	(4.1%)	(1.8%)	0.5%		5.5%
	29.05%	(3.7%)	(1.4%)	0.9%		6.0%
	26.55%	(3.3%)	(1.0%)	1.3%		6.4%

U.S. Dollar Total Return for a 91-Day Holding Period
Implied Devaluation & Peso/U.S. $ Exchange Rate at End of Period

	Implied Deval.	7.19% 11.00 Ps/$	5.45% 10.75 Ps/$	3.00% 10.50 Ps/$	0.00% 10.19 Ps/$	(1.90%) 10.00 Ps/$
	46.55%	1.2%	3.6%	6.1%		11.4%
	44.05%	1.2%	3.6%	6.1%		11.4%
CETE	41.55%	1.2%	3.6%	6.1%		11.5%
yields at	39.05%	1.2%	3.6%	6.1%		11.5%
end of	36.55%					
period	34.05%	1.2%	3.6%	6.1%		11.5%
	31.55%	1.2%	3.6%	6.1%		11.5%
	29.05%	1.2%	3.6%	6.1%		11.5%
	26.55%	1.2%	3.6%	6.1%		11.5%

assume a static U.S. Treasury curve (and therefore only simulate changes in perceived emerging markets risk), or it can include movements in the U.S. Treasury curve and thereby incorporate information relevant to making a duration decision.

Tools—Equity

Equity investing in Latin America takes on all the risks associated with domestic equity investing and adds to them currency and sovereign risk. The most appropriate approach to managing these risks is to make appropriate allocation decisions based on rigorous fundamental research. Diversification along countries, industries, and companies is a crucial element to this approach.

Hedging is costly and often impractical. As we have discussed, options and futures markets for Latin American equities are underdeveloped and may only be available over-the-counter. To hedge for periods longer than six months is difficult at best, and such short-term hedges introduce significant rollover risk.

One such over-the-counter product is a warrant on a basket of the most liquid stocks in a given market. This enables the market maker to hedge its exposure with less expense than purchasing an option on the overall index, since the low liquidity of many index components makes it difficult to cover the position. Such an arrangement introduces additional risks, such as counter-party risk; can be expensive when considering the bid/ask spread; and also creates basis risk, as the investor's exact position may not be fully hedged.

Hedging only currency exposure in an equity portfolio is problematic because it introduces a large degree of basis risk as local stock prices and the currency move divergently. (As an aside, we feel compelled to clear up a common misperception regarding ADRs. ADRs do not remove currency exposure. ADRs may settle in dollars but in reality represent local currency investments.) As a U.S. dollar-based investor in Latin America, you are buying the U.S. dollar value of future cash flows associated with a company. That dollar value is a function not only of the exchange rate but also of the currency mix of a company's costs and revenues. Simply hedging the currency exposure on the basis of country exposure fails to recognize this underlying mismatch.

In the event the investor believes that a severe devaluation is highly likely, it may be more efficient to simply exit the country than to try to hedge the currency. Historically, the increase in perceived country risk, expressed through rising discount rates, is as or more responsible for falls in equity values as the currency.

CONCLUSIONS

When considering hedging Latin American investment exposure, the investor is faced with a dilemma of timing. When risk begins to increase, not only does the price of such hedges rise but the willingness of others to offer the hedge declines dramatically. Prices bottom and availability peaks when perceived risk is at its lowest. Ironically, the time to put on a hedge is when you don't think you need it.

Effective risk management in Latin America is an exercise in dynamic asset allocation. Continual assessment of fundamental risk factors and global market conditions is the sine qua non of this approach. We have only addressed the largest and most sophisticated markets in the region in brief and advise the interested investor that responsible investing in this region requires dedicated research to understand the various complexities of each market. Latin America is a diverse region where generalities fail.

CHAPTER 18

Eastern European Risk Management

Richard Vogel
Managing Director
Eastern Heritage Capital
Geneva, Switzerland

Istvan Szoke
Managing Director
Eastern Heritage Capital
Geneva, Switzerland

Investors in eastern Europe have to face risks particular to a region in massive economic transition. This chapter is an attempt to develop a framework that captures macroeconomic and political risks and to highlight the most important micro- and transaction-related issues.

ARE TRADITIONAL RISK MANAGEMENT TOOLS EFFECTIVE?

As the full growth story of eastern Europe has unfolded over the years, investors have wondered how to capture the financial benefits of growth while mitigating short-term volatility caused by domestic or external events. Classical portfolio management theory seems to be of little value just yet. As the data below illustrate, investors can enjoy the full benefits of intraregional diversification only over a longer time period. Table 18–1 is the result of compiling correlation coefficients on weekly returns of the four main indices of the region: BUX for Hungary, WIG for Poland, PX50 for the Czech Republic, and RTS for Russia. Over the last three years, individual country characteristics and stock picks determined performance; hence the level of comovement of equity market indices has been in line with the one observed in

T A B L E   18-1

Correlation Coefficients of Weekly Returns of Indices

1/12/96–11/13/98			
	BUX	**WIG**	**PX50**	**RTS**
BUX	1.000			
WIG	0.783	1.000		
PX50	–0.107	0.402	1.000	
RTS	0.677	0.730	0.391	1.000
11/4/97–11/13/98				
BUX	1.000			
WIG	0.910	1.000		
PX50	0.922	0.845	1.000	
RTS	0.716	0.590	0.821	1.000
5/1/98–11/13/98				
BUX	1.000			
WIG	0.965	1.000		
PX50	0.965	0.971	1.000	
RTS	0.865	0.899	0.838	1.000

Source: Bloomberg.

developed markets. However, as the time period under examination shrinks, correlation of returns increases significantly. History has also shown that intraregional correlation rises and dispersion of returns tightens considerably during periods of stress, such as the period between May and October of 1998.

Although the availability of traditional tools has increased considerably in the past few years and further expansion of derivatives should follow, the regional derivative market is still in its infancy. Hungary pioneered the offering of listed futures on major currencies and on its stock market index, the BUX, achieving a daily volume of US$2 million in November 98. The Vienna Stock Exchange has also started to offer futures and options on futures on their own indices for Hungary (HTX), Poland (PTX), the Czech

Republic (CTX), and Russia (RTX). Liquidity had been improving to a peak of around US$600 million per month in early 1998 but subsided amid the turmoil later in the year. For now, however, supply and demand—rather than true fair values—determine the price development of such instruments.

Some banks have also started to offer HTX, PTX, and CTX swaps up to US$5 million notional amount. A basket of stocks or single stocks could also be swapped at lower notional amounts. The option and warrant market is not yet really developed but is improving. OTC derivatives are available from a few investment banks, but wide spreads and "overpriced" volatility make them unattractive hedging tools for the time being.

A quote (for a maximum of US$3 million notional) received from a major house on July 23, 1998, illustrates (see Table 18–2) how almost prohibitively expensive options are for risk management for the time being. After paying 13 cents to protect a dollar for six months, the Polish market had to drop 18 percent for an investor just to break even on the hedge. A fund manager would probably sell long before she would consider such costly hedging.

Investors in fixed-income instruments are not much better off. London-traded nondeliverable forward agreements (NDFs) for Poland are fairly liquid, but domestic nondeliverable swaps, fixed-rate agreements, currency options, and forwards are usually expensive and often require lengthy negotiations. Hungarian NDFs offer reasonable liquidity, but due to restrictions in the domestic market, the availability of other instruments is limited. The convertibility of the currency has made forwards, swaps, swaptions, and currency options widely traded and reasonably effective for managing Czech fixed-income risks. Instruments in

T A B L E 18–2

Five-Percent Out-of-the-Money Puts

	Maturity	
	October 23, 1998	January 14, 1999
on HTX	5.2%–7.2%	8.0%–10.5%
on PTX	7.5%–9.5%	10.5%–13.0%

Russia mushroomed over the years, but many defaulted in the aftermath of the August 1998 devaluation, destroying all the trust in any risk management tool.

Given the immaturity of the central and eastern European markets, common sense is an important ingredient in the analysis and management of risks. Lack of historical data and the rapidly changing environment make qualitative evaluation more important than in developed markets. The poor availability of risk management tools makes prevention, i.e., *ex ante* risk assessment, the focal point of managing risks in the region. Our experience shows that once the investment is made, traditional methods may not be accessible or may be inadequate to mitigate risks. The next sections will provide some help to understand and assess risks up front.

THE TOP-DOWN VIEW

Evaluating risk in central and eastern Europe requires an understanding of the historical transition process from a command economy to a capitalist market economy. The three-phase lifecycle curve model shown in Figure 18–1 describes the main points of the development process. Investing in those three different periods implies different risk profiles and hence requires different approaches.

The first phase is marked by a complete disintegration of the command economies as market prices are introduced and create a series of major macroeconomic imbalances. In this period, industrial output and GDP contract sharply, hyperinflation sets in, and currencies tend to depreciate substantially. The legal system is not yet adapted to the new economic environment, corporate law is nonexistent, and property rights are not guaranteed for all classes of assets.

Most companies operate below their break-even points, factories and facilities are in need of massive capital investments, and management often is unfamiliar with such basic business concepts as marketing and financial controls. Accounting information is sketchy at best. In this phase, two different investment approaches can be followed. The most sensible one is to take a private equity-direct investment view, assuming control of a com-

FIGURE 18–1

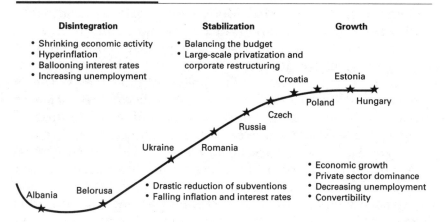

pany, and introducing western management techniques. The only option available to portfolio investors is a highly risky one, namely, to buy assets at very low valuation, based upon capacity measures, and speculate that a favorable transition to the second phase of the model will lead to a massive revaluation of assets.

As stabilization sets in, most portfolio investors focus on the analysis of macroeconomic aggregates. At this stage, however, as Czech investors experienced, a careful analysis of the structural reforms is much more relevant, since seemingly good macro figures do not guarantee a passage to phase three, i.e., the establishment of a long-term growth path. First, privatization laws must be voted and implemented at all levels of the economy. The privatization method plays an important role in that respect. Sales to foreign strategic investors, as shown in Hungary, tend to accelerate the necessary investments and generally ensure that assets will be used in a profitable manner. Second, a far-reaching reform of accounting and auditing standards must be undertaken. Accounting rules must be changed to reflect the real financial health of companies, showing the commitment of the government to expose the need to restructure companies. Here the differences between Russia ("barter accounting") on the one hand and Poland and Hungary (close to IAS) on the other could not be more striking. A third element is the legal framework. Property rights must be defined, and claims on real estate from pre-war owners must be dealt with. Modern corporate law and bank-ruptcy laws must be drafted. Just as Hungary and to a lesser degree Poland let most unprofitable companies go bankrupt at the beginning of the decade, other countries, such as the Czech Republic, still do not have enforceable bankruptcy laws. This is especially a threat to the banking system because it increases moral hazard in lending. Fourth, a functioning capital market must be established to secure proper allocation of capital. The reg-ulation of the financial markets must be designed to ensure trans-parency and proper reporting. Here again, differences between countries are huge, with Poland and Hungary at the head of the pack and Russia and the Czech Republic lagging behind in this regard. Once such a long list is drawn up, it is easy to see how demanding is the task of carrying through all those reforms with-out having periods of uncertainties.

From an investment point of view, the second phase is crucial. The paradigm must shift from an asset-based valuation to a cash-flow-based valuation, since shareholders want to see their assets producing results. For that to happen, the structural transitions must take place smoothly to underpin the rerating of valuations.

The depth and relevance of the structural reforms open the gate to the third phase, which is characterized by a sharp pickup in industrial production and GDP growth. Institutions and the legal framework are being fine-tuned, massive privatization and refurbishment of the former state monopoly takes place, and the virtuous cycle induced by foreign direct investments (FDI) starts. At this stage, FDI starts to accelerate, attracted by a large pool of educated labor, massive cost advantages compared to western Europe, and a predictable legal and macroeconomic framework. FDI triggers higher economic growth, allows the creation of a large number of small companies in the service sector, and helps correct the current account deficit. The long-term sustainability of the model rests on wise allocation of the resources generated dur-ing this first investment boom. Retained profit and tax receipts must be reinvested in projects with positive future cash flows, which is difficult because of those expenditures need to capture more value-added than the first wave of investments, which cen-tered around cheap labor and infrastructure spending.

It is now that the attention of portfolio investors should turn to macroeconomic analysis of the different countries. Since this subject has been developed in earlier chapters, we will only touch upon a few important particularities of central and eastern Europe. The level of debt of both the public and the private sectors is low. The five countries applying for European Union membership (EU5), with the exception of Hungary, meet the Maastricht criteria with respect to debt levels and budget deficits. In the private sector, the situation is similar; the loan-to-GDP ratio in those five countries is only 33 percent versus 93 percent in the European Union. The scope for inducing growth through an increase in debt levels is especially obvious in Poland, which in the next three years should see a 50 percent increase in its loan-to-GDP ratio from the current 24 percent. As liquidity pours into the system, central banks have to avoid the overheating of the economy and at the same time bring down inflation by gradually lowering nominal and real interest rates. Lower local interest rates are essential to creating an incentive for companies to borrow in local rather than in foreign currency, and therefore to limiting exposure to foreign exchange rate fluctuation. Lower interest rates should not endanger currency stability, especially during the early phase of an FDI cycle, when the current account deficit widens following imports of capital goods. Simultaneously, privatization proceeds flow through the capital account and should balance the external accounts. The management of the external account is a very delicate one, and countries that successfully laid the foundation during the second phase, i.e., the EU5 also managed to go through the crisis of August 1998 without currency devaluation or interest rate hikes. The main reasons are a relatively low exposure to foreign debt-holders and the confidence of local investors in the stability of their local currency.

Capital markets are quick to price in excessive optimism, as happened in Russia in the summer of 1997, or excessive pessimism, as in central European countries after the Russian devaluation. It is therefore crucial for an investor to understand which phase the country in which he is investing is in, and if capital markets price assets according to the risk profile of that particular phase.

THE BOTTOM-UP VIEW

Once an investor is convinced of the solid macroeconomic foundation of the countries, she can concentrate on the bottom-up analysis of the region. In the security selection process, investors' risk-reward options are going to be largely different, depending on where they are on the life-cycle curve. The further ahead a country and its companies are on the curve, the more similar their risk profile to the developed markets.

As described above, the current shape of the microeconomies in all eastern European countries has been largely determined by the privatization method the countries have opted for. Broadly speaking, the two main privatization methods were mass privatization through voucher schemes, which was seen as a fair way to distribute wealth evenly, and the sale of significant stakes to strategic or financial investors. The privatization methods have implications for corporate governance and hence should be carefully studied by portfolio investors. According to the shareholder value model, the foremost duty of managers is to maximize returns to shareholders, and all other obligations on management are derived from this duty. This is a new concept for the region, as there was no culture of real ownership in eastern Europe under the old regime, and even today, decisionmaking involves a broad range of stakeholders, creating situations where investors can become hostages of conflicting interests.

Mass privatizations in this region have rarely created real shareholders, as they resulted in employees or newly formed vehicles such as investment funds taking control of companies. Some of those groups have mostly been interested in asset stripping and short-term cash generation and have used capital markets to enhance their own return at the expense of everyone else. Companies in the Czech Republic, controlled by voucher funds, and in Russia, led by the notorious oligarchs, are the best examples of such "schemes." Other groups have rebuilt proper companies in spite of the lack of capitalist business experience and limited financial means. Management incentives have been realigned in a large number of big companies in Poland and Hungary, and very generous stock option plans have been put in place.

The other privatization route, which Hungary, for example, chose early on, was a systematic sale to strategic foreign investors. FDI has been one of the strong pillars of the transition in the region, bringing foreign know-how, new technologies, and efficiency improvement to the newly acquired companies. In an effort to boost domestic capital markets, governments have also obliged many of these companies to float a minority stake. Although the presence of a western major shareholder can be reassuring for portfolio investors, their attitude toward minority shareholders can vary. Most strategic investors treat the minority owners of their subsidiaries as well as if they were their own. Nevertheless, some western companies engage in such practices as using transfer pricing to channel profits out of their daughter companies. The ideal situation is to be invested in a company with more than one strategic investor, an approach followed by most of the telecom companies in the region.

Another issue is that strategic investors do have much longer-term objectives than portfolio managers, who typically care about short-term share price appreciation. The need for restructuring in the second part of the curve, or the race for market share in the second and/or third parts, puts management in the position of having to choose between optimizing short-term or long-term profitability. An aggressive and badly communicated expansion strategy can erode the share price in the short term. Examples include a foreign-controlled bank that launched an aggressive retail expansion and a regionwide manufacturer that has been acquiring companies and markets in dire need of restructuring.

The situation can be further complicated when the state retains part of its stake in a company. Business decisions in such companies often serve the interests of political groups. Investors in some Czech banks, for example, have seen their equity wiped out because of imprudent, politically motivated lending practices designed to support bankrupt companies.

No matter which category an investment falls into, investors have to carefully analyze how and with whom they align their interests, because corporate governance remains a risk factor for investors in central and eastern Europe.

Post-World War II state planners and other state organizations were the main users of accounting information in this region. Again, the countries at the forefront of the curve reformed their accounting standards early on, making them user-friendly to new shareholders. In the countries aspiring to EU membership, only minor differences remain between their respective local standards and IAS or U.S. GAAP standards. Most large companies in Hungary, for example, publish audited accounts in both IAS and in Hungarian Accounting Standards.

The laggards have failed to adopt proper accounting standards, so users of such accounts are exposed to the considerable risks of making decisions based on "false" information. The most notable case is Russian accounting. As barter is the most important way of trading goods in the CIS, it inflates revenues and expenses alike and makes the accounts of little use. The so-called social costs include, among others, the costs of social facilities, schools, sports venues, and holiday resorts that the companies operate for the benefit of their employees. These are often major expense burdens, yet they are booked below the reported earnings line. P/E ratios based on such reported earnings obviously loose their meaning. Another example is Romanian accounting, in which goods that are still in inventory are booked as sales, inflating top-line growth. Inflationary accounting is another issue, since high inflationary periods distort asset values and income statement items, yet few have adopted proper inflationary accounting.

TRANSACTION-RELATED RISKS

As investors become ready to cope with the macro and micro issues, market and transaction-related risks need to be addressed.

The execution-related risks can be largely eliminated by trading in depositary receipts. These securities are usually fully fungible with their underlying instruments and trade on more-liquid western markets, such as the SEAQ in London or the NASDAQ in the U.S. In addition, depositary receipts are denominated in US$ or DM, hence there is no need for an expensive foreign exchange transaction. There is little reason not to opt for a depositary receipt if available.

The different countries adopted different models for their capital markets, which in turn has a great impact on trading strategies. The positive feature of the main markets is a well-developed and transparent trading system. Nevertheless, investors have to be aware of country specifics. For example, in fear of any wrongdoing, the Poles designed a safe but somewhat rigid model in which bids and offers are entered once a day, with a maximum daily move of 10 percent. Prices are fixed in order to match the highest possible bids and asks, which leaves little room for skillful trading and artificially increases daily volatility of stock prices. In addition, it may take days to accumulate positions, since adjustments can be made only on a daily basis. The introduction of a continuous session in the afternoon is supposed to address these issues, but liquidity has been building up slowly in this segment. Since the market is designed to guard the interests of domestic retail investors, who contribute a dominant albeit decreasing share of the daily volume, the regulators have been in no hurry to make trading smoother. As the increasing role of domestic and foreign institutional investors calls for a more flexible solution, a new system is expected to be introduced by the year 2000.

At the other extreme are countries with rather lax regulations. Up until recently in the Czech Republic, most of the volume was done in the form of direct trading between individual brokers, leaving the door open for all kinds excesses. Since the introduction of the market maker-driven SPAD system in mid-1998, over 90 percent of the volume trades on it, lowering the probability of being victimized by manipulative pricing. In general, wide spreads, wild price movements, and the lack of liquidity demand active attention when buying or selling securities on any eastern European market.

Settlement procedures have improved over time, and today, most transactions settle smoothly and swiftly. Nevertheless, there are exceptions in which registration can be a lengthy process. In Russia, ownership is recorded upon physical registration at the registrar's office often at company headquarters in remote places. Although this practice makes shareholder-unfriendly actions or fraud easy to execute, in practice, such events have rarely occurred. At times of rapid price erosion, the lengthy registration process could potentially cause undercapitalized market makers to not honor confirmed purchase transactions. In a delivery against payment trade, the risk is limited to the opportunity cost of such a sale be unexecuted, which in falling markets can become a considerable risk factor. Therefore, investors should do a proper due diligence check on their counterparts and possibly do business with the better-capitalized international brokers.

Trustworthy custodial facilities are vital in any emerging market. Today, all of the global custodians are present directly or through subcustodians in most eastern European markets. Although being first in a new market has rewarded pioneer investors, they have also been required to carry out their own due diligence on the local custodian. Given that global custodians are rapidly expanding to cover the entire region, investors should consider the costs and benefits of going alone into new markets.

In summary, every stage of a transaction must be monitored closely to make sure that investment returns are not undermined by unsecure or unfamiliar systems.

The smaller the market is, the more powerful a force liquidity becomes. Therefore, at times of high volatility, monitoring fund flows is more crucial than trying to assess changes in fundamentals. Paradoxically, over a short time period, liquidity can be a curse rather than a blessing. In the aftermath of the Russian devaluation in 1998, bigger capitalization and more liquid stocks sold off heavily in other eastern European markets, although fundamentally, they were barely affected by the Russian collapse. In panic, investors sold whatever they could, which meant the big-cap, liquid names. Similarly, markets with scarce liquidity, such as Slovenia or the Czech Republic, held up pretty well. Once the storm calmed down, the liquid names recovered the most and the fastest. Low free float, and hence liquidity, can punish you, even if the investment is sound. For example, one fast-growing Polish company had impressed every investor that analyzed them. Some of them used the market mayhem to accumulate large stakes, significantly reducing the float. Although the fundamentals are now better than ever, the low liquidity dried up demand and the stock price has suffered from lack of interest.

OUTLOOK

Investing in eastern Europe requires a careful analysis of all the risks involved before making a decision. The last few years have seen a great deal of improvement throughout the region, at every level of the investment process, which in turn significantly reduces the risks. The Russian crisis shed positive light on the stability of the currencies of the countries at the forefront of the curve. The main challenge for investors is to understand where a country is positioned on the life-cycle curve and what the appropriate risk-adjusted valuation should be for their investments at that phase. Then, a properly conducted investment process will reward long-term investors not only on an absolute but also on a risk-adjusted basis.

Internet Resources for Global Investment Risk Management

Ezra Zask
Manager
Gibson Capital Management, Ltd.
Lakeville, Connecticut

GENERAL INFORMATION SITES

Center for International Business Education and Research (CIBER) at the University of Michigan: http://ciber.bus.msu.edu

Invest-o-Rama Director of Investing Resources: http://www.investorama.com/director.html

Foreign Market Advisory: http://www.investools.com

Wall Street Directory: http://wallstreetdirectory.com

Cyber Investing Guide: http://cyberinvest.com

Investor Home: http://investorhome.com/index.htm

Infomanage: http://informanage.com/investment/test.htm

Wall Street City: http://www.wallstreetcity.com

M.A.I.D. Profound: http://www.maid-plc.com

Net Guide: http://www.netguide.com

Dr. Ed Yadeni's Economics Network: http://www.yardeni.com

International Investing: http://www.investorguide.com

Global Investment Information: http://www.site-by site.com

The Global Investor: http://global-investor.com)

Worldly Investor: http://worldly investor.com

RISK MANAGEMENT SITES

Global Association of Risk Professionals (GARP):
http://www.garp.com

Applied Derivatives Trading: http://adtrading.com

BARRA: http://www.barra.com

Cambridge Risk Dynamics: http://www.riskex.com

Creditrisk+: http://www.csfp.csh.com

Contingency Analysis:
http://www.contingencyanalysis.com

Essentials of Financial Risk Management:
http://www.amex.com

IFCI Risk Watch: http://risk.ifci.ch

JP Morgan Riskmetrics: http://www.jpmorgan.com

Financial Engineering News: http://fenews.com

S&P: Global Markets: http://www.globalmarkets.com

REGIONAL SITES

Emerging Markets

Emerging Markets Companion: http://emgmkts.com

Bradynet: http://bradynet.com

Internet Securities, Inc. Emerging Markets:
http://www.securities.com

Africa

ABSA Group: http://www.absa.co.za

Asia

Asia Crisis Homepage: http://www.stern.nyu

Asia Inc. Online: http://www.asia-inc.com

Asia Business Connection: http://www.asiabiz.com

Latin America

Center for Latin America Capital Markets Research:
http://netrus.net/users/gmories

Middle East

Israel's Business Arena by Globus: http://www.globes.co.il
Middle East Business Review:
http://sun.rhbnc.ac.uk/mgt.mbr.html

Russia and Eastern Europe

Corline: http://eng.corline.com
Skate: http://www.skate.ru
Russia Online: http://online.ru
RINACO Plus: http://www.fe.msk.ru
Central and East Europe Business Information Center:
http://www.itaiep.doc.gov/eebic/eebic.html
Central Europe OnLine: http://www.centraleurope.com

Western Europe

Liffe: http://www.liffe.com
Electronic Share Information: http://www.esi.co.uk
Interactive Investor: http://www.iii.co.uk
Moneyworld: http://co.uk
Financial Information Warehouse: http://www.financial.de

ON-LINE MARKET NEWS AND PRICES

Bloomberg: http://www.bloomberg.com
Reuters: http://www.Reuters.com
Data Broadcasting Corp.: http://dbc.com
Financial Information Network: http://finetwork.com

PC Quote Europe: http://www.pcquote-Europe.co.uk
WEBS on the Web: http://websontheweb.com
American Depository Receipts: http://www.adr.com
I/B/E/S Financial Network: http://www.ibes.com
Money Market Services: http://www.mms.com
Olson Research Associates: http://www.olsonresearch.com
Global Forex Online Currency Exchange:
        http://www.forexonline.com

GLOBAL EXCHANGES

Wall Street Research Net: http://www.wsrn.com
The Financial Center On-Line: http://www.tfc.com

GLOBAL INVESTMENT VEHICLES

Micropal: http://www.micropal.com
International Fund Listing:
        http://iht.com/iht/fun/funds.html
Alternative Investments Management Association:
        http://www.aima.org
Morningstar: http://www.morningstar.com
Mutual Funds Interactive:
        http://www.fundsinteractive.com

INDEX

A

Accounting issues, 21–23, 50, 52, 52n, 264, 296
Algeria, 221
ARCH-family of models, 114–116
Argentina, 147, 150, 154, 221, 225, 270, 275, 276–277, 278
Asian markets, 245–267
  currency crisis (1997-1998), 2, 4, 9–11, 45, 56, 110, 111, 217–218, 220, 221, 248, 256–260
  extent of share price movements in, 247–249
  financial liquidity cycle and, 252–254, 257–262
  financial versus economic risks in, 254–255
  relative equity ownership and, 250–251
  (*See also names of specific countries*)
Asset allocation, 5–6, 75–107, 109–126, 171
  balanced portfolio and, 76, 83–84, 95
  currency hedging and, 67–68
  default risk and, 233–235
  equity derivatives and, 172, 173
  inflation versus volatility in, 77–83
  interest-generating versus equity investments in, 77
  interfund variation and, 29
  investment portfolio design format and, 104–105
  market timing versus, 91, 100–101
  multiple-asset-class portfolios and, 88–89, 92–104
  power of diversification and, 84–92
  tactical, 170, 172
  time horizon and, 76, 83–84
  tools of, 234–235
  top-down bottom-up approach to, 234–235
  total, 170, 172
  (*See also* Diversification)
Asset-backed securities, 40
Asset managers (*see* Investment managers)
Asset mix:
  knowledge of investments in, 17–19
  target, 17
Auditing, 21–23, 50

Average impact of currency fluctuations, 127–129

B

Baekart, G., 245–247
Balance of payments, 151–152, 271
Balanced portfolios, 70, 83–84, 95
Bankers Trust, 221
Banks:
  central, 149, 152, 154, 156
  in Eastern Europe, 289, 292
  in Latin America, 274–275, 279
Barclays Global Investors, 46
Barings Bank, 22, 50, 109
BARRA, 184
Barter accounting, 291, 296
Basis risk, 233, 284
Beers, David T., ix, 7, 139–159
Bolivia, 221
Bollerslev, Tim, 114, 116
Bond markets (*see* Global bond markets)
Brady bonds, 221
Brazil, 156, 223–224, 270, 271, 275, 276, 278, 280–281
Brokers:
  controls over, 22
  front-running by, 49
  recordkeeping and, 21
  trading risk and, 49–50, 222
  transaction costs and, 29, 68–69
Brookings Institution, 58
Bulgaria, 221
Business cycles, global bond markets and, 37
Buy-write, 181–182

C

Call on dollars, 162
Call options:
  covered call writing, 170, 174, 181–182
  naked call writing, 181
  short call hedge, 168, 184, 185
Canada, 156
Capital asset pricing model (CAPM), 245
Capital controls and currency intervention:
  currency boards, 11, 243–244, 276
  in Malaysia, 45, 49, 56, 240